William Cobbett and the United States

The Gallows rises to his view.
His steps a host of foes pursue:

From Number 164, Mathew Carey, *The Porcupiniad. . . .*
Canto II. & III. Philadelphia, 1799.

WILLIAM COBBETT

AND THE UNITED STATES

1792–1835

A Bibliography with

Notes and Extracts by

PIERCE W. GAINES

American Antiquarian Society: Worcester, Massachusetts: 1971

Copyright © 1971 by American Antiquarian Society
Library of Congress Catalog Card Number 79-168901
Standard Book Number 912296-00-3
Designed by Klaus Gemming, New Haven, Connecticut
Manufactured in the United States of America
by the Davis Press, Worcester, Massachusetts
All rights reserved

TABLE OF CONTENTS

PREFACE

THERE ARE two objectives of the present volume. The first is to present in a useful manner, bibliographically, the works of William Cobbett written in the United States and published here or abroad, or written elsewhere and published here, or written and published elsewhere but related in a major way to the United States. Also included are the writings of others published by Cobbett in this country, together with the writings of others about Cobbett written while he was here. Cobbett was in the United States from October 1792 to June 1800 and again from May 1817 to October 1819. Publications after Cobbett's death in 1835 are not included.

The second objective is to rescue, if that is the word, some of the pungent and homely style of Cobbett which lies buried in the mass of his United States writings too deep for present-day readers to wish to extract. It was the judgment of Cobbett's principal biographer, G. D. H. Cole, that of all Cobbett's pamphleteering in this country, only his *Life and Adventures of Peter Porcupine* still lived, but Professor Cole also believed that the other works contained many effective phrases and passages of distinction.* The reader, if he wishes, may see some of these in the present volume; or he may ignore them and, hopefully, find use for the descriptions of the editions, issues, and variants here set forth.

In preparing the present bibliography, at least one copy of each item described was personally examined, except in a few instances which are noted in the text. However, there was no attempt to find multiple copies, and many institutions contain important Cobbett holdings which are not mentioned. Through the kindness of Mr. Donald A. Sinclair and his staff of the Special Collections at Rutgers University Library, I had the privi-

---

Letters from William Cobbett to Edward Thornton, ed. G. D. H. Cole (London, 1937), p. xlvi.

lege of examining the extensive material gathered for a Cobbett bibliography by the late C. Rexford Davis, Professor of English at Rutgers and a great admirer of Cobbett. I found after checking that Professor Davis' bibliographical data were of a high order of accuracy. Accordingly, since librarians generally are overburdened and I wish to avoid the fate of Professor Davis of being unable to complete his work, I have in a relatively few instances, so indicated in each case, adopted Professor Davis' descriptions, rather than try to bring together again from scattered locations works which he had found. I wish to express my appreciation to Mr. Sinclair especially in this connection.

The present work is based in major part on the collections of the American Antiquarian Society, New York Public Library, and Yale. Also visited were the Boston Athenaeum, the Houghton, Kress, and Widener Libraries at Harvard, Massachusetts Historical Society, John Carter Brown Library, New-York Historical Society, New York Society Library, Columbia University Library, Fordham University Library, Rutgers University Library, American Philosophical Society, Library Company of Philadelphia, Historical Society of Pennsylvania, University of Pennsylvania (including the Philadelphia Union Catalogue), and the Library of Congress. Valuable information was furnished by the William L. Clements Library and the Peabody Institute of Baltimore, among others.

In the course of the work, I became indebted for their kindness and assistance to many people connected with the institutions named, for which I am deeply appreciative. Their courtesy was unfailing. I should like to mention a few of them in particular: at American Antiquarian Society, Messrs. Shipton, Mc-Corison, and Mooney and the Misses Brown and Clarke; at New York Public Library, Mr. Stark, Mrs. Cole, Mr. Tobin, and Mr. Mask; at Yale, Mr. Liebert, Miss Boatfield, Miss Bridgewater, and Prof. Labaree; at the Houghton Library, Mr. Bond; at Massachusetts Historical Society, Mr. Butterfield; at the John Carter Brown Library, Mr. Adams; at the William

L. Clements Library, Mrs. Haugh; at American Philosophical Society, Mr. Bell; at the Library Company, Mr. Wolf, Mrs. Tonkin, and Mr. Fraser; and at the Library of Congress, Mr. Goff. I wish also to extend thanks for valuable assistance to Mr. W. A. Taylor, City Librarian, Birmingham, England, to Dr. Julian P. Boyd, Editor of the Papers of Thomas Jefferson, and to Mrs. Marcia Williamson, who deciphered my handwriting. I am very grateful to Mr. Roger E. Stoddard, of the Houghton Library, who by his spot-checking saved me from some serious errors, and to Mr. L. H. Butterfield, who caught some more. And finally I am especially appreciative of the assistance and encouragement of Mr. Marcus A. McCorison and Mr. James E. Mooney at American Antiquarian Society, who made a reality of the book now before you.

METHODS USED

THE MAIN ENTRIES give the first editions and are arranged chronologically by date of publication. Subentries give later editions, issues, and variants of the same work, within the limitations just mentioned, and generally chronologically. If there is no conclusive evidence of priority, imprints of the same date are listed in the order of their proximity to the place of first publication. London is taken as the nearest English point for this purpose.

Following McKerrow*, an edition includes all copies printed from the same setting of type and an issue embraces copies mainly from the same setting but including matter new or differently arranged and with a new title-page. Variants involve lesser changes, such as cancels. Simultaneous publications by more than one person from the same setting of type do not create separate issues.

A brief description of the content of the main entries may be helpful, as follows: (a) item number; (b) author, if not Cobbett; (c) title transcription, not including all capitalization nor any description of type faces; (d) colophon, if any; (e) collation, including format, if laid paper, or height, if wove paper (parentheses indicate unsigned gatherings); (f) pagination, what pages are numbered and how (figures in parentheses indicate so many unnumbered pages); (g) citations; (h) locations which mean copies examined except that (repro.) indicates reproduction examined; (i) contents (a number in brackets is one supplied in normal sequence); (j) notes on publication and contents; and (k) extracts. In general, notation is made of the presence of plates, decoration, catchwords, volume numbers, press numbers, running titles, and distinguishing errata.

*Ronald B. McKerrow, *An Introduction to Bibliography* (London, 1928), pp. 175-176.

Several instances occur in the present work where titles are included although there is no extant copy known. In each case the grounds of inclusion are given, which one may discount or not as may seem proper. On the other hand, there are a number of titles of this kind described in Evans' *American Bibliography* which do not appear here. Evans did not state his basis for inclusion in the usual case, but it is evident that he sometimes relied on information which may not be adequate. I have rejected as not alone sufficient the publication of a notice that a work has been 'just published' or 'shortly will be published', and the like. As to this, we know that printers have had a way of testing potential market demand by such a notice before undertaking the risks of printing (the practice has lately been common in the case of reprints).

Evans entries which have not been described include 28438, *A Little Plain English*, Boston, 1795; 28440, *Observations on the Emigration of Dr. Joseph Priestley*, 1795 (on this, see No. 2k believed to be dated 1797); 30211, *A Letter to the infamous Tom Paine*, in 64 pages, but the letter is only 18 pages; 32731, Puglia, *The Disappointment, or Peter Porcupine in London*, advertized in *The Blue Shop* (No. 146) and in *The Political Massacre* (No. 147) as 'shortly will be published'; and 33528, *Bradford's fourth edition . . . Priestley*.

A NOTE ON WILLIAM COBBETT

WILLIAM COBBETT has earned a significant place in American history and letters. Scholars have observed that a study of his writings in Philadelphia from 1794 to 1799 is of great value in understanding the politics of the time.[1] George Washington took note of Cobbett in language which can be considered praise when he wrote of one of Cobbett's pamphlets: 'Making allowances for the asperity of an Englishman, for some of his strong and coarse expressions, and a want of official information as to many facts, it is not a bad thing.'[2] On the other hand, much of the attention Cobbett received has been understandably biased against this outspoken foreigner. This was so in the celebrated libel suit against him successfully brought by Dr. Benjamin Rush on the ground that Cobbett had maliciously attacked his treatment of yellow fever by copious blood-letting.[3] James Madison wrote of his 'satirical scurrility.'[4] Apt commentary is found in Rufus W. Griswold, *The Republican Court* (New York, 1867, p. 379): 'In 1794 the three most remarkable Englishmen in America were William Cobbett, Joseph Priestley and Thomas Cooper . . . they were all able, ambitious and persevering . . . [Cobbett's] English was admirable for purity and

[1]See James Kent, quoted in Henry T. Tuckerman, *America and Her Commentators* (New York, 1864), p. 208; Henry Cabot Lodge, *Studies in History* (Boston, 1884), pp. 110, 131; Henry M. Tinkcom, *The Republicans and Federalists in Pennsylvania 1790-1801* (Harrisburg, 1950), p. 144.

[2]Washington to David Stuart, Jan. 8, 1797, quoted in Moncure D. Conway, *The Life of Thomas Paine* (New York, 1892), p. 175.

[3]George W. Corner, editor of the *Autobiography of Benjamin Rush* (Princeton, 1948), states that Cobbett had flung at Rush the worst abuse an honest physician has ever had to bear, p[1]. Joseph Dennie agreed with Cobbett in *The Spirit of the Farmer's Museum* (Philadelphia, 1801), p. 61. Such contemporaries as Ebenezer Hazard, also criticized Rush. See Carl Binger, M.D. *Revolutionary Doctor Benjamin Rush* (New York, 1966), pp. 217, 223, 229, 241, 247. Rush believed the body of a man of average size contained about twelve quarts of blood, about twice as much as is actually the case (p. 229). Rush took 'sixty, seventy and even eighty ounces [2-1/2 quarts]' of blood. *Letters of Benjamin Rush* ed. L. H. Butterfield, (Princeton, 1951), p. 695; and see pp. 1213-18.

[4]See Moncure D. Conway, *Omitted Chapters of History* (New York, 1888), p. 347.

strength, and was used most successfully in invective, of which he was a consummate master.' Nathaniel Hawthorne had a sharp view (*Works*, 1883, XII, pp. 255-56): 'the ferocity of the true blood hound of literature—such as Swift, or Churchill, or Cobbett—which fastens upon the throat of its victim, and would fain drink his life-blood.'

John Bach McMaster in *A History of the People of the United States* (New York, 1921, II, pp. 206, 207) wrote: 'William Cobbett . . . was, of all the pamphleteers at that time in America, the most able, the most sarcastic, the most entertaining and successful . . . the vigor of his style, the felicity of his nicknames, the fearlessness of his strictures, marked him out as the chief of pamphleteers.' Abigail Adams, wife of the President, commented on Cobbett: 'There is a strange mixture in him . . . He can write very handsomely, and he can descend and be as low and vulgar as a fishwoman.'[5] The appraisal of Cobbett by Justin Winsor in *Narrative and Critical History of America* (Boston, 1888, VII, pp. 314, 515) includes the following: 'The most virulent and probably effective pamphleteering was done on either hand by William Cobbett and Thomas Paine.' More recently and colorfully, Claude G. Bowers in his *Jefferson and Hamilton* (Boston, 1925, p. 357) wrote of Cobbett: 'He could string chaste words into a scorpion lash that Swift would have envied, or stoop to an obscenity or vulgarity that would have delighted Kit Marlowe in his cups. None but a genius could have risen from his original low estate, with so little education.'

William Cobbett was born March 9, 1763, at Farnham, Surrey, England, the son of a small farmer who also kept 'The Jolly Farmer' Inn. He apparently had no formal schooling, but early learned the joy of books, and could quickly absorb whatever he wished to learn. He grew up a farm boy, but when he was twenty suddenly broke away from country life. After eight or nine months in London, as clerk to a solicitor in Gray's Inn, in utterly uncongenial surroundings, he enlisted as a private

[5]Quoted in Page Smith, *John Adams* (New York, 1962), p. 956.

in His Majesty's Service and in 1785 found himself bound for Nova Scotia and then New Brunswick. He became sergeant-major of his regiment in a highly responsible position. He returned to England in 1791, obtained his discharge and married early in 1792. In March of that year he took his bride to France, where he remained until August, which still was sufficient time for him to learn the French language well enough so that later he could write a French-English dictionary. Taking ship for America, he landed at Philadelphia in October. November found him in Wilmington. In February 1794, he moved to Philadelphia, and August of that year saw the start of his career as pamphleteer with the publication of his *Observations on the Emigration of Dr. Joseph Priestley.*

Cobbett was then thirty-one years of age. He was six feet one inch tall, a commanding height in those days, and solidly built in proportion. Mathew Carey wrote that he had a 'carotty head and Drawcansir face.'[6] Fearless, combative, opinionated, the words flowed freely and powerfully from his pen. Strongly attached to the British interest[7] and therefore opposing the French as well as 'Republican' principles, his favorite targets naturally became the Republican leaders in Pennsylvania: Thomas Mifflin, Governor, or 'Tom the Tinker' as Cobbett called him; Thomas M'Kean, Chief Justice; Alexander J. Dallas, Secretary of the Commonwealth; Albert Gallatin, Congressman from Pennsylvania, 'the Genevese' or 'Political Sinner'; and John Swanwick, merchant and Congressman, 'little duck-legged squire.' Cobbett also attacked Dr. Benjamin Rush of Philadelphia as 'Dr. Sangrado,' (the bloodletting physician in Gil Blas). Cobbett began his attacks on Rush in January 1797 because of Rush's remarks praising Republicanism in his eulogium on David Rittenhouse (Evans 31143, at p. 36), but he soon

[6]See Carey's *A Plumb Pudding for . . . Peter Porcupine* (No. 160). 'Drawcansir' is a blustering braggart.

[7]It has been charged that Cobbett received an English subsidy, but it is pretty clear this was not so. See the Cole-Thornton letters, especially the letter of May 15, 1800. Thornton, Secretary to the British legation, did help Cobbett to settle Rush's judgment.

concentrated on Rush's 'murder' of his yellow-fever patients. These attacks resulted in a judgment against Cobbett in December 1799 for the ruinous sum of $5000.

Cobbett wrote of himself in 1818 in reference to an occasion when cattle broke into his garden: 'I had nothing to wreak my vengeance on . . . there was no human being that I could blame . . . In short, I had, for once in my life, to submit peaceably and quietly . . . '8

In the period 1795 to 1797, Cobbett's pamphlets followed each other in quick succession. In May 1796 he leased a house and shop at 25 North Second Street, Philadelphia. He had broken with his first publisher, Thomas Bradford, in March and was employing Benjamin Davies on an interim basis. In July he had a formal opening of his shop, and *The Scare-Crow* (No. 18) appeared as the first work of which he was publisher. On March 4, 1797 came the first number of *Porcupine's Gazette* (No. 30), published each weekday, which thereafter occupied most of his attention until October 1799, and diminished the flow of his other works. His removal to New York in November 1799 was followed by the Rush judgment on December 14. After a few parting salvoes, including the numbers of the *Rush-light*, directed at his adversary, Cobbett left the country June 1, 1800, for Halifax and thence to England.

Despite the circumstances of his return to England, Cobbett never lost his interest in the United States. Though still an observer of American politics, his main concerns there tended more and more toward farming and gardening and conditions of interest to emigrants from Britain. He soon edited Forsyth's *Treatise on . . . fruit trees* for use in this country, which was published in Philadelphia in 1802 (No. 62), with an epitome published the following year (No. 63). His *Letters on the late war* (No. 68) and *Pride of Britannia humbled* (No. 70), articles on the War of 1812, were surprisingly sympathetic to the Ameri-

---

8*A Year's Residence in the United States of America, New York 1819* (No. 77), par. 219.

can view. *A Year's Residence in the United States* (No. 77), published 1818-19, contained much information on farming on
Long Island and on conditions in the United States generally.
This was followed by the *American Gardener*, London 1821 (No.
80). Cobbett's *Emigrant's Guide*, 1829 (No. 88), was intended
to correct the pretensions of land promoters concerning the
manner of life emigrants from Britain might expect to achieve
in various parts of the United States. As will be seen, many
other Cobbett works found publication here.

Cobbett returned to this country in 1817. He had become
the leading advocate of English government reform, attacking
the iniquitous poor laws, sinecures and placemen, the rotten-
borough system, or 'boroughmongering' as he called it, and
the compulsory tithes for the support of the clergy. His newspaper, the *Political Register*, or 'Twopenny Trash' as he called
it, was enormously popular and influential. For his temerity
in attacking the establishment, he had spent two years in Newgate prison, been fined £1000 and put under bonds of £5000
to keep the peace. His financial resources were overextended
in the Spring of 1817 when on March 4th the Habeas Corpus
Act was suspended and 'agitators' became subject to immediate
imprisonment without trial. It had become evident that Cobbett could not remain in the country unless he kept silent. He
shortly sailed from England, reaching New York in May. He
leased a farm near North Hempstead, Long Island. The house
burned in May, 1819, and he removed temporarily to New
York City. From there he sailed for the last time to England,
October, 1819. He was elected to Parliament in 1832 and died
June 18, 1835.

REFERENCES USED

A.B.

American Bibliography, a Preliminary Checklist for 1801 (−1825), compiled by Ralph R. Shaw and Richard H. Shoemaker. New York, 1958-1969. 28 volumes.

Account Book
Sale Date

This is the date of first sale as recorded in Cobbett's Account Book, as to which see the Appendix.

B.A.L.

Bibliography of American Literature, compiled by Jacob Blanck. New Haven, 1955−.

Bartlett

Bibliotheca Americana . . . Library of John Carter Brown . . . Part III. John Russell Bartlett. Reprinted. New York 1963.

Brigham

History and Bibliography of American Newspapers. Clarence S. Brigham. Worcester. American Antiquarian Society. 1947. 2 volumes.

Clark

Peter Porcupine in America: The Career of William Cobbett, 1792–1800. Mary Elizabeth Clark. Philadelphia, 1939.

Cole

The Life of William Cobbett. George Douglas Howard Cole. New York. Harcourt, Brace & Co. 1924.

Cole-Thornton

Letters from William Cobbett to Edward Thornton written in the years 1797 to 1800. Edited by G. D. H. Cole. London. Oxford University Press. 1937.

Davis

The late C. Rexford Davis of Rutgers, Cobbett research specialist.

Evans

American Bibliography. Charles Evans. Vols. IX-XIII. Chicago, for the author. 1925–1955.

Evans Supp.

Supplement to Charles Evans' American Bibliography. Roger P. Bristol. Charlottesville. University Press of Virginia, 1970.

Muirhead   An Introduction to a Bibliography of William Co-
bett. Arnold M. Muirhead. The Library. Fourth
Series. Vol. XX, pp. 1-40 (1939).

Pearl   William Cobbett. A Bibliographical Account of His
Life and Times. Morris Leonard Pearl. London.
Oxford University Press. 1953.

Reitzel   William Cobbett and Philadelphia Journalism:
1794-1800. Penn. Mag. of Hist. and Biog. Vol.
LIX (1935) pp. 223-244.

Sabin   Dictionary of Books Relating to America. Joseph
Sabin. 29 vols. New York, J. Sabin, 1868-1936.

S. T. Evans   National Index of American Imprints through
1800: The Short-Title Evans. Clifford K. Shipton.
James E. Mooney. 2 vols. American Antiquarian
Society and Barre Publishers. 1969.

LOCATION SYMBOLS

CtY	Yale University
CU	University of California, Berkeley
DCU	Catholic University of America
DLC	Library of Congress
ICU	University of Chicago
InU	Indiana University
M	Massachusetts State Library
MB	Boston Public Library
MBAt	Boston Athenaeum
MH	Harvard University
MHi	Massachusetts Historical Society
MiU-C	William L. Clements Library
MMeT	Tufts University
MoSW	Washington University, St. Louis
MWA	American Antiquarian Society
NHi	New-York Historical Society
NjR	Rutgers University
NN	New York Public Library
PCarlD	Dickinson College
PHi	Pennsylvania Historical Society
PPAmP	American Philosophical Society
PPL	Library Company of Philadelphia
PU	University of Pennsylvania
RPJCB	John Carter Brown Library

William Cobbett and the United States

Cobbett Works

1a Impeachment | of | Mr. Lafayette: | containing | his accusation, | (stated in the report of the extraordinary commission to the Na- |tional Assembly, on the 8th of August, 1792,) | supported by | Mr. Brissot of Warville; | and | his defence | by | Mr. Vaublanc: | with | a supplement, | containing the letters, and other authentic pieces relative thereto. | [rule] | Translated from the French, | by William Cobbett. | [rule] | [one line of French from] Marmontel. | [rule] | Philadelphia: | Printed by John Parker, No. 259, North Second-Street. | [rule] | M,DCC,XCIII.

[A]–N⁴=52 leaves, 8 vo; (3)iv(1)6–84(1)86–89(1)91–97(1)99; 100(1), 102(1), 104 ¶ Evans 25497; Pearl 3; Sabin 38583 ¶ cty; MWA

Contents: Title, blank, To the Citizens of the United States [iii] iv, subscribed 'William Cobbett. Wilmington, Feb. 19, 1793'; Impeachment [5]–84; Supplement [85]–104; foot of p. 104 3 line errata. Running titles, catchwords. Type ornaments top p. [5]. Catchword p. 59 'exist-' for existence'; p. 84 'supple-' for supplement'. The Federal Gazette and Philadelphia Daily Advertiser, February 14, 1793: 'This day is published...translated by William Crobbet [corrected in later printings] of Wilmington, Delaware...' In the foreword, Cobbett says his purpose is 'to do justice to La Fayette as well as to those who have persecuted him.'

Some errors noted: p. iv, l. 4 has a period instead of a comma; p. 22, l. 28 'La Fayatte'; p. 28, l. 28 in 'the' the type is broken; p. 47, l. 8 the question mark is misplaced; p. 50, l. 24 in 'La Fayette' the y is gone; p. 55, l. 3 word 'it' missing; p. 81, l. 20, improper comma after 'austere'; p. 83, l. 7 'fantom'.

1b ———. A variant in that the errors on p. iv and p. 55 are corrected. ¶ MWA; NN

1c Impeachment | of | Mr. La Fayette: | containing | his accusation, | (stated in the report of the extraordinary com- | mission to the National Assembly, on the | 8th of August, 1792,) | supported by Mr. Brissot; | and his defence by Mr. Vaublanc; | with | a supplement. | containing the letters, and other authentic pieces | relative thereto | [rule] | Translated from the French, | by William Cobbett. | [rule] | [two lines from] Marmontel. | [rule] | Hagerstown, | printed by Stewart Herbert. | M,DCC,XCIV.

[A]–K⁴[L]¹=41 leaves, 8 vo; (5)6–68(1)70–81(1) ¶ Evans 26996 ¶ MWA

Contents: title; blank; [row of type ornaments] To the citizens of the United States, subscribed William Cobbett, Wilmington, February 19, 1793; blank; [row of type ornaments] Impeachment | of | Mr. La Fayette [5]–68; [rule] Supplement [69]–81; blank.

2a Observations on the emigration of Dr. Joseph Priestley, and on the several addresses delivered to him on his arrival at New York. Published for the purchasers. Philadelphia: Printed by Thomas Bradford, No. 8 South Front Street. [August, 1794].

Conjectural title; no copy known ¶ Evans 26777; Sabin 13899; Pearl 4

In 'Porcupine's Works', London, 1801 (No. 59), the running title for the 'Observations' is 'August, 1794.' In the 'Political Censor' for September 1796 (No. 20a), Cobbett wrote (p. 70) that the first pamphlet the Bradfords published for him was issued in August 1794. In Mathew Carey's 'Plumb Pudding for...Porcupine' (No. 159a), p. 11, Carey wrote that he purchased 36 copies of the Observations from Bradford August 23, 1794. Dunlap and Claypoole's American Daily Advertiser, July 25, 1794: 'This day is published | and sold by | Thomas Bradford, | price one fifth of a dollar | Observations on the Emigration of Dr. | Joseph Priestley, and on the several | addresses delivered to him on his arrival in New- | York &c. July 25.' Also Gazette of the United States, same. S.T. Evans, Vol. 1, p. 157.

As to the wording of the title, in the 'Life and Adventures of Peter Porcupine' (No. 19a) Cobbett wrote (p. 40) that the 'Observations' were 'Published for the Purchasers' by Thomas Bradford. Samuel F. Bradford, Thomas' son, in his 'The Impostor Detected' (No. 136), on p. 14 of 'A Refreshment' annexed, states that the first edition of the 'Observations' contained the following 'at the bottom of the title page' viz. 'Philadelphia: printed by Thomas Bradford, No. 8, South Front Street.' Evans in his reconstruction of the title added the words 'By Peter Porcupine.' However, these words are not in the New York and London reprints (Nos. 2b and 2c), nor in Cobbett's next work 'A Bone to Gnaw' (No. 3a). The first use of the pseudonym is believed to be in 'A Kick for a Bite' (No. 4a), which is dated March 6, 1795.

The Observations are a bitter attack on Priestley because he was representing himself as a victim of English persecution. Priestley's home, manuscripts, and apparatus had been burnt by a mob in Birmingham, England. Cobbett felt that Priestley got his just deserts, having attacked hereditary monarchy, praised the French revolutionaries, claimed that trinitarians were idolatrous, and advocated that dissenters should share in tithes. Cobbett asserted that Priestley's scientific reputation was founded on plagiarism and his writings were below mediocrity.

2b Observations | on the | emigration | of | Dr. Joseph Priestly [sic], | and on the several addresses delivered | to him, on his arrival at New-York. | [rule] | [four lines of verse from] | Boileau | [rule] | Philadelphia, printed:-New-York, re-printed, | M,DCC,XCIV.

[A]–E^4=20 leaves, 8vo; (3)4–40 ¶ Evans 26778 (Evans inserted 'by Peter Porcupine' in the title); Pearl 4 ¶ cty; MH

Contents: title, blank, 'Observations, &c.' [3]–40. Type ornaments top p. [3].

Some errors noted: p. 9, third last 'guillontine'; p. 18, l. 1 'sit' for 'sat'; p. 20, l. 10 'Amercian'; p. 25, l. 6 'tetaliation'. p. 32, sub-title 'The Pot-Shop A Fable.' In the title the first 'n' is broken. 'Priestly' is used throughout.

2c Observations | on the | emigration | of | Dr. Joseph Priestley, | and on the several addresses delivered | to him, on his arrival at New-York. | [rule] | [four lines of verse from] | Boileau. | [rule] | Philadelphia, printed: | London: re-printed for John Stockdale, | Piccadilly. | [rule] | 1794. | [Price One Shilling and Six-pence.]

[A]–H^4=32 leaves, 8vo.; (3)4–63(1); second leaves signed A2 etc. ¶ cty; BRIT MUS (repro)

Contents: title, blank, 'Observations, &c.' [3]–63, blank. On p. 50 subtitle: 'The Pot-Shop, a Fable'. On p. 63: 'Finis'. The text is the same as the previous entry. In the British Museum copy there apparently is no catchword on page 28. Reviewed in Gentleman's Magazine, London, June 1795.

2d Observations | on the | emigration | of | Dr. Joseph Priestley, | and on the several addresses delivered | to him on his arrival at

New-York | [rule] | [four lines of verse from] Boileau. | [rule] | New edition | [rule] | Philadelphia, printed: | London: re-printed for John Stockdale, | Piccadilly. | [rule] | 1794. | [Price One Shilling and Six-pence.]

Same description as previous entry but a new setting of type, with different press numbering. Pp. [2] and [64] contain advertise-ments, and the catchwords are missing on pp. 17 and 20. ¶ cty; nn

2e   Observations | on the | emigration | of | Dr. Joseph Priestley, | and on the | several addresses | delivered to him on his arrival at New York. | [rule] | [four lines of verse from] | Boileau. | [rule] | Philadelphia: | Printed by Tho. Bradford, No. 8, South Front-Street,–1794. | London, Re-printed; | and sold by W. Richarson, Cornhill, G. Kearsley, Fleet- | Street, and J. Debrett, Piccadilly, opposite Burlington- | House; Swinney & Co. Birmingham; Haz-ard | and Meyler, Bath; and Bulgin and |Sheppard, Bristol [1794].

[A]–H⁴=32 leaves, 21 cm; (3)4–63(1); second leaves signed A2 etc. ¶ Birmingham Reference Library (repro.)

Contents: title, blank, 'Observations, &c' [3]–63, blank. On page 50 subtitle: 'The Pot-Shop, a Fable.' Text same as previous entries.

2f   ———. [π]¹ A,B⁷=15 leaves; (3)4–30. Third leaf, fourth leaf signed A3; tenth leaf B2; eleventh leaf B3 ¶ cty; mb (Readex Mi-croprint for Evans 26777).

Contents: title, blank, 'Observations, &c.' [3]–30. Text same as preceding entries. P. 25, l. 3, subtitle 'The Pot-Shop, a Fable'. Foot of p. 30 'The End'. Last word on p. 6: 'unpadronable'.

2g   ———. Same description as 2f except the date 1794 is added to the foot of the title page. 22.5 cm. ¶ cty.

Note: Pearl 4 suggests there were Birmingham and Liverpool editions in 1794. These have not been located.

2h   Observations | on the | emigration | of | Dr. Joseph Priestley, | and on the several addresses delivered to him, on | his arrival at New-York, | with additions; | containing many curious and interest-ing facts on | the subject, not known here, when the | first edition was published: | together with | a comprehensive story | of a | farmer's bull | [rule] | The Third Edition | [rule] | [four lines of verse from] Boileau. | [rule] | Philadelphia: | Published by Thomas Bradford, No. 8, South- | Front-Street | [rule] | 1795. [Printed by Richard Folwell-Evans].

[A]–L⁴=44 leaves, 8 vo; (3)4–6(1)8–81(2)84–88. Second leaves signed except H2, I2 and L2 ¶ Evans 28439; Sabin 13899; Pearl 4 ¶ ctY; MWA; NN

Contents: title, blank, Introductory Address, | to the Gazetteers of the City | of Philadelphia. [3]–6; Observations, &c. &c. [7]–81; Copyright secured [82]. 'The | Short but comprehensive | Story | of | a Farmer's Bull' [83]–88. Dated at foot of p. 6: 'Philadelphia | Feb. 8th 1795'. At p. 50 subtitle 'The Pot-Shop, a Fable': At p. 62 swelling rule. On p. 88 'Finis'. Beginning with p. 62 the matter is new in this edition, as well as the 'Introductory Address', and notes pp. 9, 26, 35, 42, 52, 53 and 56.

Some errors noted: p. 49, 6th line from bottom, 'seratch'; p. 72, 10th line from bottom, 'usuage'; p. 75, l. 18 'Purgerers'; p. 79, l. 11 'propable'; p. 88, l. 2 'cows-lips.'

Eighty-fourth Pennsylvania district copyright issued to Thomas Bradford, January 30, 1795.

In the Introductory Address, Cobbett, with mock humility, chides the newsmen for their harsh judgment of the first edition. He concludes: 'If...I am doomed to suffer your applauses, I trust, that he who is preparing me the chastisement, will give me fortitude to bear it like a man.' [p. 6].

There are a few small word changes and in one instance a charge is softened. In the first paragraph on p. 10 the words: 'and doctrines were there held forth subversive of all civil and religious order' became: 'Here it was that the Doctor beat his drum ecclesiastic, to raise recruits in the cause of rebellion.' In the new matter beginning on p. 62, Cobbett says Priestley fled England rather than reply to charges by Harrington of plagiarism in regard to his theory of the composition of water.

In the Story of a Farmer's Bull, Cobbett shows his farmboy humor. The peaceable bull is goaded by a troublesome fellow until it breaks loose and does great damage. After it is finally confined, the fellow 'set to work bottling up his own f--ts, and selling them for superfine inflammable air, and what's still worse, had the impudence to want a patent for the discovery....' [p. 87]. When he was exposed as a fraud, one dark night he moved into the next parish.

2i   Bradford's Fourth Edition | [rule] | Observations | on the | emigration | of | Dr. Joseph Priestley, | and on the several addresses delivered to | him, on his arrival at New-York, | with additions; | containing many curious and interesting facts on | the subject, not known here, when the | first edition was published: | together with | a comprehensive story, | of a | farmer's bull | [rule] | by Peter Porcupine | [rule] | [four lines from] | Boileau | [rule] | Philadelphia: | published by Thomas Bradford, | printer, book-seller & stationer, | No. 8, | South-Front-Street. | 1796.

[A]–L⁴=44 leaves, 8vo; (3)4–6(1)8–81(2)84–88. Second leaves signed C2–G2, K2 ¶ Evans 30218 ¶ cty; mwa; nn

Contents: title, blank, Introduction [3]–6, Observations & [7]–81, Copyright-secured, The | Short but Comprehensive | Story | of | a Farmer's Bull. [83]–88. P. 50, subtitle 'The Pot-Shop, A Fable'; P. 62 thick-thin rule; p. 88: rule, 'FINIS', rule.

This is a faithful reprint of the third edition, with, however, new matter making up pp. [3]–6. It represents a new setting of type. For example, all page-numbers are from a different font, and there are very many different line endings, etc. An extract from the English 'Gentleman's Magazine', pp. 4–6, is unfavorable to Priestley and flattering to Cobbett.

2j   Observations | on the | emigration | of | Dr. Joseph Priestley, | and on the several addresses delivered | to him, on his arrival at New-York. | [rule] | [four lines of French from] Boileau. | [rule] | [rule] | Philadelphia: | Printed by Thomas Bradford, No. 8, South- | front street, | M,DCC,XCVI.

[A]–E⁴G⁴G,H⁴=32 leaves, 8 vo; (3)4–64 ¶ Evans 30217 ¶ cty; mwa; nn

Contents: title, blank, Observations &c [3]–64. P. 52, subtitle 'The Pot-Shop, a Fable.' The text may go back to that of the first edition, which has been lost. Omitted is the story of the Farmer's Bull, added the previous year, 1795.

Some errors noted: P. 5, l. 24 'of' for 'from'; p. 8, l. 21 'Priestly's'; p. 9, l. 1 'honses'; p. 31, l. 2 'intented'; p. 58, l. 22 'solecims'; p. 59, l. 9 'spectable.'

2k   Observations | on the | emigration | of | Dr. Joseph Priestley: | to which is added, | a comprehensive story | of a | farmer's bull [rule | [four lines from] Boileau | [rule] | [Philadelphia: Printed by Richard Folwell, No. 33 Carter's Alley. 1797.]

[A]–L⁴=44 leaves, 8 vo; pages as in No. 2h, and of a similar description. ¶ cty; mwa

This pamphlet is found separately and as a part of Volume 1 of Porcupine's Works, 1797 (No. 34c). In the copies seen, each signature has 'Vol. 1' alongside to the left. This would indicate a publication in 1797, and that Evans 28440 and Pearl 4 are not correct in assigning 1795 as the publication date. Printing is assigned to Folwell on the basis of his advertisement at the end: 'Printing | done with | Fidelity, Expedition and Care, | by | Richard Folwell, | No. 33, Carter's Alley.'

2l   Observations | on the | emigration | of | Dr. Joseph Priestley, | and on | the several addresses | delivered to him, on his arrival at New York. | with additions; | containing many curious and interesting facts on the subject, not | known when the former editions were published: | together | with a comprehensive story | of a | farmer's bull. | [rule] | By Peter Porcupine. | [rule] | The fourth edition. | [rule] | [four lines from] Boileau. | [rule] | Printed at Philadelphia. | London: | re-printed for J. Wright, opposite Old Bond Street, | Piccadilly; | 1798.

[A]–E⁸F²=42 leaves, 8 vo.; (5)vi,vii(2)2–68(1)70–73(2)2. Second, third and fourth leaves signed B–E; also F2 ¶ Pearl 4; Sabin 13899 ¶ rpjcb

Contents: half-title, blank, title, blank, introductory address [v]–vii; blank, Observations [1]–68; The | short but comprehensive | story | of a | farmer's bull [69]–73; blank; cheap political tracts [1]2. The tracts comprise 10 titles, including Democratic Principles, part the first, and same, part the second. Subtitle page 38. Swelling rule page 49.

Errors noted: Pages 57, 58 'Francklin'; page 68 the catchword is 'Th' for 'The.'

2m   ———. A variant in which the error on page 68 is corrected and in the title page quotation, last line, 'nest' has a semi-colon above. ¶ rpjcb.

2A   La | Nomenclature | Anglaise. | contenant, | 1⁰. une liste des verbes Anglais qui sont suivis | des particules, avec un exemple en

Anglais | et en Français contre chaque particule. | 2⁰. Une liste alphabétique de tous les verbes irré- | guliers | [four descriptive lines] | 3⁰. Une liste des verbes qui ne prennent | point de to avant l'infinitif qui suit. | avec | une introduction et des notes utiles. | [rule] | Philadelphie: | Imprimé par Thomas Bradford, N⁰. 8, Front | street, (sud.) | 1794.

[A]–F⁶E⁴=40 leaves, 12 mo; (3)ii–iv,5–63(2)66–76(1)78. Second and third leaves signed A2 A3–F2 F3 ¶ Evans 27418 ¶ MWA

Contents: title; blank; [rule] Introduction [in French] [i]–iv; Liste des verbes [text vertical] 5–63; blank; [row of type ornaments] | Liste des verbes irrégulieres [in three vertical columns] [65]–75; [row of type ornaments] | Liste des verbes. 76; [row of type ornaments] | Notes [77]78.

3a   A | Bone to Gnaw, | for the | Democrats; | or, | Observations | on | a pamphlet, | entitled, | 'The Political Progress of Britain.' | [rule] Philadelphia: | printed for the purchasers. | [rule] | 1795.

[A]–I⁴=36 leaves, 8 vo; (3),iv,v,(2),2–66. Second leaves signed A2 etc. except in C. ¶ Evans 28431; Pearl 5; Sabin 13875 ¶ CtY; MWA

Contents: title, blank, Preface [iii]–v, blank, caption: 'A | Bone to Gnaw, | for the | Democrats'. [1]–66. Dated at end of Preface: 'Philadelphia, Jan. 10th, 1795.' On page 66: 'FINIS.' The printer was Thomas Bradford. 85th Penna. District copyright issued to Thomas Bradford 30 January, 1795. Running title 'Preface' on iv. and v. Dated in Porcupine's Works, (No. 59) 'January, 1795' Gazette of the United States, January 16, 1795: 'This day was published [price 25 cents] and for sale at T. Bradford's book store...'

Errors noted: p. 2, l. 1 'phamphlet'; p. 2, l. 22 'wether'; p. 4, l. 7 from foot 'corrrespondent'; p. 17, footnote last word, 'he', above the line; p. 31, l. 2 'New Hamshire'; p. 36, last line 'east' for least'; p. 53, l. 21 'wetted' for 'whetted'; p. 55, l. 10 'lilly'; p. 55, l. 14 'batterred'.

The ostensible target of this work, 'The Political Progress of Britain,' was by James Thomson Callender. Originally published in Edinburgh in 1792, it resulted in his flight from England as a political refugee. It was republished by Callender in Philadelphia November 1794 (Evans 26725; see No. 130). Cobbett does not spend many pages on Callender. His principal thrust is on American public affairs: the democratic societies, slavery, Thomas Paine, Bache's Aurora and Andrew Brown's Philadelphia Gazette, Madison's resolutions on commerce with Britain, the Whiskey Insurrection of 1794, and so forth. It is a vigorous plea for the English point of view.

Extracts: 'Reader, if you have a shop to mind, or any other business to do, I advise you to go and do it, and let this book alone; for, I can assure you, it contains nothing of half so much importance to you, as the sale of a skein of thread or a yard of tape.' p. [iii]. '...my work answers to its title, and consequently, nobody but the Democrats can have any thing to do with it. Nor does it court their approbation; I throw it in amongst them, as amongst a kennel of hounds; let them snarl and growl over it, and gnaw it and slaver it; the more they wear out their fangs this way, the less dangerous will be their bite hereafter.' p. v. As to Callender: 'Is it anything to us whether he prefers Charley to George, or George to Charley, any more than wether [sic] he used to eat his burgoo with his fingers or with a horn spoon?' p. 2. As to *'the mania reformatio'*: 'if this malady is not stopped at once, by the help of a hempen necklace, or some other remedy equally efficacious, it never fails to break out with Atheism, Robbery, Unitarianism, Swindling, Jacobinism, Massacres, Civic Feasts and insurrections.' p. 5. As to allegations by the Democrats of a British influence: 'Reader, when you were a little boy, did you never carry on a secret correspondence with the pies and tarts; and, when, by the rattling of the plates or some other accident, you were like to be caught at it, did you never raise a hue and cry against the poor dogs and cats? Those who look upon the conduct of our Democrats as unnatural, forget their own little roguish tricks.' p. 25. 'The truth is, those among us who have made the most noise, and have expressed the most rancour against Great Britain, seem to have done it only to cover their enmity to the Federal Government'. p. 27. On slavery: 'Oh! happy Carolina! happy, thrice happy Virginia! No tyrannical aristocrat dares to lord it over the free born swains who cultivate the delicious weed, that adorns, first thy lovely fields and then the lovelier chops of the drivling drunkard! After having spent the day in singing hymns to the Goddess of Liberty, the virtuous Democrat gets him home to his peaceful dwelling, and sleeps, with his *property* secure beneath his roof, yea, sometimes in his very *arms*; and when his *"industry"* has enhanced its value, it bears to a new owner the proofs of his Democratic Delicacy!' p. 48. On Thomas Paine: *'The Political Progress* [No. 130] is in politics, what Mad Tom's *Age of Reason* is in religion, and they have both met with encouragement from some people here, from nearly the same motive.

Had not the last mentioned piece been suppressed in England, there is every reason to believe, that it would never have rivaled the Bible among us, in so many families as it does. What a preposterous thing!' p. 52.

The following refers to Pennsylvania Congressman John Swanwick: 'He has taken it into his head to run dangling from one Boarding School to another, in order to acquire by the art of speechifying, a reputation for which nature seems to have disqualified him. My imagination cannot form to itself anything more perfectly comic than to see a diminutive superannuated bachelor, cocked up on a stool, and spouting out compliments to an assembly of young Misses.' p. 56. As to a report quoting Madison that in the event of a revolution in Britain, he expected the Peerage would come here and he would receive them: "'Tis a pity the poor devils are not apprised of all this. It would certainly be an act of humanity in our good Citizen to let them know what blessings he has in store for them: they seem attached to their Coronets and Coach-and-sixes at present; but were they informed that they can have as much homony and fat pork as they can gobble down (once every day of their lives,) liberty to chew tobacco and smoke all the week, and to ride out on the meeting-going mare on Sundays, it might tempt them to quit their baubles and their poor bit of an Island without a struggle, and fly to the free State of Virginia.' p. 59. As to England: 'Let us open our eyes; it is pretty near time, if we do not wish to be led blindfolded [by the French] to the end of the farce, and even after it is over-...Because a war once existed between the two countries is that a reason that they should now hate one another? They had their battle out; let them follow the good old custom, drink and shake hands, and not suffer themselves to be set together by the ears by a parcel of out-landish butchers.' p. 64.

Cobbett was intentionally deceptive in writing [p. 60]: 'For my part, the English are no favourites of mine; I care very little if their Island were swallowed up by an Earthquake....' This statement embarrassed him later and was used effectively against him and Federalists generally. See National Intelligencer & Washington Advertiser, Aug. 28, 1809, p. 3, col. 2, where the quotation is slightly altered.

3b   A | Bone to Gnaw, | for the | Democrats; | or, | observations | on | a pamphlet, | entitled, | 'The Political Progress of Britain' | [rule] | The Second Edition, Revised | [rule] | [two lines from] | La

Pompadour. | [rule] | Philadelphia: | Printed by Thomas Bradford, No. 8, South | Front Street. | [rule] | 1795.

[A]–I⁴=36 leaves, 8 vo; (3),iv,v,(2),41,3–66 Second leaves signed A2, D2–I2 ¶ Evans 28432; Pearl 5; Sabin 13875 ¶ cty; mwa; nn

Contents: title, blank, Preface [iii]–v, blank, caption 'A | Bone to Gnaw, | for the | Democrats' [1]–66. Dated at end of Preface: 'Philadelphia. Feb. 19th, 1795'. Foot of page 66: 'Finis | The Copy Right | Secured ac | cording to | law: | 1795' | As noted, page '41' for '2'. A new setting of type. Page numbers are in brackets instead of parentheses. Page 43, note, 'two thousand five hundred heads' is changed to 'two hundred & fifty thousand heads.' Running title in preface.

Errors noted: p. [2], l. 1 'phamphlet'; p. 4, l. 7 from bottom 'corrrespondent'; p. 11, note l. 8 'Unatarian'; p. 15, l. 2 'çaira' for 'ça ira'; p. 25, l. 21 'thatthere'; p. 27, last line 'fiften'; p. 44, par. 2 'Maddison'; p. 55, l. 10 'lilly'.

3c ⸺. Here the only second leaves signed are A2 and D2. The note formerly on p. 43 is on p. 44. At the foot of p. 66: 'FINIS | Copy right secured according to law'. Page numbers in brackets except 66 in parentheses. Page 41 for page 2. Errors noted on pages 4 and 11 corrected. This would appear to be a new setting of type except the first signature. ¶ njr (as part of bound volume—see 34e)

3d ⸺. The title is the same as 3b, except 'Third' replaces 'Second' before 'Edition'. 8 vo. Same collation, except A2 not signed. Same contents, with same errors, except dated at the end of the Preface, Philadelphia, March 10th, 1795. ¶ Evans 28433 ¶ cty; mwa

This is a reissue of 3b with, however, signatures [A] and F reset and also G1 and H1. Samples of differences:

Sig.	Page	3d	3b
[A]	[iii]	Short rule below 'Preface'	No such rule
	[1]	Ornamental swelling rule 3.8 cm.	Plain swelling rule 3.3 cm.
	2	Numbered correctly	Numbered 41
F	35, l. 4	Ends 'strum'	Ends 'strumpets'
	37, l. 1	Begins 'nance'	Begins 'tenance'
	39, l. 26	'Tyger'	'Tiger'
	41 note	'Payne'	'Paine'
G	43 note, l. 13	'Liberty of the French'	'French Liberty'
H	51 last	'sates'	'States'

Use of the same type on other pages is indicated by the common errors and also peculiarities of type. For example, p. 52, l. 24, the word 'met' has a broken 'm' in both issues.

3e   A | Bone to Gnaw, | for the | Democrats; | or, | observations | on | a pamphlet, | entitled, | 'The Political Progress of Britain.' | [rule] | by Peter Porcupine | [rule] | The fourth edition, with additions by the author. | [rule] | [two lines from] La Pompadour | [rule] | Philadelphia: | Printed by Thomas Bradford, No. 8, South | Front-Street. | [rule] | 1796.

[A]–I⁴=36 leaves, 8 vo; (3)iv–vi;(1)2–66. Leaf D2 signed. ¶ Evans in 30234 (No. 9e), second title ¶ cty; mwa

Contents: title, blank, Preface [iii]–vi; A | Bone to Gnaw | for the | Democrats. [1]–66. At foot of p. 66. 'Finis. | Copy right secured according to law.' Dated on p. vi 'Philadelphia. March 10th, 1795.'

This edition is completely reset and contains a number of textual changes, including these: p. 7, 3rd l. from bottom, added, 'as the girls say,'; p. 9, first footnote revised; p. 10, footnote omits reference to Scotch in the American war; p. 27, final word 'from' is missing; p. 30 note 'Algierines' is corrected but 'Potuguese' is then misspelled; pp. 36, 37, new note added on Mifflin and Brissot; p. 39 l. 6 'Curia' becomes 'Cloacina' and text is rearranged as to 'nosegays of straw'; p. 40, note is new; p. 57, revised note identifies the 'democrat'; and p. 66, note is omitted as to the burning of the British flag.

3f   A | Bone to Gnaw, | for the | Democrats; | or, | observations | on a | pamphlet, | entitled, | 'The Political Progress of Britain'. | [rule] | The third edition, revised. | [rule] | [two lines of French from] La Pompadour. | [rule] | Philadelphia: | Printed by William Young, | for William Cobbett, opposite Christ's Church. | [rule] | 1797.

[A]–I⁴=36 leaves, 8 vo; (3)iv,v(2)41,3–66. Second leaf signed D2 only. ¶ Evans 31945; Sabin 13877 ¶ cty

Contents: title, blank, preface [iii]–v, dated Philadelphia Feb. 19th, 1795; blank; A | Bone to Gnaw | for the | Democrats. [1]–66 p. Foot of p. 66 Finis | Copyright secured according to law.

3g   ———. [M]–U⁴=36 leaves, 8 vo.; (3)92,93(2)96–160 ¶ cty; mwa

Contents: title, blank, preface [91]–93 dated Philadelphia, Feb. 19th, 1795; blank; A bone to gnaw [95]–160. Running title in preface.

Second title in Porcupine's Works. Vol. 1, 1797, No. 34a. A new setting of type, with new pagination. Errors noted: p. 109, l. 2 'caira'; p. 134, l. 17 'tyger'.

3h   A | Bone to Gnaw | for the | Democrats. | By Peter Porcupine; | author of the Bloody Buoy, etc. etc. | [four lines of verse] | [rule] | To which is prefixed | a rod, | for the | backs of the critics; | [five descriptive lines] | By Humphrey Hedgehog. | melius non tangere. | [rule] | London: | Printed for J. Wright, opposite old Bond-Stseet [sic], | Piccadilly. | [rule] | 1797.

[π]^{2}a–e^6[f]–h^6;[A]–P^6=140 leaves, 12 mo; (5)ii–lxxiii;lxxiii–lxxv;lxxvii–xcv(1);(3)iv,v,(2),8–88;(3),92–96;95–175(3) Second and third leaves signed except p. 93. P. lxxxl for lxxxi. ¶ Pearl 5, Sabin 64161 ¶ ctY

Contents: half-title, blank, title, blank, A Rod [i]–xcv; Table of Contents; title 'A Bone...'; blank; Preface [iii]–v, dated Philadelphia, Feb. 19th, 1795; blank; A Bone [7]–88; Title: 'A Bone...Part II'; blank, Preface [91]–96,95,96; A Bone 97–147; Democratic Memoirs 148–175; 3 pages of New Publications. P. 159 the note is pied and signature O3 reversed.

Pearl identifies Humphrey Hedgehog as John Gifford [i.e. John Richards Green], 1758–1818, English author, editor. The 'Rod' is a vigorous defense of Cobbett against his English critics. The 'Bone' and 'Bone...Part II' follow the 1795 American editions. The eleven 'New Publications' listed include: 5. The Bloody Buoy...Third Edition; 6. Memoirs of the Life and Adventures of Peter Porcupine; 7. The Life of Thomas Paine; 8. A Letter to the Infamous Tom Paine; 9. Observations on the Debates of the American Congress.

3i   ———. A variant in which the errors noted on page 159 have been corrected ¶ NN

4a   A | Kick for a Bite; | or, | review upon review; | with a | critical essay, | on the works of | Mrs. S. Rowson; | in | a letter | to the editor, or editors, | of the | American Monthly Review. | [rule] | By Peter Porcupine, | Author of the Bone to Gnaw, for the Democrats. | [rule] | 'Autant de traits que d'ennemis.' | [rule] | Philadelphia: | Printed by Thomas Bradford, No. 8, South | Front Street. | [rule] | 1795.

[A]–D^4=16 leaves, 8 vo; (5)6–31(1) ¶ Evans 28436; Pearl 6, Sabin 13866 ¶ ctY; NN

Contents: title, blank, 'Advertisement', blank, caption: 'To the Editor'. [5]–31, page of Bradford advertisements. Dated at foot of page 31 'March 6th, 1795.' 90th Penna. District Copyright issued to Thomas Bradford, 17 March 1795. Dated in Porcupine's Works, London 1801 (No. 59), 'February, 1795.' P. 18, l. 9 'pontentate.' p. 21, l. 1 'you' for 'your'; 'loo' for 'look', foot p. 27.

This work marked the first use of the name 'Peter Porcupine' by Cobbett. It is mainly a reply to a review of Cobbett's 'Bone to Gnaw' which appeared in the February 1795 issue of the 'American Monthly Review.' The editor of the 'Review' was Samuel Harrison Smith (1772–1845) and Pearl says he wrote the piece Cobbett is here objecting to. Apparently Smith's review was in fact rather mild and he had written of Cobbett: 'His magical pen throws every object into a ludicrous light.' (Quoted in Clark, page 28). The discussion of Mrs. Rowson begins at page 20 and she is dealt with rather severely.

The Bradford advertisements on the final page include as 'just published': 'a third edition, revised, of the Bone to Gnaw for the Democrats...also a third edition of the 'Observations on the Emigration of Dr. Joseph Priestley.'

Extracts: '...if you should see a person with one ear hanging down upon his cheek, like the ear of an old sow, that is Peter Porcupine, at your service.' p. 10. 'When I see you flourishing with a metaphor, I feel as much anxiety as I do when I see a child playing with a razor.' p. 12. 'Now comes the agreeable part of my task.— How pleasant is it to pass from censure to commendation! It is like turning from the frowns of surly Winter, to behold the smiling Spring come dancing o'er the daisied lawn, crowned with garlands and surrounded with melody. Yes, Sir, I cannot deny that there is one thing in your *critique* that has my entire approbation; I mean its brevity.' p. 15. '...what excuse have you for having omitted to take notice of the voluminous productions of the celebrated *Mrs. Rowson?*...when a lady tunes her lyre, he must be a sniveling devil of a critic whose bow remains unstrung.' p. 20. 'Who knows but our present house of Representatives, for instance, may be succeeded by members of the other sex ? What information might not the Democrats and grog-shop politicians expect from their communicative loquacity!...If the speaker should happen to be with child that would be nothing odd to us, who have so long been accustomed to the sight; and if she should even lie in, during the sessions, her place might be supplied by her aunt or grandmother.' p. 24. '...let us not damp a genius that promises such ample encouragement to our infant manufactories of ink and paper.' p. 29.

Susanna Haswell Rowson (1762–1824) was a favorite actress in the Philadelphia theatre at the time. Twenty of her writings are listed in Evans. In the introduction to her 'Trials of the Human Heart' published in four volumes in April 1795, she noticed that 'a kind of loathsome reptile...lately crawled over' some of her works. (See R.W.G. Vail, Susanna Haswell Rowson, Worcester 1933, p. 39).

4b ————. A variant in which at the foot of p. 27 'loo' has been corrected to 'look'; page 29, line 2 has 'that that' instead of 'that;' line 30 has 'literary' instead of 'Literary'. Except for page 29, the type seems to be the same setting. ¶ cᴛʏ

4c A | Kick for a Bite; | or, | review upon review; | with a | critical essay, | on the works of | Mrs. S. Rowson; | in | a letter | To the editor, or editors, | of the | American Monthly Review. | [rule] | Second edition. | [rule] | By Peter Porcupine, | [rule] | 'Autants de traits que d'ennemis'. | [rule] | Philadelphia: | printed by Thomas Bradford. | [rule] | 1796.

[A]–D⁴=16 leaves, 8 vo; (5)6–31(1) ¶ Evans 30210 ¶ cᴛʏ; ᴍᴡᴀ; ɴɴ

Contents: title, blank, Advertisement, blank, To the Editor [5]–31, blank. Dated at foot of p. 31 'March 6th 1795.' Follows the text of the first edition. It appears to be reset except for signature D. Some comparisons:

Page	First Edition	Second Edition
[1]	'Review upon Review,' 7.8 cm.	Same, 6.4 cm.
9, l. 33	'twitched'	'twiched'
18, l. 9	'pontentate'	'potentate'
20, l. 29	'shown'	'shewn'
24, l. 11	'not'	'not not'
27 last	'loo'	'look'

4d ————. A variant in which the final page advertises books 'just published' by Bradford, including a third edition of Bone to Gnaw and a third edition of Observations ...Priestley. ¶ cᴛʏ

5a Le | Tuteur Anglais, | ou | grammaire regulière | de la | langue anglaise | en | deux parties. | premiere partie, contenant une ana-lyse | des parties de l'oraison. | Seconde partie, contenant la syntaxe complete | de la langue anglaise, avec des thèmes, | analogues aux différens sujets | qu'on y a traités | [rule] | par William Cobbett. | [rule] | A Philadelphie: | chez Thomas Bradford, libraire, | Première Rue Sud, No. 8. | [rule] | 1795.

[A]–XX^4=176 leaves, 8 vo.; (3),iv,(1),vi,(3),ii,(1)2–78(1)80–82(1)84–187(1)189–340,(2). Colophon page 340: 'Imprimé par Thomas Bradford.' Second leaves signed except C,G,T,Hh,Ll,Nn, Pp-Tt,Xx ¶ Evans 28441; Pearl 7 ¶ MWA

Contents: title, 'entered according to law', Preface [iii], iv; Table des matieres [v]vi; Premiere Partie; blank, Introduction [i]ii, text [1]–340, 2 pages of advertisements. The advertisements include 'La Nomenclature Anglaise' (No. 2A). In a contemporary calf binding with a label on the spine lettered 'Grammaire | de Cobbett'. Page 74 for 274. A text in French on English grammar, giving the parts of speech and rules for the formation of grammatical sentences in English. 89th Pennsylvania District copyright issued to Thomas Bradford 17 March 1795.

In the second part of 'The Impostor Detected' (No. 136) page 13, Thomas Bradford's son wrote that Cobbett received for Le Tuteur 'a considerable sum of money...together with two hundred copies of the work.' Later editions: Paris 1801 (No. 5c) as 'Le Maitre d' Anglais' and Philadelphia 1805 (No. 5d); many other editions; by 1861, the 35th edition was reached (Muirhead, p. 7).

5b   ———. A variant in which p. [viii] contains 'Faut à corriger', namely, that on p. 22 at the foot 'that' should be 'these'. In a contemporary calf binding with red leather label on the spine reading: 'Grammaire de Cobbett'. ¶ NN

5c   Le | Maitre Anglais, | ou | grammaire raisonée, | pour faciliter aux français | l'étude de la langue anglaise; | par William Cobbett: | ouvrage élémentaire, adopté par le Prytanée Français. | seconde édition, | soigneusement corrigée, et augmentée | notamment d'une table alphabétique des matières; | par F. Marguery, professeur de belles-lettres. | [rule] | à Paris, | chez [bracket] Fayolle, Libraire, rue Honoré, No. 1442. | Warée, Libraire, au Louvre. | Masson, Besson et Bossange. | AN 1X.—1801.

[π]^{6}1–21^{8}22–30^{4}31^3=213 leaves, 19.6 cm; (5)vi–viii(1)x–xii(1) 2(1)4–414 except 76,79,341,392,395 ¶ NjR

Contents: half-title, imprimerie de Laran, title, blank, advertisse-ment [v]–viii, chapitres [ix]–xii: Introduction [1]2; text [3]–394; Table [395]–414. Lettered on spine 'Grammaire Anglaise'. There were further Paris editions in 1803 and 1810.

5d   Le Tuteur Anglais, | ou | grammaire regulière | de la | langue Anglaise | en | deux parties. | Premiere partie, contenant | une ana-lyse des parties de l'oraison. | Seconde partie, contenant | la syntaxe complete de la langue Anglaise, avec | des thèmes, analogues aux différens sujets qu'on | y a traités | [rule] | par William Cobbett. | [rule] | Seconde édition: | corrigee sur celle qui a été imprimée à Paris sous l'inspec- | tion du prytanée français, et terminée d'une liste alphabé- | tique des explications et règles contenues dans cet ouvrage | [rule] | à Philadelphie: | chez Thomas et William Brad-ford, libraires, première | rue sud. No. 8 | [rule] | 1805.

[A]–Tt⁴=168 leaves, 21.5 cm; (6)7,8(1)2(1)4–72(1)74,75(1)77–288(1)290–316(1)318–328 ¶ A.B. 8202 ¶ MWA; NN

Contents: title, copyright, Preface, avertissement [4],[5]; Table [6]–8; Introduction [1],2; première partie [3]–72; second partie [73]–316; Liste [317]–328.

The MWA copy is in contemporary calf with a red leather label on the spine lettered 'Grammaire | par | Cobbett.'

6a   Part II. | [rule] | A | Bone to Gnaw, | for the | Democrats; | containing, | 1st. Observations on a patriotic pamphlet. | entitled, | 'Proceedings of the United Irishmen.' | 2dly. Democratic principles exemplified by example. | 3dly. Democratic Memoires; or, an ac-count of some re- | cent feats performed by the Frenchified ci- | tizens of the United States | of America. | [rule] | By Peter Porcu-pine | [rule] | [4 lines of verse] | [rule] | Philadelphia: | Printed & sold by Thomas Bradford, No. 8, South | Front Street | [rule] | 1795.

[A]⁴[B]–G⁴G⁴I⁴K²=38 leaves, 8 vo; (3)iv–viii(1)2–66,(2). Sec-ond leaves signed B2–E2,I2 ¶ Evans 28434; Pearl 5; Sabin 13866 ¶ CtY; MWA

Contents: title, copyright secured, Preface [iii]–viii, caption 'A Bone to Gnaw, &c. Part II [1]–66; 2 pages of advertisement. Catch-words on pages 20 and 42. Running titles pages iv–viii. Captions on p. 21: 'Democratic Principles, | Illustrated by Example' and on p. 43 'Democratic Memoires'. Dated at end of preface 'May 28, 1795.' p. 5, l. 3 'of motto' for 'motto of'; p. 26, last line : 'in chat case';

page numbers 65 and 66 in parentheses instead of brackets. Dated in Porcupine's Works, (No. 59): March, 1795. However, a note on page 45 refers to the Philadelphia Gazette of 16th May, 1795.

In the Preface Mrs. Rowson is again criticized (see 4a) as well as her defender, John Swanwick. There are passing swipes at 'Tom the Tinker' (Thomas Mifflin) and Samuel Harrison Smith. Pages [1] through 20 attack the pamphlet 'Proceedings of the Society of United Irishmen of Dublin. Philadelphia, printed for Thomas Stephens by Jacob Johnson. 1795' (Evans 28590) Says Cobbett, 'I am much mistaken if it will ever be used any where but in the *temple of Cloacina.*' (p. 3). Cobbett's attitude on democracy: '...universal suffrage...is the master wheel in the machine of reformation, as it transfers the power from the hands of the rich into the hands of the poor...' (p. 7). Pages 21 to the end consist mainly of descriptions of the savagery of the French democrats, particularly in the butchery of the citizens of Lyons, France. As to Cobbett's 'puff indirect' for this work, see The Impostor Detected (No. 136).

6b ————. same transcription.

[A]⁴[B]–I⁴K², 8 vo; second leaves signed B2–E2, I2 ¶ cty; mwa; nn Pagination and contents same.

6c Part II | [rule] | A | Bone to Gnaw, | for the | Democrats; | containing, | [as in first edition] America. | Second edition, | with a new preface, to which is subjoined | a song, to be sung by the Democrats | at their future nocturnal meetings. | [rule] | By Peter Porcupine. | [rule] | Philadelphia: | printed & sold by Thomas Bradford, No. 8, South | Front Street | [rule] | 1795.

[A]⁴[B]–I⁴K²=38 leaves, 8 vo; (3)iv–vii(2),2–66(2). Second leaves signed B2–E2, I2 ¶ Evans 28435 ¶ cty; mwa

Contents: title, blank, Preface [iii]–vii, copyright secured, A Bone to Gnaw &c. Part II [1]–66, 2 pages of advertisements. Running titles pages iv–vii. Catchwords on pages 20 and 42 and captions on pages 21 and 43 as in first edition. 100th Pennsylvania District copyright issued to Thomas Bradford 27 May 1795.

This second edition represents a new setting of the first signature. The new preface of three and one half pages is followed by a poem of six four-line stanzas, which have a swing to them. Cobbett reports that the first 'very numerous edition has been sold off in the space of six weeks.' He has scornful things to say on the premature release of the Jay Treaty by Senator Mason, 'the Blabbing Senator,' and B. F. Bache. He concludes: 'Oh, the pleasures of a second edition!' (p. vi).

6d ———. Same transcription.

[A]⁴[B]–G⁴G⁴I⁴K²=38 leaves, 8 vo, as in 6a. Second leaves signed B2–E2, I2 ¶ cty

Pagination and contents as in 6a, with same errors as noted, and ornamental swelling rule on p. [1].

6e ———. Same transcription.

[A]–G⁴G⁴I⁴K¹=37 leaves, 8 vo. Second leaves signed C2–E2, I2 ¶ cty

Pagination and contents same except no advertisements. Signature B is a new setting of type. Thus on page [1] in the preceding entry '&c' is used and the second swelling rule is ornamental. In the present entry, '&c' is used and the swelling rule is plain; the error on page 5 is corrected; etc. In second signature G, which was H, page number 56 is enclosed by brackets instead of by a bracket and a parenthesis.

6f Part II. | [rule] | A | Bone to Gnaw, | for the | Democrats; | containing, | 1st, observations on a patriotic pamphlet | entitled, | 'Proceedings of the United Irishmen.' | 2dly, Democratic Memoires; or an ac- | count of some recent feats per- | formed by the Frenchified citi- | zens of the United States | of America. | [rule] | By Peter Porcupine. | [rule] | Philadelphia: | Printed by William Young, | for William Cobbett, opposite Christ's Church. | [rule] | 1797.

[A]¹B–I⁴K¹=34 leaves, 8 vo; (3) 2–66. Fourth title of No. 34a ¶ cty; MWA; PPL

Contents: title, blank, 'A Bone to Gnaw &c. | Part II. [1]–66. Catchwords on pages 20 and 42 and captions on pages 21 and 43 as in two 1795 editions. New setting of type. The second 1795 edition (No. 6c) is followed except for the omission of prefatory matter and advertisement, and except that the title enumerates two subjects instead of three. Page numbers in parentheses instead of brackets.

Some errors noted: p. 3 l. 5 and 18, 'archieves'; p. 34 l. 16, 'sacraligious'; p. 48 l. 14, 'hording'; p. 52 second note: 'unreasanable'; p. 56 l. 2, 'veangeance'; l. 2, 3, 'vengeace'.

6g   Part II | [rule] | A Bone to Gnaw | for the | Democrats; | containing, | 1st, observations on a patriotic pamphlet, | entitled, | 'Proceedings of the United Irishmen.' | 2dly, Democratic memoirs; or an account of | some recent feats performed by the | frenchified citizens of the United | States of America. | [rule] | By Peter Porcupine. | [rule] | Philadelphia: | Printed by William Young, | for William Cobbett, opposite Christ-Church. | [rule] | 1797. ¶ Evans Supp. B9898 ¶ cty; ppl

Except for the title page, this appears to be identical with the preceding entry. There are several differences in the title page, notably 'memoirs' vs 'memoires', four lines instead of five in '2dly' and 'Christ' vs 'Christ's'. It could be argued that this is the earlier, and that 'memoires' represents a correction, in that the subtitle on page 43 begins 'Democratic Memoires...'.

6h   A Bone to Gnaw for the Democrats Part II occupies pp. [89]–175 of the London 1797 edition of A Bone to Gnaw, No. 3h supra.

7a   A Little | Plain English, | addressed to | the people of the United States, | on the | treaty, | negociated with his Britannic Majesty, | and on the conduct of | the President | relative thereto; | in answer to | 'The Letters of Franklin.' | with a supplement | containing an account of the turbulent and fac- | tious proceedings of the opposers of | the treaty | [rule] | By Peter Porcupine | [rule] | [8 lines from] | Shakespeare | [rule] | Philadelphia: | Published by Thomas Bradford, Printer, Bookseller, | and Stationer, No. 8, south front street | [rule] | 1795.

[A]–P⁴=60 leaves, 8 vo; (5),6–8(1)2–111(1). Second leaves signed B2 through O2 ¶ Evans 28437; Pearl 8; Sabin 13895 ¶ cty; mwa; nn

Contents: half-title, copyright secured, title, blank, Preface [5]–8. 'A Little | Plain English [1]–102, Supplement 103–110, Postscript 111, blank. Dated at end of preface: 'Philadelphia, August 10th 1795'. At foot of p. 111 'Finis'. 108th Pennsylvania District Copyright issued to Thomas Bradford 15 August 1795. Dated in Porcupine's Works (No. 59) 'August, 1795.'

Some errors noted: p. 9, ll. 20, 21, 'to to'; p. 26, l. 4, 'irreconcialition'; p. 54, l. 15, 'Beause'; p. 64, l. 32, 'Constiution'; p. 67. l, 16, 'incapaciating'; p. 75, ll. 17, 18, 'inteference'; p. 75, ll. 20, 27, 'intefere'; p. 76, l. 22, 'should should'; p. 96, l. 28, 'apprroved'; p. 101, l. 27, 'tripple'; p. 105, ll. 6, 7, incapaciate'; (and see next entry).

The 'Letters of Franklin' (No. 132), to which this work is largely an answer, were first published in Eleazer Oswald's 'Independent Gazetteer' in Philadelphia beginning March 9, 1795 and ending June 12, 1795. The preface as published in pamphlet form is dated June 18, 1795. It is often attributed to Oswald, but is more likely by Alexander James Dallas. In Porcupine's Works (No. 59), Vol. II, page 355 note, Cobbett identifies 'Franklin' as Dallas. In A New-Year's Gift (No. 10a), p. 68, Cobbett had asserted that the Letters were 'originally the work of' the French Minister Fauchet.

Dallas was at a disadvantage in attacking the treaty, which was being kept secret pending Senate action and Presidential signature. Before the latter occurred Stevens T. Mason, Virginia Senator, gave the text to Benjamin Franklin Bache of the Philadelphia 'Aurora.' An abstract of the Treaty appeared in the Aurora on June 29 and two days later was published in full as a pamphlet. Cobbett of course had the full text when he wrote. Dallas penned other, more effective attacks on the Treaty, notably 'Features of Mr. Jay's Treaty' published anonymously in five parts in the American Daily Advertiser July 18 to August 7, finishing just before the present work appeared.

In the Preface Cobbett asserts he is an Englishman and very proud of it. He has selected the 'Letters of Franklin' to answer since it is a fair sample of the opposition to the Treaty. In the text the first attack is on the motives of 'Franklin', a demagogue of the French faction and 'fawning mob orator.' (p. 2). Proceeding to the 'Letters' he gives them a character: 'the first seems to be the overflowings of passion bordering on insanity, and each succeeding one the fruit of a relapse' (p. 4). He analyses the three principal objections of Franklin: (1) that a commercial treaty with Great Britain is unnecessary and dangerous, (2) that the Treaty is disadvantageous, humiliating and disgraceful and (3) that the conduct of the President in regard to the Treaty has been improper and even monarchical. The 'Letters' are quoted not always exactly. James Madison is attacked: 'War was his object' (p. 9). The French are 'those men of blood, those profligate infidels, who, uniting the frivolity of the Monkey to the ferocity of the Tyger, can go dancing to the gallows, or butcher their relations to the air of ah, ca ira.' (p. 15) Great Britain is defended against charges that she let the Indians and the Algerines loose upon our citizens (p. 30). Also discussed are the failure of Great Britain to surrender the western posts and the non-payment of British merchants. (pp. 36–40). The Treaty articles are considered seriatim. In summation at one point, Cobbett says that the terms of the Treaty 'are as advantageous as you ought to have expected.' (p. 62).

A spirited defense of Washington is made, concluding with mock concern that he had not consulted the democratic society of Pennsylvania: 'Mightily "alarming," indeed, that the President should not consult this club of butchers, tinkers, broken huksters, and transatlantic traitors! Had he wanted a fellow to fell an ox or mend a kettle, to bilk his creditors or blow up an insurrection, he would have done well to address himself to the democratic society of Pennsylvania for advice; but to ask their advice in the appointment of an Envoy Extraordinary would have been as preposterous as consulting the devil in the choice of a Minister of the Gospel' (p. 70).

Some random phrases are revealing of Cobbett's viewpoint. 'The ingratitude of republics and republicans has long been proverbial' (p. 74). '...the absurdity of a government's being founded upon the presumption that the people are capable of governing themselves.' (p. 87). A long attack on the French Minister Genet occupies pp. 91–99. In the Supplement the democratic societies are further attacked. Concerning a meeting of Philadelphia citizens to protest the treaty Cobbett wrote: 'It would be useless to describe the stupid stare, the dirty shirts, and long beards, of these sovereigns, or the *patriotic* strut and imaginary consequence of their chairman and committeemen.' (p. 109). In conclusion, Cobbett points to the danger of rule by 'the lower orders of the people' and exhorts 'every honest man, every man of property, to give his hearty and sincere support to the General Government' (p. 110).

Pearl 8 suggests there were New York and Boston editions in 1795, locating no copies. Gazette of the United States, May 6, 1796, has a favorable review of this and other Cobbett works.

7b ——. Same transcription, format, collation and so forth, as the preceding entry. ¶ cty

Signatures L, N and O have been reset at least in part. Thus, there is no page number 103 and no rules above and below the word 'Supplement' on that page. The same errors appear as mentioned in the prior entry through p. 67. A comparison after that follows:

Page	7a	7b
75, l. 17, 18	inteference	inteference
l. 20	intefere	interfere
l. 27	do	do

Page	7a	7b
l. 31	of	of of
l. 31	interfere	intefere
76, l. 22	should should	should should
89, last	that	tha
96, l. 28	apprroved	approved
101, l. 27	tripple	tripple
105, l. 7, 8	incapaciate	incapaciate

This appears as the fifth title in Bradford's The Works of Peter Porcupine, D.D. (No. 9b) published in 1796. It is therefore probably later than 7a above.

7c ———. A variant in that the last word on p. 89 has been corrected to 'that' ¶ cty

7d A Little | Plain English, | addressed to the | people of the United States, | on the | treaty | negociated with his Britannic Majesty, | and on the conduct of | the President | relative thereto; | in answer to | 'The Letters of Franklin.' | With a Supplement, | containing an account of the turbulent | and factious proceedings of the | opposers of the treaty. | [rule] | By Peter Porcupine, | author of Observations on Dr. Priestley's Emigration to America, | A Bone to Gnaw for the Democrats,&c. &c. | [rule] | [8 lines from] Shakespeare | [rule] | Philadelphia, printed: | London, reprinted: | for F. and C. Rivington, No. 62, St. Paul's Church | Yard; and sold by all the booksellers. | 1795.

[A]⁴B⁸D⁸D–H⁸=60 leaves, 8 vo; (5),6–8,(1)2–111(1). Second, third, and fourth leaves signed commencing B2 except the first D3. ¶ Sabin 13895; Pearl 8 ¶ cty; mwa

Contents: half title, blank, title, blank, Preface [5]–8, 'A Little Plain English' [1]–102, Supplement, 103–110, Postscript 111, blank. Dated at end of preface 'Philadelphia, August 10th 1795.' Catchwords pp. 80 and 96.

This faithfully follows the Philadelphia edition with one notable exception. On page 7 of the Preface there is a reference to 'Tom the Tinker, toping, bawling and dancing *à la canibale* round the altar of *La Liberté*....' In the present edition only, there is a footnote identifying Tom as 'Mr. Mifflin, Governor of the State of Pennsylvania.'

7e A Little | Plain English, | addressed to | the people of the United States, | on the | treaty, | negociated with his Britannic Majesty, | and on the conduct | of the President relative thereto; | in answer to | 'The Letters of Franklin.' | With a supplement | containing an account of the turbulent and factious | proceedings of the opposers of the treaty. | [rule] | By Peter Porcupine. | [rule] | Second edition. | [rule] | [8 lines from] | Shakespeare | [rule] | Philadelphia: | From the free and independent | political & literary | press of | Thomas Bradford, | printer, bookseller & stationer, | No. 8, South Front Street | [rule] | 1796.

[A]–L⁴=44 leaves, 8 vo; (5),4,5,(2),2–70(1)72–77(3) ¶ Evans 30214; Sabin 13895 ¶ cty; mwa

Contents: half-title, 'copyright secured', title, blank, Preface [3]–5, blank, 'A Little Plain English' [1]–70; 'Supplement' [71]–76, 'Postscript' 77, blank (3). Dated on page 5 'Philadelphia, August 10th 1795.' At foot of page 77 'FINIS'.

The text follows that of the first Philadelphia edition. (No. 7a). Included as the fifth title of Vol. 1 of Porcupine's Works, (No. 34a). Some errors noted: Preface p.4 l. 4: 'defende', for 'defended'; p.4 last l.:' alter', for altar of'; p.16 l. 3: 'ond' for 'and'; p.22 l.6: 'on' for 'an'; p. 22 l.28: 'taka' for 'take'; p.32 l.5: 'excected'; p.32 l.17: 'debs'; p.34 l.35: 'exemple'; p.37 l.20: 'independence' for 'dependence'; p.44 l.2: 't' for 'to'; p.56 l.9: 'axactly'; p.67 l.10: 'governmennt'; p.74 l.3: 'couutry'.

Advertised as 'in the press' in 'A Congratulatory Epistle' (No. 143), which was advertised as published October 4, 1796.

7f ———. A variant in which p. 16, l. 3, has 'and' ¶ nn

8a   Martens, Georg Friedrich von 1756–1821.

Summary | of the | Law of Nations, | founded on | the treaties and customs | of the | modern nations | of | Europe; | with | a list of the principal treaties, | concluded since the year 1748 down to the present time, | indicating the works in which they are | to be found | [rule] | by Mr. Martens, | Professor of law in the University of Gottingen. | [rule] | Translated from the French | by William Cobbett. | [rule] | Philadelphia: | published by Thomas Bradford, printer, | bookseller & stationer, | No. 8, South Front Street. | [rule] | 1795.

[a],b⁴c²B–Aaa⁴Ccc²Bbb⁴=200 leaves, 8 vo; (3),iv,(1),vi–viii,(1) x–xix,(2)2–21(2)24–45(2)48–66(1)68–120(1)122–174(1)176–183 (2)186–194(1)196–263(2)266–338(1)340–342(1)344–372(1)374–379(1). Second leaves signed except 3d leaf is A2; D, 2d leaf is D3; G, Gg and Mm second leaves not signed. Rr is signed Rr2 ¶ Evans 29025; Pearl 9 ¶ cty

Contents: title, blank, dedication [subscribed Thomas Bradford] [iii]iv; Preface [v]–viii; Table of Contents [ix]–xix; entered according to law; Introduction [1]–21; blank; Text [23]–342, with blank pages at [46], [184] and [264]; List of treaties [343]–372; Subscribers [373]–379; blank. Page 36 for 136; 37 for 372.

The dedication is dated 'Philadelphia Dec. 1795'. Clark, page 38, writes that Bradford's dedication was actually written by Cobbett. Cobbett so stated in the Political Censor for September (No. 20a), at page 70, which see as to the composition. 118th Pennsylvania District Copyright to Thomas Bradford as proprietor 4 December 1795. Gazette of the United States, January 6, 1796: 'Martans [sic] Law of Nations' for sale by Bradford.

8b ———. A variant in which page number 136 is corrected, whereas, in page number 285, the 5 is above the line ¶ cty; NN

8c ———. A variant in which page numbers 136, 285 and 372 are corrected. ¶ MWA

8d A | Compendium | of the | law of nations, | founded on the | treaties and customs | of the | modern nations of Europe: | to which is added, | a complete list | of all the |treaties, conventions, compacts, declarations, &c. | from | the year 1731 to 1788, inclusive, indicating the | several works in which they are to be found. | [rule] | By G. F. von Martens, | Professor of public law in the University of Gottingen. | [rule] | translated, and the list of treaties, &c. brought down to June, 1802, | by William Cobbett. | [rule] | London: | published by Cobbett and Morgan, Pall-Mall. | [rule] | June 1802.

[a],b⁸B–Ff⁸Gg³=243 leaves 20.4 cm.; (3)iv(3)viii–xi(2)xiv–xxxii(1)2–21(2)24–45(2)48–67(2)70–122(1)124–178(1)180–187 (2)190–198(1)200–270(1)272–352(1)354–454. Page 366 for 266. Second, third and fourth leaves signed A2–4 through Ff2–4, except C3 and O4. Gg2 also signed ¶ Pearl 9 ¶ cty; MH

Contents: title, blank, dedication [iii]iv, dated Pall-Mall 4th June 1802; Advertisement, blank, author's preface [viii]–xi, blank, Table of Contents [xiii]–xxxii; Summary of the Law of Nations [1]–356; List of the principal treaties [357]–454.

Running titles, except p. iv; 'ceremonial' p. 226. Catchwords, except pp. iv, [v],21,67,171,178,187,270. cty copy has final advertising leaf dated June 11, 1802.

8e   The | law of nations: | being | the science of national law, | covenants, power, &c | founded upon the | treaties and customs of modern nations | in Europe. | [rule] | By G. F. von Martens, | Professor of public law in the University of Gottingen. | translated from the French, by | Wm. Cobbett. | [rule] | to which is added, | a list of the principal treaties, declarations, and other | public papers, from the year 1731 to 1788, by the | author; and continued by the translator | down to November, 1815. | The fourth edition. | [rule] | London: | published by William Cobbett, | 183, Fleet Street. | [rule] | 1829.

Colophon: Printed by Mills, Jowett, and Mills, Bolt Court, Fleet Street.

[a],b⁸B–GG⁸HH¹=249 leaves; (3)iv(2)vii–xxxii(1)2–354,357–468. Page 613 for 316 ¶ cu (Davis).

9a   The | Works | of | Peter Porcupine, D.D. | a new edition. | [rule] | Philadelphia: | published by Thomas Bradford, | printer, | bookseller and stationer. | No. 8, Southfront [sic] street. | [rule] | 1795.

¶ Pearl 10 ¶ Bodleian (Pearl); pcarlᴅ (Davis).

Contents: title page, blank, and the following pamphlets:
    I. A Bone to Gnaw...third edition (No. 3d)
    II. Part II, A Bone to Gnaw (No. 6a)
    III. A Little Plain English (No. 7a)
    IV. Observations...Priestley...third edition (No. 2h)
    V. A Kick for a Bite (No. 4a)

Per Davis, the Dickinson copy lacks the fourth title, and is therefore incomplete. Bradford would hardly have omitted his best seller. Gazette of the United States, January 6, 1796 'P.P.s works Compleat', for sale by Bradford.

9b   The | Works | of | Peter Porcupine, D.D. | [rule] | A new edition. | [rule] | [three lines quoted] | [rule] | Philadelphia: | published by Thomas Bradford, | printer, | bookseller, and stationer. | No. 8, South Front-street. | 1796.

¶ Evans 30234 similar; Pearl 10 ¶ ɪɴu (Davis)

Contents: title, blank, and the following pamphlets:
    I. Bradford's fourth edition. Observations...Priestley (No. 2i)
    II. A Bone to Gnaw...second edition (No. 3b)
    III. Part II. A Bone to Gnaw (No. 6b)

IV. A Kick for a Bite (No. 4a)

V. A Little Plain English (No. 7b)

VI. A New Year's Gift (No. 10a)

The entries under 9 might well be called 'Bradford's remainders'. The present volume includes the pamphlets published by Bradford for Cobbett except 'A Prospect from the Congress Gallery'. It is advertised on the wrapper of 'A Prospect' (No. 11a).

9c ———. Same as the preceding entry except that the final pamphlet is: Second Edition. A New Year's Gift (No. 10f) ¶ cty

9d ———. Here II is the third edition (No. 3d) ¶ Seven Gables Bookshop.

9e The | Works | of | Peter Porcupine | [rule] | Fourth Edition | [rule] | revised, altered & corrected | by | the Author | [rule] | Philadelphia: | published by | Thomas Bradford, printer, | bookseller & Stationer, | No. 8, | South Front Street | [rule] | 1796.

8 vo ¶ Evans 30234 ¶ DLC

Contents: title, blank, and the following pamphlets:

I. Bradford's fourth edition, Observations...Priestley (No. 2*i*)

II. A Bone to Gnaw...fourth edition (No. 3e).

III. Part II. A Bone to Gnaw...second edition (No. 6c).

IV. A Little Plain English (No. 7a).

V. Second edition. A New Year's Gift (No. 10d).

10a A | New-Year's Gift | to | the Democrats; | or | observations | on | a pamphlet | entitled, | 'A Vindication | of | Mr. Randolph's Resignation.' | [rule] | By Peter Porcupine. | [rule] | 'For gold defiles by frequent touch; | 'There's nothing fouls the hand so much. | 'But as his paws he strove the scower, | 'He washed away the chemic power; | 'And Midas now neglected stands, | 'with asses ears and dirty hands'. | Swift. | [rule] | Philadelphia; | Published by Thomas Bradford, Printer, | Bookseller & Stationer, | No. 8, | South Front-Street. | [rule] | 1796.

Enclosed in grey paper wrapper entitled 'Porcupine | Versus | Randolph. | [rule] | Sold at | The Political Book-Store, | South Front-Street, | No. 8.', with advertisement on each side of back cover.

[A]–I⁴=36 leaves, 8 vo; [3]iv,(1),6–71[1]. Second leaves signed A2 etc. ¶ Evans 30215; Pearl 12; Sabin 13896 ¶ cty; MWA

Contents: title, blank, Preface [iii]iv; 'A |New Year's Gift, &c.'
[5]–71; Advertisement of T. Bradford. Preface dated 1st January,
1796. Running title p. iv. The works advertised by T. Bradford on
page [72] include Peter Porcupine's works; Marten's Law of Nations, a new work; Bone to Gnaw, 1st and 2d parts; Plain English.
Some errors noted: p. 6, l.29 'apparant'; p.11, l.17, 'faultering'; p.
24, 4th, 5th from foot, 'mushroon'; p. 32, last word of note missing,
'me;' p.34, l.25, 'fradulent'. 124th Pennsylvania district copyright
issued to Thomas Bradford January 6, 1796. Dated in Porcupine's
Works (No. 59) 'January 1796.' In the preface to 'A Prospect from
the Congress-Gallery' (No. 11). Cobbett says he wrote 'New Year's
Gift' in five days during the session of Congress which began
December 7, 1795. 'Prospect' covered proceedings in the House to
January 5, 1796. Gazette of the United States, January 9, 1796:
'this day is published...'

The Vindication of Mr. (Edmund) Randolph's Resignation (from
the position of Secretary of State) was written by him and published,
so Cobbett writes on p. 7 of the 'Gift', on December 18, 1795 (see
No. 133). Cobbett strongly attacks it. Some extracts follow:

'The French... have ransacked the coffers of the rich, stripped
poverty of its very rags, robbed the infant of its birth-right, wrenched
the crutch from the hand of tottering old age, and joining sacrilege
to burglary, have plundered even the altars of God, in order to
possess themselves of the means of corrupting degenerate foreign-
ers.' (p. 5). 'The people might have remained in this delusive confidence...had it not been for the accidental interception of the letter,
that has led to the *Vindication*...(p. 7) 'Should it appear, at last, that
the Vindicator is to share in the profits of the work, he will have
the honour of introducing an improvement into the art of vindicat-
ing: men have often been known to barter their reputations; but to
derive profit from a public sale of the proofs of their having done
so, is as yet without an instance on the annals of corruption' (p. 12)
'...had he sent his copy to his gazeteer, Mr. [Andrew] Brown...two
or three thousand copies of it would have been distributed through
the dark lanes and alleys of Philadelphia in the space of forty-eight
hours... The windows of Paddy's filthy cabin, and even the crannies
of citizen Pompey's hovel, might have exhibited as clear and unde-
niable proofs of Mr. Randolph's innocence as the French archives.'
(p. 14.) 'Here, then, this worthy statesman was endeavouring to
render a most important service to his country. His only object
being to dive into the machinations, that the English minister and

his Congress were hatching against the United States. A very laud-
able pursuit.—This story has something in it so flattering to human
nature, that it is a pity it should be the most abominable falshood
that ever issued from the procreant brain of a petty fogging politician.' (p. 42) 'I leave any one to guess at the low ebb to which he
must be reduced, when he was obliged to throw himself on the
purity of the French nation, for want of a little of the ready to purchase the *'consciences* of the *pretended* patriots of America,'* which
were just going off as cheap as neck-beef, or damaged goods at
vendue!' (p. 61.) 'There was, indeed, one difficulty; and that was,
the Treasury of the Convention was nearly as empty as Father
Joseph's [Fauchet's] purse or the pouch of his mendicant pilgrim
[Randolph]...however,...they had only to set the national razor at
work for two or three days, upon the heads of the bankers and merchants, to collect the sum required: or, if these should be grown
scarce, a drowning of four or five thousand women might bring
them in ear-bobs and other trinkets sufficient to stir up fifty town-
meetings, and to cause two thirds of the Federal Senators to be
roasted in effigy'. (pp. 65,66.) 'Thus has the Vindicator failed in all
his attempts. On the article of corruption, of which we before
doubted, we now doubt no longer; and as to his indirect accusation
against the President, it only serves to show that one who, with un-
blushing front, can ask a bribe, will never be ashamed to publish his
ingratitude and apostacy.' (pp. 70,71).

Of this pamphlet Madison wrote to Jefferson January 10, 1796:
'Randolph's "Vindication" has just undergone the lash of the author
of the "Bone to Gnaw." It is handled with much satirical scurrility,
not without strictures of sufficient plausibility to aid in the plan of
running him down'. (Quoted in Moncure D. Conway, Edmund Randolph p. 347. Conway termed it: 'this outburst of Cobbett's vulgar
malice'.)

10b ————. A variant in which on the title page, next to last line,
the 'h' in 'South' is dropped markedly; p. 32, last line of note, the
'me' has been added; and p. 47, l. 3 of the poem has the asterisk ¶ cty

10c ————. A further variant in which the title page is corrected
¶ NN

10d Second Edition | [rule] | A | New Year's Gift | to | the Demo-
crats; | or | observations | on | a pamphlet, | entitled, | 'A Vindication |

of | Mr. Randolph's Resignation.' | [rule] | By Peter Porcupine | [rule] | [six lines from] | Swift. | [rule] | Philadelphia: | published by Thomas Bradford, printer, | book-seller & stationer, | No. 8, | South Front-Street. | 1796.

[A]–I⁴=36 leaves, 8 vo; (3)iv(1)6–71(1). Second leaves signed except F2 ¶ Evans 30216 ¶ CTY; MWA

Contents: title, blank, Preface [iii], iv; 'A | New-Year's Gift &c' [5]–71, blank. Follows the first edition (No.10a) except that there are no advertisements. Running title page iv. The edition represents a new setting of type. Some of the many differences between the two:

Page	Second edition	First edition
[5]	Second rule, swelling	Second rule, thick-thin
6, l. 29	apparent	apparant
14, l. 6, 7	ga-zeteer	ga-zetteer
14, l. 8	gazettte	gazette
37, l. 2	so-	socie-
39, l. 19	ci-	Ci-
41, l. 4, 5	ab-vanced	ad-vanced
47, poem, l. 3	asterisk	no asterisk
49, l. 14	h at an angle in 'the'	———
64 last	no comma after 'else'	comma
71	Gap between 'Finis' and 'Entered According to Law' is 2 cm. in the second and 1.5 cm. in the first edition.	

10e ———. A variant in which p. 22, l. 36, begins 'ticipate' instead of 'participate.' ¶ NN

10f ———. A variant in which signature D, at least, has been reset. The distance between the parentheses around page number 25 is 1.7 cm. as against 1.5 cm. in the preceding two entries ¶ CTY Other differences:

Page	Preceding entries	This entry
26, l. 18	No quotation marks	Marks
28, l. 1	their	thei
29, l. 14	at end, comma	at end, semi-colon
31, l. 28, 29	com-mitted'	'con-mitted'

10g ———. Here page 14 is corrected: l. 8 'Gazette' and l. 29 'alleys' instead of 'allies' ¶ CTY

10h A | New Year's Gift | to the | Democrats; | or, | observations on a | pamphlet, | entitled, | 'A vindication of Mr. Randolph's resignation.' | [rule] | By Peter Porcupine. | [rule] | [six lines from] | Swift. | [rule] | The third edition. | [rule] | Philadelphia: | published by William Cobbett, opposite | Christ Church. | 1798.

[A]–I⁴=36 leaves, 8 vo; (3)iv(1)6–71(1). Second leaves signed C2E2 only ¶ Evans 33527 ¶ MWA

This edition follows the second edition, but is a new setting of type. The errors noted have been corrected. The second rule on page [5] is like the first edition.

11a   A | Prospect | from the | Congress-Gallery, | during the | Session, | begun December 7, 1795. | containing, | The President's speech, the addresses of both Houses, some of the | debates in the Senate, and all the principal debates in the House of | Representatives; each debate being brought under one head, and | so digested and simplified as to give the reader the completest view | of the proceedings with the least possible fatigue. | With | occasional remarks, | [rule] | by Peter Porcupine. | [rule] | Philadelphia: | Published by Thomas Bradford, printer | bookseller & Stationer, | No. 8, | South Front-Street, | 1796.

[A]–H⁴I²=34 leaves, 8 vo; (3)iv(1)2–12,17–68 ¶ Evans 30229; Pearl 13; Sabin 14010 ¶ CtY; MWA; NN

Contents: title, blank, Preface [iii]iv, 'A Prospect, &c' [1]–12, 17–68. P. 68: 'End of the First Number'.

Gazette of the United States, February 24, 1796: 'This day is published....' 127th Pennsylvania District copyright issued to Thomas Bradford, February 24, 1796, Dated in Porcupine's Works (No. 59) 'January 1796'.

In a printed wrapper entitled: No. 1 | [rule] | A | Prospect | from the | Congress-Gallery, | during the | Session | Begun December 7th, 1795 | with | occasional remarks | [rule] | by Peter Porcupine | [rule] | Philadelphia: | Sold at | The Political Book-Store, | South Front-Street. | No. 8. On verso 'Entered according to Law'. Back Cover: 'Political Publications, | for sale at present | at No. 8 South Front-Street', include Peter Porcupine's Works (No. 9). On verso, advertisement for Martens, 'A Summary of the Law of Nations' (No. 8a).

Some errors noted: p.[iii] last word 'to'; p.6, l.36 'scites'; p.10, l.22, 'as' for 'was'; p.18, last l. 'it'; p. 19, l.11 'cccasions'; p.19, l.42 'commmunication'; p.25, l.14 'committe'; p.33, last line 'intire'; p. 44, l.31 'bottommest'; p.59, l.11 'Heavan'.

The pamphlet has value as a spectator account of Congressional debates. On the President's speech in the House: 'The President is a timid speaker....This was the first time he had ever entered the walls of Congress without a full assurance of meeting a welcome from every heart....' (p. 7). In the reply of the House to the President, the words 'the undiminished confidence of your fellow citizens' were stricken. Cobbett strongly objects (p.33). There is a full discussion of the debate on the attempts by Randall and Whitney to bribe congressmen in the matter of title to Western lands. Cobbett criticizes Dayton in this regard (p.38). As to Giles: 'the manner of his proceeding might, if adopted, become a very evil precedent.' (p.43). It was improper to suggest British influence (p.45). As to the flag sent by the French: 'Mr. Swanwick (don't smile reader) saw, at once, the impropriety of postponing the consideration...who told you, my dear little orator...' (p.66).

11b   A | Prospect | from the | Congress-Gallery [continues as in first edition except 'th' for 'the' before 'debates'] By Peter Porcupine | [rule] | The second edition | [rule] | Philadelphia: | Published by Thomas Bradford, printer, |bookseller & stationer, | No. 8, | South Front-Street | [rule] | 1796.

[A]–H⁴I²=34 leaves, 8 vo; (3)iv,(1)2–64 ¶ Evans 30230 ¶ ctY; MWA

Contents: title, blank, preface [iii]iv, A Prospect &c[1]–64. On page 64: 'End of the First Number.'

The work represents a new setting of type. It is apparently a faithful copy, with corrections, of the first edition. Examples of corrections, p.2, last line 'unadjusted' becomes 'unjustified'; page 20, l.17 addition of 'a'; the type errors noted in the first edition have been corrected, except that on p.6.

12a   The | Bloody Buoy | thrown out as | a warning to the political pilots of America; | or a | faithful relation | of | a multitude of acts of horrid barbarity, | such as the eye never witnessed, the tongue never | expressed or the imagination conceived, | until the commencement of | The French Revolution, | to which is added | An Instructive Essay, | tracing these dreadful effects to their real | causes. | [rule] | Illustrated with four striking copper-plates. | [rule] | By Peter Porcupine. | [rule] | [four lines from] Abbe Maury's speech to the National Assembly. | [rule] | Philadelphia: | printed for Benjamin Davies No. 68. High-Street. | MDCCXCVI.

[A]–U⁶=120 leaves, 16.5 cm; (5)vi–viii(1)x–xii(1)16–139(1) 141–241(1). Third leaves signed A2–U2 ¶ Evans 30205; Pearl 14 ¶ cty; MWA

Contents: title, blank, Dedication, blank, Table [v]–viii; Introduction [ix]–xii; The Bloody Buoy &c [15]–139; An Instructive Essay [140]–241; advertisements. Two line errata note p. viii. On p.241 'copyright secured according to Act of Congress.' Running titles pp.vi–viii,x–xii. Four Plates: Heads of three assassins, signed by [James] Smither; republican marriages, men and women tied naked together being drowned; 405 prisoners going to be drowned, with a soldier carrying a child on his bayonet; the guillotine, with piles of heads.

129th Pennsylvania District copyright issued to Benjamin Davies March 8, 1796. Dated in Porcupine's Works (No. 59) 'February 1796'. Claypoole's American Daily Advertiser, March 18, 1796: 'published this day'.

Errors noted: p.80, l.7 'nex'; p. 83, l.3 'neck' for 'deck'.

The introduction states that the object is to show the horrible effects of anarchy and infidelity. It is necessary because the public prints have concealed events in France. The facts are taken from French publications and the illustrations copied from French engravings. The Bloody Buoy is a compendium of barbarities, listed in the Table.

Subtitle, p.140: 'An | instructive essay, | tracing all the horrors of the French Revolu- | tion to their real causes, the licentious poli- | tics and infidel philosophy of the present | age'. Charles Fox is attacked as 'this humane and honest swindler', p. 145; defence of William Pitt, p.147 et seq; the 'detestable principle' of equality, p. 161; the lies and blasphemies of Voltaire, Rousseau a thief and adulterer, p.165; the word 'Republic' is a delusion, p.233; the attacks on Washington show a faction here to be feared, p.240.

12b   The | Bloody Buoy, | thrown out as a | warning to the political pilots | of America; | or, a | faithful relation | of a | multitude of acts of horrid barbarity, | such as | the eye never witnessed, the tongue never | expressed, or the imagination conceived, | until the commencement of | the French Revolution. | Illustrated with four striking copper-plates. | [rule] | The second edition; | with additional notes, and a copious appendix | [rule] | By Peter Porcupine. | [rule] | [four lines from] Abbe Maury's speech to the National Assembly. | [rule] | Philadelphia: | Printed for, and sold by, Benjamin Davies, | No. 68, High-Street, and William Cobbett, | No. 25, North Second-Street. | M,DCC,XCVI.

[A]–U⁶X–Gg⁶=180 leaves, 24 mo; (3)iv–vi(1)viii–xii(1)16–342 (1)344–362. Third leaves signed A2–Gg2. ¶ Evans 30206 ¶ ctʏ; MBAt; MWA; NN

Contents: title; blank; table [iii]–vi; Introduction [vii]–xii; The Bloody Buoy, &c [15]–342; Appendix [343]–362. Four plates as in first edition. Running titles in preliminaries. Catchwords, except in preliminaries and on pp. 53,161,197 and 345–62. Catchword on p. 24 is omitted on p. 25. Gazette of the United States, July 11, 1796: 'This day is published…'

The text substantially follows the first edition, with a new setting of type. The principal changes are omission of the dedication, a longer introduction, new quotations pp. 191–194 and the addition of 14 notes, of which 10 make up the new appendix containing other instances of barbarity. The introduction on page xi refers to the 'rapid sale' of the first edition, Benjamin Davies is cited on the authenticity of the sources and the conclusion is stated that the eyes of the people have been opened. New notes are on pp. 32,53, 220,221,225,232,260,269,281,306,313,323,325,327. Other minor changes found on pp. 20,33,65,71,84,179,195.

12c ———. Here the plates are omitted. Page numbers 175 and 273 illegible ¶ DLC

12d ———. Transcription the same except for the omission of the reference to plates ¶ Evans 30207 ¶ DLC

There is a frontispiece, a man holding two severed heads, entitled: 'Phillipe cuts off the heads of | his father & mother, as a proof of | his patriotism. See page 35'. On page xi the reference to plates is omitted. Otherwise, this appears to be from the same setting of type as 12b and 12c. On thin paper.

12e The | Bloody Buoy, | thrown out as a | warning to the political pilots of America; | or a | faithful relation | of a | multitude of acts of horrid barbarity, | such as the eye never witnessed, the tongue never | expressed, or the imagination conceived, | until the commencement of | the French Revolution. | To which is added, | an instructive essay, | tracing these dreadful effects to their real |

causes. | [rule] | by Peter Porcupine | [rule] | [four lines from] Abbe Maury's Speech to the National Assembly. | [rule] | Philadelphia printed. | London reprinted, and sold by J. Owen, | No. 168, Piccadilly. [1796?]

[A]–U⁶=120 leaves, 12 mo; (5)viv(2)x–xii(1)14–239(1). A3 signed; second and third leaves signed B2B3 et seq. except G2 ¶ Pearl 14 ¶ cty

Contents: title, blank, dedication, blank, table [v],vi,v, blank, introduction [ix]–xii; the Bloody Buoy [13]–239, blank. Running titles in preliminaries.

12f Die | Blut-Fahne | ausgestecket zur warnung politischer | wegweiser in America, | oder | eine getrue erzählung | einer grossen anzahl handlungen der abschenlichsten | grausamkeiten, solche als nie ein auge gesehen, nie | eine zunge ausgesprochen, oder die einbildungskraft | gedacht, ehe die | frauzoische revolution | ihren anfang genommen hat. | welchem | ein unterrechtender versuch | der diesen schrecklichen thatsachen bis auf ihren wahren | ursprung nachforschet, beygefügt ist. | [rule] | Ausgezieret mit vier treffenden kupferstichen. | [rule] | Von Peter Porcupine. | [rule] | [six lines] | (aus des abt Maury's rede vor der National-Assemblie: | [rule] | Reading; | Gedruckt bey Gottlob Jungmann und Comp. | 1797.

[π]⁶A–Bb⁴=106 leaves, 8 vo; (13)2–198(2). Second leaf *2; fifth leaf ††; second leaves A2–Bb2 ¶ Evans 31944 ¶ cty; mwa

Contents: title, blank, copyright, blank, dedication, blank, contents (3), preface (3), text [1]–186; appendix 187–198; translators notes (2). Four plates with captions in English. P. 198 'Finis' in ornamental scroll. 181st Pennsylvania District copyright issued to Benjamin Davies June 1, 1797. Advertised in Porcupine's Gazette July 13, 1797 with a note that of 3000 copies printed, 'but a few hundreds remain unsold, although the impression is but two weeks from the press.' dlc has a modern pamphlet by Joseph A. Donahue aiming to describe this work, Wilmington, n.d. The title is translated 'The Blood-Flag', etc.

12g The | Bloody Buoy, | thrown out as a | warning to the political pilots of all nations. | or a | faithful relation | of a | multitude of acts of horrid barbarity, | such as the eye never witnessed, the tongue never ex- | pressed, or the imagination conceived, until | the commencement of | The French Revolution. | To which is added, | an instructive essay, | tracing these dreadful effects to their real | causes. | [rule] | By Peter Porcupine. | Third edition, | with additional facts, and a preface addressed | to the people of Great Britain. | [rule] | [four lines from] Abbé Maury's speech to the National Assembly. | [rule] | Philadelphia printed. | London reprinted, and sold by J. Wright, No. 169, | opposite old Bond-street, Piccadilly | [rule] | 1797.

[A]^{8}B–L^{12}M^{6}N^4=138 leaves, 12 mo.; 18.8 cm. in wrappers; no plates. (3)iv–vi(3)x,xi(2)xiv–xvi(1)2–125(1)127–227(2)230–259 (1). Second leaf A2; fourth leaf A3; B through K, second through sixth leaves signed; ninth leaf of B signed C3; fifth leaf of I signed I3; L second through fifth leaves signed; M second and third leaves signed; N second leaf signed ¶ Pearl 14 ¶ cty; MWA

Contents: title; blank; Preface [iii]–vi; Dedication; blank; Table [ix]–xi; blank; Introduction [xiii]–xvi; The Bloody Buoy, &c. [1]–125; An Instructive Essay [126]–227; blank; Additional Facts [229]–259; Advertisement: 'This day is published, price one shilling, Memoirs of the Life of Peter Porcupine...'. Running titles iv–vi,x,xi,xiv–xvi; on p. v, 'Preeace'.

In general, the text follows the first edition. For example on p. 125 reference is made to a plate opposite, not present in this edition. The new publisher's preface concludes that the author 'is now established as a Bookseller in Philadelphia, where all his efforts are exerted to prevent the introduction of French principles, and to exhort the inhabitants of the United States to maintain the bonds of friendship with Great Britain.' Omitted are two paragraphs concerning 'private parts' appearing on page 129 in the original. Also omitted on pages 130, 131 and 133 are highly uncomplimentary remarks about Charles Fox appearing on pages 144, 145 and 147 of the original.

In the London 1797 edition of A Bone to Gnaw (No. 3h) the Editor, 'Humphrey Hedgehog', writes p. iii that he wrote the preface to the 'Bloody Buoy', Third Edition. Humphrey is identified as John Gifford (i.e. John Richards Green,) English author.

12h   Annals of Blood; | or, | an authentic relation | of | various acts of horrid barbarity, | committed by the | authors and abettors | of | the French Revolution. | to which is added | an instructive essay, | tracing these effects to their | real causes. | [rule] | By an Ameri-

can | [rule] [seven lines quoted from] | Milton P.L. XI 675 | [rule] |
Cambridge: | printed and sold by F. Hodson, | sold also by G. & T.
Wilkie, Paternoster-row, | London; and by J. Deighton, Cam-
bridge. | 1797 | [rule] | price eighteen pence.

[A]²B–O⁶=80 leaves, 12 mo; (2)iii(2)2–154(2) ¶ Sabin 13874+.
¶ British Museum. (Davis)

Contents: title, blank, advertisement, blank, text [1]–82, An Instructive essay 83–154, blank leaf.

12i   The | Bloody Buoy, | thrown out as a |warning to the political
pilots of all nations. | or, a | faithful relation | of a multitude of |
acts of horrid barbarity, | such as the eye never witnessed, the
tongue expressed, or | the imagination conceived, until the com-
mencement of | the French Revolution. | To which is added, | an
instructive essay, | tracing these dreadful effects to their real causes |
[rule] | By Peter Porcupine | [rule] | Fourth edition | [rule] | [four
lines from] Abbé Maury's speech to the National Assembly | [rule] |
London. | Printed for J. Wright, No. 169, opposite old Bond- |
Street, Piccadilly. | [rule] | 1798.

[a]²b⁶B–L¹²M⁶[N]⁴=138 leaves, 12 mo; (5)vi–ix(1)xi–xiii(1)xv,
xvi(1)2–125(1)127–227(2)230–259(1). Second leaf signed a3; fifth
leaf b3; B through L second through sixth leaves signed; M second
through fifth leaves signed; [N] second leaf signed N2. Press numbers
on eight pages ¶ cty

Contents: title; blank; Dedication; blank; Preface [v]–ix; Introduction [x]–xiii; Table [xiv]–xvi; The Bloody Buoy &c. [1]–125;
An instructive essay...[126]–227; blank; Additional facts [229]–
259; blank. This is a faithful copy of the English edition of the previous year, completely reset. On p. 157 next to last line has 'preceived'. On p. 252 a two-line note on Carnot is omitted. Running
titles in preliminaries. Catchword on p. 227.

In a copy in half-calf, a leather label on the spine reads 'Porcu-
pine | on the | French | Revolution'.

12j   The | Bloody Buoy, | abridged. | [rule] | thrown out as | a
warning to Britons, | at the present important period: | containing |
a faithful relation of a multitude | of | acts of horrid barbarity, | such
as the eye never witnessed, the tongue expressed, or the | imagina-
tion conceived, until the commencement of | the French Revolu-
tion. | [rule] | By | Peter Porcupine. | [rule] | It is essential to the

cause of justice and humanity, to recal [sic] | the minds of every
Englishman, that these dreadful recitals ar [sic] | not the effusions
of party malice, but absolute facts, faith- | fully extracted from the
State Trials of France, and taken | from the formal depositions, de-
livered upon oath, of eye wit- | nesses, or indirect accomplices, of
the criminal deeds which | they describe. These facts are written in
characters appropri- | ate to the genius and spirit of their legitimate
parent, the Republic | of France, the deformed offspring of perjury,
plunder, and as- | sassination: they are written in characters of
blood, | which can never be effaced ! ! ! | [rule] | eleventh edition. |
[rule] | London. | printed for J. Wright, No. 169, Piccadilly. 1798. |
[rule] | (price 3d. Twelve for 2s 6d or one guinea per hundred.)

[B]¹²=12 leaves, 12 mo. 16.3 cm (trimmed); (3)4–24. The
second through sixth leaves are signed B2–B6 ¶ MH

Contents: title, address to the reader, the Bloody Buoy, &c. [3]–
24, in 74 numbered divisions, some containing two to four paragraphs. On page 24 are listed seven 'cheap political tracts, just published', including Cobbett's Democratic Principles, and same, part
the second. Press numbers on pp. 4 and 23.

Apparently in earlier editions the type errors noted in the title do
not occur, except 'recal [sic] to'. (MB-Davis-fourth edition).

12k   The | Bloody Buoy, | thrown out as a | warning to the political
pilots of America; | or, a | faithful relation | of a | multitude of acts
of horrid barbarity, | such as | the eye never witnessed, the tongue
never expressed, | or the imagination conceived, until the | com-
mencement of the | French Revolution. | [rule] | The third edition; |
with additional notes, and a copious appendix. | [rule] | By Peter
Porcupine. | [rule] | [3 lines quoted from] Abbe Maury's speech to
the National Assembly. | Philadelphia: | printed for, and sold by,
P.M. Davis. | 1823.

[π]¹[A]–S⁶[T]¹=110 leaves, 17.7 cm; (2)(3)iv,v(2)viii–x(1)12–
27(1)29–36(1)38–208(1)210–217(1). Third leaves signed A2–S2 ¶
Sabin 13874. ¶MWA

Contents: blank, plate, title, blank, table [iii]–v, blank, introduction [vii]–x, The Bloody Buoy [11]–208, Appendix [209]–217,
blank. The plate, on thin paper, shows a man holding two heads,
with a caption beginning 'Phillipe cuts off the heads of his father
and mother...' (See No. 12d).

12l The | Bloody Buoy, | thrown out as a | warning to the political
pilots of | America; | or a | faithful relation | of a | multitude of acts
of | horrid barbarity, | such as | the eye never witnessed, the tongue
never expressed, or the | imagination conceived, until the com-
mencement of | the French Revolution. | [rule] | The second edi-
tion; | with additional notes, and a copious appendix. | [14 aster-
isks] | By Peter Porcupine | [14 asterisks] | [three lines from] Abbe
Maury's Speech to the National Assembly. | [reference marks] |
Paradise [Penna.]: | Printed by Henry Witmer. | 1823.

[A]²B–O⁴P²=56 leaves, 20 cm; (3)viii(1)10–109(1)111–116. ¶
cty; PPL

Contents: title, table, Introduction [vii]viii; The | Bloody Buoy,
&c [9]–109; Appendix [110]–116.

The text follows that of the second Philadelphia edition (No.
12b), but there are no plates. P. 13, line 20 'exhibtied'; p. 23 last,
'justise.'

12m ———. The transcription is the same as the preceding entry
except for omission of the words 'thrown out as a warning to the
political pilots of America.'

[A]²B–O⁴P²=56 leaves, 23.5 cm; (5)10–109(1)111–116 ¶ PPL

Contents: title, table, introduction [7][8], The | Bloody Buoy, &c
[9]–109, appendix [110]–116.

13a The | Political | Censor, | or | monthly review | of the | most
interesting political occurrences, | relative to | the United States |
of | America. [for March 1796] | [rule] | By Peter Porcupine. |
[rule] | Philadelphia: | Printed for Benjamin Davies, No. 68, High-
Street | MDCCXCVI.

[A]–I⁴=36 leaves, 8 vo; (3)iv–vi(3)8–70. Printed wrappers ¶
Evans 30219; Pearl 15; Sabin 14001 ¶ cty; mwa

Contents: title, blank, Introduction [iii]–vi, blank leaf, The Political Censor [7]–70. Running title pp. iv–vi.

130th Penna. District Copyright issued to Benjamin Davies as
proprietor, 4 April 1796. Dated in Porcupine's Works (No. 59)
'March 1796.' The earliest session of Congress referred to is January 19th and the latest is February 29th. Claypoole's American
Daily Advertiser, April 7, 1796: 'this day is published and sold by
Benjamin Davies.' The wrapper, front recto: The | Political | Cen-
sor, | or | Monthly Review | for | March 1796, | [hand] This work

will be published on the last day of every | month. Six Censors will make a volume, the sixth will | therefore contain a general Index and a Table of Contents. | The one ending the year will contain a chronological Ta | ble of all the remarkable events in the Political world. | [rule] | by Peter Porcupine | [rule] | Philadelphia. | Printed for Benjamin Davies, No. 68, High-street. | MDCCXCVI. Verso: Copyright secured according to law. Rear recto: blank. Verso: advertisements, including the Bloody Buoy.

Some errors noted: p. 9, l. 36: 'appropiations'; p. 13, l. 17, 'were' for 'where'; p. 43, five lines up, 'hvae'; p. 44, l. 18, 'scized'.

In the Introduction, Cobbett writes he will combat the public papers '...I shall take a review of the political transactions of the past month; give an account of every democratic trick...unravel the windings of the pretended patriots, and more particularly those of the flour-merchants...' (pp.v,vi). '...by the indiscretion (to give it the mildest term) of our Ambassador [Monroe, concerning the flag] have we been degraded in the eyes of even Italians....' (p.8) On the debate whether the House could refuse an appropriation for the Mint: 'Mr. Sedgwick (from Massachusetts)' who thought not, against 'Mr. Gallatin (from Geneva)' who thought so. 'The principle was, that this House has a right by withholding appropiations [sic] when they see fit, to stop the wheels of Government.' (p.9). '...Mr. [Edward] Livingston, whom we shall by-and-by see making a considerable figure in the field of opposition to the government, made a motion for striking out the whole appropriation for the Mint'. (p.11). 'He could have striken the salaries of the President, Vice President and Senate and the government of the United States might have been changed into a National Convention....' (p.13). 'Some members object to having any printers publish abstracts of speeches'. (p.23). Cruelty of the members 'to my poor Caledonian friend, Callender...how was his Register torn to pieces!...Oh! gentlemen from Virginia! how could you so belabor this imported patriot?' (pp.26,27). Debate on a motion to adjourn ½ hour on Feb. 22nd to congratulate the President, which lost 50 to 38. 'Mr. Parker, the blooming and accomplished Mr. Parker, the honest and virtuous Mr. Parker of the free State of Virginia...' is attacked in this regard. (p.29). Likewise 'The gentleman from Whiskyland [Gallatin] ...an intruding foreigner, a mere adventurer...what are the services Mr. Gallatin ever rendered America?' (pp.30,31). Debate on a loan for Washington City: Giles thought the President's house too grand; the houses for Congress not grand enough.

(p.38). Remarks on that (p.43). On calling 'Congress House' a 'Capitol' '...While we are swaggering about in our consular robes, we shall care but little whether we are called ambitious buffoons or not.' (p.46). Removal to the Potomack will be fatal because of the neighborhood (p.47). Debate on the impressment of seamen discussed. Doggerel against Livingston, '...So weak, so haughty, pompous, proud and mean, |Indeed so black, so shameful and obscene...' (p.62). Defense of Hamilton, with the implication Livingston had caused his stoning (p.63). As to impressment charges against Britain, '...is it thus we treat our poor old mother in the hour of her distress?' (p.65). Article on the supposed suicide of the Argus in New York, by a french knife, in despair at news from England, with a farewell letter to 'his Sister and only relation, the Aurora of Philadelphia' (pp.67–70. The Argus, published by Thomas Greenleaf, continued to 1800).

13b   The | Political | Censor | or | monthly review | of the | most interesting political occurrences, | relative to | the United States | of | America [for March 1796] | [rule] | By Peter Porcupine. | [rule] | The second edition. | [rule] | Philadelphia: | printed for, and sold by, William Cobbett, No. 25, | North Second Street, opposite Christ-Church | M.DCC.XCVI.

   $[\pi]^1 A^2 B-I^4 = 35$ leaves, 8vo; (3)4–6(1)8–70 ¶ Evans 30220 ¶ cty; mwa

   Contents: title, blank, Introduction [3]–6, The Political Censor for March, 1796, [7]–70. Running title pp. 4–6. At foot of page 70: 'Owing to a new arrangement of the matter | in the second edition, the number of the first page | of the April Censor does not immediately follow that | of the last page of this Censor.' Two rows of type ornaments at the top of page [3]. The errors noted in the first edition have been corrected.

13c   The | Political | Censor, | or | monthly review | of the | most interesting political occurrences, | relative to | the United States | of | America. [for March 1796] | [rule] | By Peter Porcupine. | [rule]. | The third edition. | [rule] | Philadelphia: | Printed for, and sold by, William Cobbett, No. 25, | North Second Street, opposite Christ Church. | M.DCC.XCVI.

   $[\pi]^2 A^2 B-I^4 = 36$ leaves, 8vo; (5)38–40(1)42–104 ¶ cty; mwa; nn

   Contents: title, 3 blanks, Introduction [37]–40; The | Political | Censor, | for March, 1796 [41]–104. Running title in Introduction.

This edition faithfully follows the first but is completely reset. The errors are corrected. Some other comparisons:

First edition		*Third edition*	
p. [iii]	ornamental rule	p. [37]	swelling rule
iv. l. 24	'expence'	38	'expense'
8	'the' in 1st line of caption	42	'the' in 2d line of caption
16	ornamental rule, 3 ovals	50	rule has 5 ovals
21	'Stenographer'	55	'stenographer' lower case 4 out of 5
49	caption in italics	83	caption in bold, leaded. Extra lines pp. 98,102,103.

14a   The | Political | Censor, | or | monthly review | of the | most interesting political occurrences, | relative to | The United States | of | America [for April 1796] | [rule] | By Peter Porcupine | [rule] | Philadelphia: Printed for Benjamin Davies, No. 68, High-Street | MDCCXCVI.

[A]²B–N⁴O²=52 leaves, 8 vo; (5)72–158,158–165,167–169(1). Plate ¶ Evans 30221; Pearl 15 ¶ MWA

Contents: blank, plate, title, blank, 'The | Political | Censor | for April, 1796' [71]–169, blank. Plate pictures a man above the waist, pointing, with a guillotine behind him, over the caption 'Stop the Wheels of Government'. (Evans states the man is Thomas Paine, but it is no doubt Albert Gallatin. See No. 13a, 'Censor' for March, p.9). Dated in Porcupine's Works (No.59) 'April, 1796'. Gazette of the United States, May 5, 1796: 'This day is published...'

Some errors noted: p.73, l.1 Parenthesis before 'faction'; p.74, l. 10 'Precident'; p.77, ll. 22,23 'Perswaded'; p. 82, l.37 'parts' for 'parties'; p.91, l.13 'sevaral'; p.98, l.29 'r' in 'for' reversed; p.99, l.12 'gived'; p.112, l.7 'fifty five' (p.121 it is 62); p.137, l.23 'preample'; p.139, l.18 'relinguishment'; p.150, l.24 'nothern'; and p.157, l. 4 'you' for 'your'.

The work is an attack on the Congressmen, and on their arguments, who sought in the House to annul the British (Jay) Treaty. It will be recalled that the House passed a resolution requesting the President to supply information on the Treaty negotiations, which Washington declined to do, and that the Republicans then sought to prevent appropriations necessary to carry the Treaty into effect. Pages 73–112 contain an important summation of the debate on the treaty power. The attacks on some of the members, especially Gallatin, Giles, Livingston, Madison and Swanwick, descend to personalities. The work, concluding with a supposed letter dated April 21, 1796, went to press before the decisive vote of April 29, 1796 favoring the Treaty (Censor for May, No. 17a, p. 172).

As to impressment of Americans by the British: 'tyrannical...the effect of that overbearing insolence which is the characteristic of but too many among their subaltern officers....' (p.72). As to the Treaty: 'the outlandish gentlemen, such as Mr. Gallatin for example, may experience serious difficulties [in understanding it].' (p.114.) 'Some of the members of opposition...did not want light.... That profound politician patriot Madison found out five different constructions of one single clause of the constitution....' (p.115). '...the Livingstons harbour a mortal hatred against the family of his Excellency Governor Jay, which hatred is undoubtedly paid back with contempt. The characters of the parties sufficiently explain the cause' (p.117). '...their plan is nothing short of driving the President of the United States from the post he now fills.' (p.118). 'Now where has the patriot [Madison] been...I should be very sorry to suppose that he has drank at the fountain that poisoned his countryman Randolph....' (p.124). 'Indeed, as Mr. Giles observed, the conduct of his State [Virginia] has been uniform...a continual disaffection to the government of the United States, sometimes concealed under the mask of hypocrisy and base crawling flattery, and sometimes breaking out in open opposition....' (p.141). 'Those who have read Mr. Randolph's Vindication, as it was humourously called, have seen how narrowly the President escaped from the plots of that gentleman....' (p.144). 'Mr. Swanwick...has taken upon him to pronounce me a hired English scribbler....I never snapped at the hand that gave me bread.... I am the base and cringing flatterer of no man....' (pp. 146–147). 'I have heard of a sturdy young Lord in England, who got himself elected through the interest of the wives and daughters of his constituents; Mr. Swanwick will never be suspected of *this kind of corruption*; but whether be ought to be suspected of no other kind, is more than I will pretend to determine. Grog is cheap, and its influence is mighty.' (p.148). 'Thus is this opposition bottomed on *dishonesty, corruption* or *ignorance*, and, probably, on all three together.' (p. 151).

A supposed interview is given between Gallatin and Lord Grenville—extract: 'Mr. Gallatin. Insurrection! Me Lort! vy it is de very first article in de bill of rights. I have made von insurrection in de mountains of Pennsylvené, dat is vy I am representative.' (p. 156). (Lord Grenville) 'Can it be possible that the Americans are so poor in talents, so debased in principle, as to entrust their public affairs to an European adventurer, the leader of an insurrection!' (p.158).

'The enemies of peace, in the House of Representatives, are with two honourable exceptions, to be found almost solely in the southern States. Can it be imagined, that the honest and industrious people of the north will suffer themselves to be dragged down to perdition, merely to satisfy the unprincipled vengeance of a nest of fraudulent debtors? Can it be imagined, that the New Englanders will tamely suffer the *lords* of Virginia to sport with their prosperity and happiness, as they do with their barrels of rice and tobacco at a cock-match? Common sense forbids us to believe any such thing.' (pp.164–165.)

14b ———. A variant in which the pages are correctly numbered. The other errors noted have not been corrected. ¶ cty; mwa; nn

14c The | Political | Censor, | or | monthly review | of the | most interesting political occurrences, | relative to | the United States | of | America. [for April 1796] | [rule] | By Peter Porcupine. | [rule] | The second edition | [rule] | Philadelphia: | printed for, and sold by, William Cobbett, No. 25, | North second street, opposite Christ Church. | M.DCC.XCVI.

[A]³B–D⁴F⁴F–I⁴=35 leaves, 8 vo; (5)106–169(1). Plate same as in first edition, 14a ¶ mwa; nn

Contents: blank, plate, title, blank, The | Political | Censor, | for April, 1796 [105]–169, blank.

This edition is a new setting of type. Omitted is the discussion of the debate on the treaty power appearing on pp. 77–112 of the original. On p.156, l.23, the phrase 'first article in de bill of rights' (quoted under 14a) becomes 'first article in de rights of man.' The N.B. on page 169 is omitted. The presidential message is given in full on pp. 111,112. In general the typographical errors are corrected, and the text is a faithful copy of the original.

14d The | Political | Censor; | or | review | of the | most interesting political occurrences, | relative to | the United States | of | America. [for April 1796] | [rule] | By Peter Porcupine. | [rule] | Philadelphia: | Printed for, and sold by, William Cobbett, North | Second Street, opposite Christ Church. | M.DCC.XCVI.

[Second title] The | Political | Censor, | or | monthly review | of the | most interesting political occurrences, | relative to | the United States | of | America | [rule] | By Peter Porcupine. | [rule] | The second edition. | [rule] | Philadelphia: | Printed for, and sold by, William Cobbett, No. 25, | North Second Street, opposite Christ Church. | M.DCC.XCVI.

[A]–D⁴F⁴F–I⁴=36 leaves, 8 vo; (7)106–169(1). The plate is re-engraved ¶ Evans 30222 ¶ cty

Contents: title, blanks (2), plate, title, blank, The | Political | Censor, | for April 1796 [105]–169, blank. The plate pictures a man above the waist (Albert Gallatin) pointing, with a guillotine behind him, a balloon 'Stop de wheels of Government', over the caption 'a Political Sinner'. The figure and the guillotine follow the first edition.

14e   The | Political | Censor, | or | monthly review | of the | most interesting political occurrences, | relative to | The United States | of | America. [for April, 1796] | [rule | By Peter Porcupine | [rule] | The Third Edition | [rule] | Philadelphia: | printed for, and sold by, William Cobbett, No. 25, |North second street, opposite Christ Church. | M.DCC.XCVI.

[A]³B–D⁴F⁴F–I⁴=35 leaves, 8 vo; (5)106–169(1) ¶ NN

Contents: blank, plate, title, blank, 'The | Political | Censor, | for April 1796' [105]–169, blank. The plate is the same as in the second edition. The text appears to be from the same setting of type as the second edition.

14f   ———. A variant in which the plate is on heavy wove paper (rest laid paper) inserted after the title page, so that the first signature is [A]² and the contents begin: title, blank, 'The Political Censor' etc. ¶ Evans 30233 second title ¶ cty

14g   Porcupine's | Political Censor, | for April, 1797. [i.e. 1796] | [rule] | Containing, | Page | Debates in the House of Representatives continued 67/ on papers relative to the Treaty with Great Britain 69 | President's Message to the House of Representatives in reply to | their request of a copy of his instructions to Mr. Jay 73 | Peter Porcupine's remarks on the same 75 | Resolution by way of protest against the President's message, | with remarks 85 | Resolution for setting aside the British Treaty 100 | Peter Porcupine's remarks on the same 101 | Traiterous advertisement of the bankrupts of Virginia 104 | Loyal address of the Virginians to the King of Great Britain in | the year 1769 106 | Review of Monsieur Swanwick's titles and his poetical writings 111 | Lord Grenville's reception of citizen Gallatin, envoy extraor- | dinary to the court of Great Britain 120 | Letter from cousin Hedge-hog of New-York to Peter Porcu- | pine 131 | [rule] [Philadelphia 1797].

[π]¹[A]–I⁴=37 leaves, 8 vo; (5)68–134(2). 'Apr. 96' to left of B; 'Apr. '96' to left of C. Plate as reengraved in 14d ¶ CTY; NN; MWA

Contents: blank, plate, title, blank, 'Debates | in the | House of Representatives, | continued' [67]–134, blank leaf.

Errors noted: p.72, l.19 'negocations'; p.84, under 'Ayes', 'Baiyl' for 'Baily'.

This is a faithful copy of the third edition, from a new setting of type.

15a   Moreau de Saint-Méry, M.L.E., 1750–1819.

A | topographical and political | description | of the | Spanish part | of |Saint-Domingo, | containing, | general observations on the climate, population, | and productions; on the character and man- | ners of the inhabitants; with an account of | the several branches of the government: | to which is prefixed, | a new, correct, and elegant map of the | whole island. | rule | By M.L.E. Moreau de Saint-Méry. | member of the Philosophical Society of Philadelphia, &c. | rule | Translated from the French | by William Cobbett. | [rule] | Vol. I [–II] | [rule] | Philadelphia: | printed and sold by the author, printer and book- | seller, No. 84, South Front-Street. | [rule] | 1796.

[Vol. II does not have a comma after 'Saint-Domingo', nor a dash after 'book'.]

Vol. I—[π]⁴a⁴a–f⁴g³A–T⁴V⁴X–Qq⁴Rr¹=192 leaves, 8 vo;(3)4–8 (1)2–8(1)ii–liv;(1)2–314. 'Vol. I' to left of signatures except first a and except S has only 'Vol.' Map following title page. Running titles (pp. 199, 239 have 'Spainsh'). Vol. II—[A]–T⁴V⁴X–Rr⁴=160 leaves, 8 vo; (3)4–239(2)242–318(2). Second leaves signed except first signature, N2 and Nn2. 'Vol II' to left of main signatures. Running titles. Catchwords p. 16 and each fourth page 48–232 except 224, and a few in index. ¶ Evans 30818; Pearl 11. ¶ CTY; MWA [map lacking]

Contents: Vol. I. Title, blank, [map], List of subscribers [3]–8. Advertisement [1]–8; Historical Summary [i]–liv; Description [1]–

314. Foot of p. 314, 'Entered according to law.' The map is described in Wheat and Brun, Maps and Charts Published in America
before 1800: 693, 694.

Vol. II. Title, blank, Description [3]–239, blank, contents [241]–
318, errata, blank. Page 198, running title 'Descrtption'. Note p.
[241] 'This table is not a translation of Mr. Cobbett.' 123d Pennsylvania District Copyright issued to Saint-Méry January 2, 1796.
Gazette of the United States, May 9, 1796, 'This day is published...'
Volume One.

15b ————. Here the transcription is the same except as follows:
'Saint-Domingo' is followed by a semi-colon; there is no comma
after 'population'; the three lines concerning the map are omitted;
and the date is 1798 instead of 1796. The transcription for Volume
II is the same as for Volume I, except of course the volume number.
Except for omission of the map, the collation, pagination, contents,
etc. are the same as in the preceding entry. The reference to the
map remains in the advertisement, page 8 ¶ Evans 34138 ¶ MWA

16a Burke, Edmund, 1729–1797.
A Letter | from the right honourable | Edmund Burke | to | a
noble lord, | on the | attacks made upon him and his pension, | in the
House of Lords, | by the | Duke of Bedford, | and the | Earl of Laud-
erdale, | early in the present sessions of Parliament. | [rule] | The
first American edition, with a preface, by | Peter Porcupine. |
[rule] | Philadelphia: | Printed for B. Davies, H. & P. Rice, and | J.
Ormrod. [1796].

[A]–H⁴,(I)¹=33 leaves, 8 vo; (3)ii–iv(3)2–58 ¶ Evans 30143,
Pearl 25 ¶ MWA; PPL (repro)

Contents: title, blank, 'Preface to the American Edition' [i]–iv,
blank leaf, 'A Letter, &c.' [1]–58. The last line on page iii begins
'rich merchants'. Subscribed on page iv 'Peter Porcupine'. The
PPL copy has handwritten on the title page 'W. Rawle May:96'.
Gazette of the United States, May 10, 1796: 'This day is published...25 cents...'

Errors noted: p.17, l.34, 'expenee'; p.33, l.13, 'condititions'; p.
38, l.27, 'puplic'; p.54, l.1, 'at' for 'as'; p.58, l.8, upside-down 'a' in
'have'. In the four page Preface, Cobbett sketches the background
of the Letter. It is, he says, a warning to the wealthy sansculottes in
America who depend on the stability of the government yet are en-

deavoring to shake it to the ground. 'Take care then, you rich, fat-brained, round-headed demagogues...' (p.iv).

16b ———. An issue in which the first signature has been reset.
[A]–H⁴I¹=33 leaves, 8 vo; (5)ii–iv(1)2–58 ¶ cty
Contents: blank leaf, title, blank, Preface [i]–iv, A Letter, &c. [1]–58. The latter rule on the title page is 6.9 cm. as against 8.4 cm. in 16a. The first line on p.iv begins 'rich merchants'. 16b has the same errors as noted in 16a. Except for the first signature, it is believed to be from the same setting of type.

16c ———. A variant from 16b in which the blank leaf follows p. iv ¶ NN

17a The | Political | Censor, | or | monthly review | of the | most interesting political occurrences, | relative to | The United States | of | America. [for May 1796] | [rule] | By Peter Porcupine | [rule]. | Philadelphia: | printed for Benjamin Davies, No. 68, High-street, | MDCCXCVI.
[A]²B–I⁴K²=36 leaves, 8 vo; (5)173–239. Plate ¶ Evans 30223, Sabin 14001 ¶ cty
Contents: blank, plate, title, blank, 'The | Political | Censor | for May, 1796' [172]–239. Plate same as for April Censor, original edition, 14a.
The work in divided under the following subtitles: 'Proceedings in the House of Representatives' [on the Jay Treaty] p.[172]; 'Paine's Age of Reason' p. 195; 'Epitaph on Tom Paine' p.206; 'French Generosity' p.208; 'Remarks on the poetical works of John Swanwick of Philadelphia' p.213; 'French fraternity' p.218; 'New discoveries in the regions of corruption' p.225. Under the first title the following men are discussed particularly: p.183, Gallatin; pp. 184–9, Livingston; pp. 189–93, Swanwick; and p.194, Madison. Dated in Porcupine's Works (No. 59) 'May 1796'. Gazette of the United States, May 31, 1796: 'This day published...'
The following errors noted: p.180, l.18 'least' for 'lest'; p.184, l.5 'Somerwille' for 'Somerville'; p.187, l.15 'Plyfair' for 'Playfair'; l.18 'hey' for 'they'; p.199, l.19 'mistery'; p.213, final line 'ri' in 'written' is dropped down; p.234, final line 'h' in 'with' dropped down.
Extracts: on the pending vote on the treaty with Great Britain: 'Terror had seized on all those who had something to lose; they knew not whether...their ships were safest in the harbour or out at

sea; the sans-culottes began to grind their teeth and whet their couteaux, while the heads of the aristocrats seemed to totter on their shoulders, and hang as it were by a bit of skin.' (p.172) On Muhlenberg's vote deciding the affirmative: 'What an excellent political weather-cock! He tacks with ten times the celerity of the Indian on top of his Sugar-house.' (p.175) 'How the Clerk of the House [John Beckley] came to miscount...well worth asking.' (p. 176) The memorial of the Merchants and Traders of Philadelphia [reproduced] was decisive (p.180). 'With what art did the *Genevese* [Gallatin] approach! how did he twist and turn...how did his eyes glisten!...' (p.183) '...the *Long-man* from New York [Livingston]... who labours under an extreme poverty of talents.... His head is generally thought to be as empty as his purse ever was.... (p. 184). What is he to do!—Jog back quietly to daddy's, make the most of his personal charms, ogle the fair sex in place of grinning at General Washington, and content himself with reading billets doux instead of state papers.' (p.189) '...the little duck legged Squire [Swanwick].... 'Tis as gentle a little creature as you ever set eyes on... (p.189) he is more an object of ridicule than...poor Gulliver astride the nipple of the Brabdingnagian maid of honour.... That a vain man should condescend to cajole the mob, to grease the hands of the leaders of a club or society, that he should crawl to news-printers... is not so very surprising; but that he should...profess himself the periodical declaimer at the breakings-up of a boarding school...is what no mortal could ever have expected, no, not from John Swanwick.' (p.191). 'Epitaph' [on Tom Paine]: 'When the wight, who here lies beneath the cold earth, | First quitted the land that had given him birth, | He commenc'd the apostle of bloodshed and strife, | and practis'd the trade to the end of his life, | ... And at last, to the sorrow of all the beholders, | He march'd out of life with his head on his shoulders.' (pp. 207, 208). On John Swanwick as poet: 'small-beer verses...the little whiffling poetastor...a sneer contracts the muscles of my nose....' (p.217). On Noah Webster: '...a high reputation for candour and understanding...a bold and able defender of the British treaty....' (pp. 227, 228). 'The insurrection in the Western Counties of Pennsylvania...was imputed to the machinations of Great Britain...but...the appearance of Citizen Fauchet's intercepted letter..."clapped the saddle on the right horse".' (p.234)

17b ———. A variant in which the errors noted on p. 184, p. 187 l.18, and p.213 are corrected ¶ MWA; NN

17c The | Political | Censor, | or | monthly review | of the | most interesting political occurrences, | relative to | The United States | of | America. [for May 1796] | [rule] | By Peter Porcupine | [rule] | The second edition | [rule] | Philadelphia: | Printed for, and sold by, William Cobbett, No. 25, |North second street, opposite Christ Church. | M.DCC.XCVI.

[A]²B–I⁴K²=36 leaves, 8 vo; (5)174–240. No plate ¶ Evans 30224 ¶ cty; NN

Contents: title, 3 blanks, The | Political | Censor, | for May, 1796 [173]–240. This edition is a new setting of type. It is apparently a faithful copy of the first edition, with the errors corrected, new pagination and different ornamental rules. Some comparisons:

First edition		*Second edition*	
Page [172], last of caption		Page [173] 'SENTATIVES'	
'PRESENTATIVES'			
213	'delphia'	214	'ladelphia'
225	ornamental rule	226	no rule

17d The | Political | Censor, | or | monthly review | of the | most interesting political occurrences, | relative to | the United States | of | America [for May 1796] | [rule] | By Peter Porcupine | [rule] | The third edition | [rule] | Philadelphia: | Printed for, and sold by, William Cobbett, No. 25, | North Second Street, opposite Christ Church. | M.DCC.XCVI.

The description is the same as for the second edition ¶ cty; MWA

17e ———. A variant which begins with the blank leaf ¶ NN

18a The | Scare-Crow; | being | an infamous letter, | sent to Mr. John Oldden, | threatening destruction to his house, and violence to | the person of his tenant, William Cobbett; | with | remarks on the same | [rule] | By Peter Porcupine. | [rule] | Philadelphia: | Printed for, and sold by, William Cobbett, | North Second street, opposite Christ Church. | M.DCC.XCVI.

[A]–C⁴=12 leaves, 8vo; (3)4–23(1) ¶ Evans 30231, Pearl 16 ¶ cty; MWA; NN

Contents: title, blank, The Scare-Crow &c. [3]–23, blank. P. 23: | 'From the free Press of | William Cobbett, | July 22d, 1796. | End.' At the top of page [3] are two lines of printers ornaments. Catchword 'when' on page 9. Dated in Porcupine's Works (No. 59): 'July, 1796'.

Error noted: p.22, l.7 begins 'tithe' instead of 'the'. And see 18c. Account Book Sale Date July 23, 1796. The Book records sales of 425 copies at 12½¢. Claypoole's American Daily Advertiser, July 23, 1796: 'This day is published by William Cobbett...'

A threatening letter to Oldden is quoted, dated July 16th 1796 (pp.3, 4) and then discussed (p.5): 'If I am right in my guess, the family of the author of this powder blunderbuss makes a considerable figure in the Tyburn Chronicle...his *papa* came to the southern part of these States on his travels, by the direction of a righteous judge and twelve honest men.' He defies criticism of his shop-window display of Earl Howe: 'The print is not sold, nor shall it be. I will keep it in my windows as long as any violence is talked of...'. (p.11) 'I have a right reverend Father in God in one corner of my window, and if I could procure that right irreverent Father in the Devil, Tom Paine, I would hoist him up in the other; for want of him I have Doctor Priestley, who, upon a shift, is very capable of supplying his place.' (pp.14,15). '...all the stink pots of all the democrats in the Western hemisphere shall never drive me from America, nor make me take coach in disguise, as the Birmingham philosopher [Priestley] did.' (p.18). 'If they [the democrats] despised my "miserable productions", why not laugh at them, as I do at theirs? Why not suffer them to rot on the shelf, like the political [sic] Progress of Britain [No. 130], or be kicked about the street, like the Aurora [of B. F. Bache]?' (p.22) '...I will continue to publish and expose for sale whatever I please, and that I will never cease to oppose, in some way or other, the enemies of the country in which I live, so long as one of them shall have the impudence to show his head. Hitherto I have given acids only, I will now drench them with vinegar mixed with gall.' (p.23).

Cobbett's use of 'from the free press of William Cobbett' was ridiculed by Samuel F. Bradford in 'The Impostor Detected.... Supplement', p.12 (No. 136). He said Cobbett had no press. Cobbett replied in the Political Censor for September 1796 (p.77) that he had 'two [presses] now at work for me, and the printers are always paid the instant their work is done.'

18b ———. A variant in which the word 'tithe', p.22, l.7, has been corrected to 'the'. The last six lines on page 21 are reset; last line begins 'mocratic'. ¶ MWA

18c The | Scare-Crow; | being | an infamous letter, | sent to Mr. John Oldden, | threatening destruction to his house, and violence to | the person of his tenant, William Cobbett. | with | remarks on the same | by Peter Porcupine. | [rule] | The second edition | [rule] | Philadelphia: | printed for, and sold by, William Cobbett, | North Second Street, opposite Christ Church. | M.DCC.XCVI.

[A]–C⁴=12 leaves, 8 vo; (3)4–23(1) ¶ Evans 30232, Pearl 16, Sabin 14016 ¶ cty; mwa; nn

Contents: title, blank, The Scare-Crow, &c[3]–23; blank. Two lines of printer's ornaments at the top of page [3]. On page 23: 'From the free Press of | William Cobbett, | July 22d 1796. | END.' Catchword "when on p. 9. A faithful copy of the first edition but a new setting of type. Some comparisons:

	First edition 18a	*Second edition 18c*
p. 5, last	this	this
p. 7, l.23	Fouchet	Fauchet
p. 8, l.1	harrangues	harangues
p.13, l.21	line begins, the	begins, "the
p.15, l.15	angels	Angels
p.19, l.28	he	,he
p.21	The last six lines of 18c correspond with 18b.	

19a   The | Life and Adventures | of | Peter Porcupine, | with | a full and fair account | of | all his authoring transactions; | being a sure and infallible guide for all enterprising young | men who wish to make a fortune by writing | pamphlets. | [rule] | By Peter Porcupine Himself. | [rule] | "Now, you lying Varlets, you shall see how a plain tale will | "put you down." | Shakespeare. | [rule] | Philadelphia: | Printed for, and sold by, William Cobbett, at No. | 25, North Second Street, opposite Christ Church. | M.DCC.XCVI.

[A]–G⁴H²=30 leaves, 8 vo; (3)iv–viii(1)10–58(2) ¶ Evans 30212, Pearl 17, Sabin 13892 ¶ cty

Contents: title, blank, Preface [iii]–viii; 'The Life and Adventures of Peter Porcupine' [9]–58; 'Proposals'; blank. Running title in the Preface. On p.58 'Copyright secured according to law.' The 'Proposals' are for publishing The History of Jacobinism, by William Playfair, with an appendix By Peter Porcupine. Type misaligned last two lines of p.19 in 'but' and 'Ports'

144th Pennsylvania District Copyright issued to William Cobbett August 5, 1796. Dated in Porcupine's Works, (No. 59): 'August 1796.' Gazette of the United states, August 8, 1796: 'This day is published by William Cobbett...' Account Book Sale Date August

8, 1796. The Book records sales of 513 copies at 31¢. In the 'Blue Shop' (No. 146) the publication date is given as August 8th.

In brief, the work describes Cobbett's boyhood; flight to London; clerkship to an attorney; career in the army, mainly in New Brunswick, 1784–1791; discharge as Sergeant Major; marriage; to France in March 1792; to New York October 1792; letter from Jefferson November 5, 1792; his dispute with Thomas Bradford; the payments made to him by Bradford, ending in March 1796; accusations he was in British pay.

Extracts: '...I little expected that the harmless essays from my pen would have conjured up against me this numerous and stupid host...their ignorance lessens the honour conferred by their envy, hatred and malice' (p.iii). 'Let them write on, till their old pens are worn to the stump.... If ever they hear me whine or complain, I will give them leave to fritter my carcass and trail my guts along the street....' (p.viii). His grandmother's house: 'It was a little thatched cottage with a garden before the door. It had but two windows: a damson tree shaded one, and a clump of filberts the other. Here I and my brothers went every Christmas and Whitsuntide, to spend a week or two, and torment the poor old woman with our noise and dilapidations. She used to give us milk and bread for breakfast, an apple pudding for our dinner, and a piece of bread and cheese for supper. Her fire was made of turf, cut from the neighboring heath, and her evening light was a rush dipped in grease.'

'How much better is it, thus to tell the naked truth, than to descend to such miserable shifts as Doctor Franklin has had recourse to, in order to persuade people, that his fore-fathers were men of wealth and consideration' (p.10). 'Every one will, I hope, have the goodness to believe, that my grandfather was no philosopher. Indeed he was not. He never made a lightning rod nor bottled up a single quart of sun-shine in the whole course of his life. He was no almanac-maker, nor quack, nor chimney-doctor, nor soap-boiler, nor ambassador, nor printer's devil; neither was he a deist, and all his children were born in wedlock...if his descendents cannot point to his statue over the door of a library, they have not the mortification to hear him daily accused of having been a whoremaster, a hypocrite and an infidel' (p.11).

'My first occupation was, driving the small birds from the turnip seed, and the rooks from the peas. When I first trudged a-field, with my wooden bottle and my satchel swung over my shoulders, I was hardly able to climb the gates and stiles....' (p.12) '...I perceived that the [recruiting] Captain thought I had eloped on account of a bastard. I blushed, and that confirmed him in his opinion; but I declare to the reader, that I was no more guilty of such an offense than Mr. Swanwick, or any other gentleman who is constitutionally virtuous. No; thank heaven, I have none of the Franklintonian crimes to accuse myself of; my children do not hang their hats up in other men's houses; I am neither patriot nor philosopher.' (p.19). 'Gracious heaven! if I am doomed to be wretched, bury me beneath Iceland snows, and let me feed on blubber;...nay, if it be thy will, suffocate me with the infected and pestilential air of a democratic club room; but save me from the desk of an attorney!' (p.23)

'...I was fool enough to imagine that the press was really free for every one. I had not the least idea, that a man's windows were in danger of being broken, if he published anything that was *not popular*. I did, indeed, see the words *liberty* and *equality*, the *rights of man*, the *crimes of kings*, and such like, in most of the bookseller's windows; but I did not know that they were put there to save the glass...' (p.39). 'Even the *Bone to Gnaw for the Democrats*... was "Published for the Purchasers." It was not till long after the public had fixed the seal of approbation on these pamphlets, that they were honoured with the bookseller's name [Bradford]. It was something curious that the second and third and fourth editions should be entitled to a mark of respect that the first was not worthy of. Poor little innocents! They were thrown on the parish like foundlings; no soul would own them, till it was found that they possessed the gift of bringing in the pence. Another singularity, is, they got into better paper as they advanced. So the prudent matron changes the little dirty ragged wench into a fine mademoiselle, as soon as she perceives that the beaux begin to cast their eyes on her.' (pp.40, 41). 'And if I have given way to my indignation when a hypocritical political divine [Priestley] attempted to degrade my country, or when its vile calumniators called it "an insular Bastile", what have I done more than every good man in my place would have done?... When a man hears his country reviled, does it require that he should be paid for speaking in its defence?' (pp.51,52). '...Yes, in spite of envy, malice and falsehood, I say, my numerous and respectable friends, who, I trust, will be well pleased to find, that there is nothing in the history of Peter Porcupine to raise a blush for the commendations they have bestowed on his works, or to render them unworthy of their future support.' (p.58).

19b ———. A variant in which the misaligned type on page 19 is corrected ¶ cty; mwa; nn

19c The | Life and Adventures | of | Peter Porcupine, | with | a full and fair account | of | all his authoring transactions; | being a sure and infallible guide for all enterprising young | men who wish to make a fortune by writing | pamphlets. | [rule] | By Peter Porcupine himself. | [rule] | [two lines from] Shakespeare. | [rule] | Second Edition | [rule] | Philadelphia: | printed for, and sold by, William Cobbett, North | Second Street, opposite Christ Church | [rule] | Oct. 1796.

[A]–G⁴=28 leaves, 8 vo; (3)iv–viii(1)10–56 ¶ Evans 30213 ¶ cty; mwa

Contents: title, blank, Preface [iii]–viii; The Life [9]–56. On page 56 'END' and, between rules, 'Copy right secured according to law.' Running title in preface.

This edition is a new setting of type. It follows the first edition. One change is noted: 'had my salvation depended on a compliance', on p. 44 of first edition, becomes 'had my life' etc. on p.43, l.11. Page viii, l.6 of 19a begins 'ed' and of 19c begins 'in'. Page [9] last line of 19a begins 'one' and of 19c begins 'died'. Thereafter the last lines are different except that on p.32 of 19a and p.31 of 19c it is 'kind to excess'. P.11, l.32 of 19a 'mathematicks' and p.11, l.27 of 19c. 'mathematics'

19d The |Life and Adventures | of | Peter Porcupine, | with | a full and fair account | of | all his authoring transactions; | being a sure and infallible guide for all enterprising young | men who wish to make a fortune by writing | pamphlets. | [rule] | By Peter Porcupine himself. | [rule] | [two lines from] Shakespeare. | [rule] | Philadelphia: | Printed for, and sold by, William Cobbett, at | No. 25, North Second-Street, opposite Christ Church. | London reprinted, and sold by J. Wright, No. 169, | opposite old Bond-Street, Piccadilly. | [rule] | 1797.

[A]²a⁴B,C¹²,D⁶=36 leaves, 12 mo; (5)iv v iv vii–ix(2)2–58(2). Leaves signed a2, B2–6, C2–6, D2,3 ¶ cty; nn

Contents: half-title, blank, title, blank, Preface [iii]–v,iv,vii–ix, blank, The Life [1]–58, blank leaf. Running titles.

A faithful rendition of the first edition. Some variations noted: p.7, l.4 'free, happy, or industrious' for 'industrious, happy or free';

p.17, last line 'pettifogging' added before 'attorney'; p.37, l.3 'out' instead of 'in'; p.39, l.5 'enormous' added.

Some errors noted: p.3, l.21 'green sword'; p.16, l.12 'doy'; p.24, l.22 'Cobbet'; p.39, l.7 'Sate' for 'State'; p.56, l.11 'Pit' for 'Pitt'; p.58, running title, the 'OF' is inverted.

19e ———. A variant in which the running title on p.58 is corrected, while on p.57 the running title is 'Perer Porcupine' ¶ cty; MWA

19f The | Life and Adventures | of | Peter Porcupine, | with a full and fair account | of | all his authoring transactions; | being a sure and infallible guide for all enterprising | young men who wish to make a fortune by writing | pamphlets. | To which is added. | his will and testament. | [rule] | By Peter Porcupine himself. | [rule] | [two lines from] | Shakespeare | [rule] | Glasgow: | printed by D. Niven; | and sold by A. Cameron, D. Niven, and J. Murdoch, | booksellers, Trongate. | 1798.

[π]²A–D⁶E⁴=30 leaves, 12 mo; (5)iv–viii(1)10–46(1)48–57(1). ¶ cty

Contents: half-title, blank, title, blank, preface [iii]–viii; Life [9]–46; will [47]–57; advertisement. The will is taken from the Political Censor for March 1797 (No. 31).

19g The | life | of William Cobbett. | [rule] | By Himself. | [rule] | intended as an encouraging example | to | all young men of humble fortune; | being a proof of what can be effected | by steady application and honest efforts. | [rule] | London: | printed by B. McMillan, Bow Street, Covent Garden; | for T. Purday & Son, No. 1, Paternoster-Row. | [rule] | 1809. | [price three shillings.] ¶ Colophon: London: printed by B. M'Millan, | Bow Street, Covent Garden.

[A]¹B–H⁴I³=32 leaves, 21.7 cm; (3)2–61(1). Second leaves signed, except D2. ¶ Pearl 71 ¶ NJR; NN (lacks title).

Contents: title, blank, the life [1]–61, advertisements. Running titles. The text is slightly abridged from the original Life. (Pearl)

19h The | Life | of | William Cobbett, | author of the | Political Register. | [rule] | written by himself. | second edition. | [rule] | London: | printed for W. Hone, 55, Fleet Street, | and 67, Old Bailey, | (three doors from Ludgate Hill.) | 1816. | [price fourpence.] | [rule] | printed by Macdonald and Son, 46, Cloth Fair.

Colophon: printed by Macdonald and son, 46, cloth fair, London.
[A]⁸=eight leaves, 21.5 cm; (2)3–16. Second leaf signed A2. ¶
Pearl 86 ¶ NJR

Contents: title, The Life of William Cobbett [2]–16. On page 16
'The end'.

There were many other later editions of the 'Life'. A handsome
edition was published by the Nonesuch Press, London 1927, with
an introduction and notes by G.D.H. Cole.

20a   The | Political | Censor; | or | review | of the | most interest-
ing political occurrences, | relative to | The United States | of |
America [for September 1796] | [rule] | By Peter Porcupine. |
[rule] | Philadelphia: | printed for, and sold by, William Cobbett,
North | Second Street, opposite Christ Church. | M.DCC.XCVI.

[A]–K⁴=40 leaves, 8 vo; (3)4–49(2)52–79(1) ¶ Evans 30225,
Pearl 15 ¶ CtY; MWA; NN

Contents: title, blank, heading: The | Political | Censor, | for
September, 1796. | [rule] | Life | of | Thomas Paine...[3]–49, blank,
heading: 'Remarks | on the Pamphlets lately published against |
Peter Porcupine' [51]–79; advertisement, which concludes: '...he
makes a very great allowance to those who take by the dozen or
more.' Foot of page 79: 'The History of Jacobinism will be published in the course of the next month, after which, the Political
Censor will be continued monthly, without interruption'. On page
[80] are advertised two books: 'An answer to Paine's Rights of
Man' by H. Makenzie 'in the press'; and also 'William Cobbett has
just published 'a new drawing book, from the best masters'; price
1 D. 25 Cts.'

Error noted p.71 next to last line 'you' for your'. 153rd Pennsylvania District copyright issued to William Cobbett September 24,
1796. Dated in Porcupine's Works (No. 59) 'September 1796'.
Account Book Sale Date September 26, 1796. The Book records
sales of 664 copies at 31¢. Gazette of the United States, September
26, 1796, 'this day is published by William Cobbett'.

The Life of Paine consists largely of excerpts from that of
Francis Oldys (George Chalmers). There is only a remote resemblance to the facts of Paine's life as presently accepted.

Some of Cobbett's comments: 'Paine's humanity...is of the spec-
ulative kind. It never breaks out into action.' (pp.10,11). On
Rousseau: 'He writes for the human race, his heart bleeds for the

distresses of the human race, and, in the midst of all this, he sends his unfortunate bastards to the poor-house, the receptacle of misery!' (p.11). On Laurence Sterne: 'Certainly nothing is so disgusting as this, except it be to see the humane and sentimental Sterne wiping away a tear at the sight of a dead jack-ass, while his injured wife and child were pining away their days in a nunnery, and while he was debauching the wife of his friend.' (p.11). Cobbett quotes from Zephaniah Swift, 'A System of the Laws of the State of Connecticut', II, 324 note, to the effect that Congress dismissed Paine for breach of trust. (p.26) He charges that Paine had a part of monies misapplied by Franklin in selling to the United States arms which had been given by France. (p.27). 'Let us now return to the hoary blasphemer at the bottom of his dungeon. There he lies! Manacled, besmeared with filth, crawling with vermin, loaded with years and infamy. This, reader, whatever you may think of him, is the author of the Rights of Man....' (pp.47,48). Cobbett concludes as to Paine: 'How Tom gets a living now, or what brothel he inhabits, I know not, nor does it much signify to anybody here or anywhere else. He has done all the mischief he can in the world, and whether his carcass is at last to be suffered to rot on the earth, or to be dried in the air, is of very little consequence. Whenever and wherever he breathes his last, he will excite neither sorrow nor compassion, no friendly hand will close his eyes, not a groan will be uttered, not a tear will be shed. Like *Judas* he will be remembered by posterity; men will learn to express all that is base, malignant, treacherous, unnatural and blasphemous, by the single monosyllable, *Paine.*' (pp.48,49.)

The second part of the pamphlet deals with Cobbett's critics and begins: '"Dear Father, when you used to set me off to work in the morning, dressed in my blue smock-frock and woollen spatterdashes, with my bag of bread and cheese and bottle of small beer swung over my shoulder on the little crook that my old God-father Boxall gave me, little did you imagine that I should one day become so great a man as to have my picture stuck in the windows, and have four whole books published about me in the course of one week."—Thus begins a letter which I wrote to my father yesterday morning, and which, if it reaches him, will make the old man drink an extraordinary pot of ale to my health.' (p.51.) He then discusses the 'Roaster', by Sim Sansculotte, i.e. John Swanwick,(No. 150); 'The Blue Shop', by James Quicksilver, i.e. Santiago Puglia, (No. 146); the caricature of Porcupine (No. 145); History of a Porcupine, by A Henderson, actually 'The Adventures of a Porcupine' (No. 142) and 'A Pill for Porcupine', by James Carey, (No. 138.) As to 'The Impostor Detected', by Timothy Tickletoby, i.e. Samuel F. Bradford, (No. 136) the comments are mainly directed to the father of the author, printer Thomas Bradford. 'The Bradfords are booksellers died in grain. Heaven is with them worth nothing, unless they can get something by it.' (pp.64,65). 'This *hatter-turned-printer*, [Samuel] this sooty-fisted son of ink and urine, whose heart is as black and as foul as the liquid in which he dabbles, must have written, if he did write, at the special instance and request of his father....' (p.65). The Bradfords 'were never out of my debt, from the moment they published the first pamphlet, which was in Aug. 1794....' (p.70) 'Martens' Law of Nations [No. 8a,] a work I translated...The dedication was written by me..."give the old boy [Washington] a little more oil", said he [Bradford]. This greasing I refused to have any hand in....' (p.75). 'Bark away, hell-hounds, till you are suffocated in your own foam.' (p.79). Claypoole's American Daily Advertiser, September 13, 1796, Cobbett advertises for sale: 'grub sheet pamphlets vomited forth against Peter Porcupine'.

20b   An | Antidote | for | Tom Paine's | theological and political poison: | containing | 1. Tom's Life, interspersed with remarks and reflections | by P. Porcupine. | 2. An apology for the Bible, in a series of letters ad- | dressed to Paine by the Bishop of Landaff. | 3. An apology for Christianity, by the same learned, | elegant writer. | 4. An answer to Paine's anarchical nonsense, commonly | called, the Rights of Man. | [rule] | Philadelphia: | Printed for, and sold by, William Cobbett, North | Second Street, opposite Christ Church. | [rule] | Oct. 1796.

[A]–K⁴=40 leaves, 8 vo; (3)4–49(2)52–79(1) ¶ Evans 30204 ¶ DLC

Contents: title, blank, 'The Political Censor, for September 1796 | [rule] | Life of Thomas Paine' [3]–49, blank, 'Remarks | on the pamphlets lately published against | Peter Porcupine' [51]–79; advertisement. Foot of page 79, 'End of Censor for September' and four line note.

This work is the same, except for the title-page, as the Political Censor [for September 1796], No. 20a, but on finer paper and priced at $1.25, with 20¢ for binding. Account Book Sale Date December 5, 1796. The Book records sales of only 56 copies.

20c   Porcupine's | Political Censor, | for Sept. 1796. | [rule] | containing, | page | The Life of Tom Paine, interspersed with | remarks and reflections 251 | Remarks on 'A Roaster for Peter Porcupine' 301 | 'The Blue Shop' 301 | 'Porcupine, a Print' 302 | 'History of a Porcupine' 305 | 'A Pill for Porcupine' 306 | 'The Impostor detected;' with anec- | dotes of the family of Lord Bradford 309 | [rule] | Philadelphia: | Published by William Cobbett, opposite Christ Church; | where all letters to the publisher are desired to be | addressed, post-paid. [1797].

[A]–K⁴=40 leaves, 8 vo; (3)252–298(1)300–327(1). Signatures have 'Vol. II [Sept.]' alongside to the left, except that on B '[Sept.]' is to the right ¶ Evans 31948 ¶ CtY; MWA

Contents: title, blank, heading 'Porcupine's | Political Censor, | for September, 1796 | [rule] | Life | of | Thomas Paine' [251]–298; heading: 'Remarks | on the Pamphlets lately published against | Peter Porcupine.' [299]–327, concludes 'End of the Censor for September', blank.

This is a new setting of type which faithfully follows the 1796 edition.

Changes and errors noted: p.257, l.1, 'timely' was 'timeful'; p. 262, l.11, 'wilful' was 'wilfully'; p.263, l.25, 'tabacco'; p.290, l.18, 'King's' was 'Kings'; p.292, l.5, 'when' was 'time'; p.296, l.23, 'cavilion' was 'civilian'; p.320, l.14, 'your' was 'you'; p.320, l.21, 'accknowledgement'; p.326, l.6, 'arugment'.

20d   The | Life | of | Thomas Paine, | interspersed with | remarks and reflections, | by | Peter Porcupine, | author of the Bloody Buoy, | etc. etc. | [rule] | [two lines from] | Churchill. | [rule] | Philadelphia, printed, | London, reprinted for J. Wright, opposite Old | Bond Street, Piccadilly. | [rule] | 1797.

[π]¹A–D⁶E⁵=30 leaves, 12 mo; (3)4–60. Second and third leaves signed. ¶ Pearl 20 ¶ NN

Contents: title, blank, Life | of | Thomas Paine,... [3]–60. 'Finis' on p. 60. Running titles: on p. 23 has 'HTOMAS'; p. 47 the 'of' is repeated; p. 51 it is 'Payne'. Taken from the September Censor. Perhaps this is the basis for Sabin 13894, S. T. Evans 48090 (p.157col.1) and Evans Supp. B9897.

20e   Cobbett's | review | of | the life | of | Thomas Paine. [two vignettes 3.9 cm., that on the left entitled above] Thomas Paine. [and that on the right entitled above] William Cobbett | sold by

Howard, 33, Gray's Inn Lane. | [rule] | Price Two-pence. | [rule]
[Caption title. np.nd.]

Colophon: R. Gilbert, Printer, St. John's Square, London.

[A]¹²=twelve leaves, 17.4 cm. (trimmed); (1)2–24. Fifth leaf
signed A5 ¶ DLC

Running title. Press numbers pages 10, 12. Taken from the
September Censor.

20f   The life | of | Thomas Paine, | interspersed with | remarks and
reflections | [rule] | by William Cobbett. | [rule] | [two lines from] |
Churchill | [rule] | London; | printed by S. M'Dowall, | No. 95,
Leadenhall-street, | and sold at No. 1, Paternoster Row. | [rule] |
Price half-a-crown. [n.d.]

[A]¹B–D⁸E⁵=30 leaves; (3)2–57(1) ¶ MB [Davis]

Contents: title, blank, text [1]–57, blank.

20g   The | life | of | Thomas Paine, | author of the 'Age of Reason',
&c. | as published with | the observations | of | William Cobbett: |
to which are subjoined, | some additional facts, | describing his last
years and miserable | end. | [rule] | Durham: | printed by F. Humble
and Co. Market-Place, | and sold by all the booksellers. | [rule]
1819. | price threepence.

[A],B⁶C⁴=16 leaves, 17.3 cm; (3)iv(1)6–32. ¶ Not located
[Davis]

Contents: title, blank, to the reader [iii]iv, text [5]–32.

21   No entry.

22   Mackenzie, H[enry], 1745–1831.

An | Answer | to | Paine's Rights of Man. | [rule] | By H. Maken-
zie [sic] Esq. of Edinborough | [rule] | to which is added | a |
letter from P. Porcupine | to Citizen John Swanwick, an English-
man, | the son of a British waggon-master, and member of Con-
gress | for the City of Philadelphia. | [rule] | Philadelphia: | Printed
for, and sold by, William Cobbett, North | Second Street, Opposite
Christ Church. | [rule] | Oct. 1796.

[A]–M⁴=48 leaves, 8 vo; (3)iv–vii(2)10–91(2)94–96. ¶ Evans
30727, Sabin 43429, Pearl 19 ¶ CtY; MWA

Contents: title, blank, Dedication, To Doctor Joseph Priestley
[iii]–vii, blank, An Answer [9]–91, blank, A Letter to Citizen John

Swanwick [93]–96. Running title in the Dedication. Row of printer's ornaments at the top of page [3]; rules, ornamented at the ends, at the top of page [93]. Advertised in 20a as 'in the press'.

Errors noted: p.13, l.22 'Saib' for 'Sahib'; p.83, l.10 'tripple'. Account Book Sale Date October 18, 1796. The Book records sales of 399 copies at 37½¢. Claypoole's American Daily Advertiser, October 18, 1796 'this day is published'.

The dedication is an attack by Cobbett on Priestley, accusing him of betrayal of his mother country, Britain. 'The father of a family, attacked by a band of ruffians, may have so behaved as to merit but little compassion from the spectators; but should his own children join with the assailants, resentment and every other hostile feeling against the parent, is lost in detestation of his unnatural offspring'. (p.vii).

Mackenzie's work, written in 1792 (see p.64, l.17,18), spends very little time on Paine. It is a defence of the English form of government, as contrasted with that of France, and with republican government generally, excepting America because of its few citizens, thinly scattered.

The letter addressed to Swanwick attacks him, particularly as having hired a 'Scotch Runaway' [J. T. Callender] to write a pamphlet, to promote Swanwick's election to Congress, which boasted of Swanwick's charitable donations. This pamphlet is 'British Honour and Humanity' (No. 137.) Cobbett suggests to Swanwick 'furnishing the churches with chafing-dishes to keep the females comfortable, while in the performance of their devotions, and thus undermine them, as it were, with...generosity'. (p.95). But he fears that the women of Philadelphia would not vote for Swanwick. Swanwick replied to Cobbett in 'a Roaster; or a check to the progress of political blasphemy...' (No. 150).

23 The | Gros Mousqueton Diplomatique; | or | diplomatic | blunderbuss. | containing, | citizen Adet's notes to the Secretary of | State. | As also his | cockade proclamation. | with a | preface, | by Peter Porcupine. | [rule] | Philadelphia: | Printed for, and sold by, William Cobbett, | Opposite Christ Church. | [rule] | Nov. 1796.

[A]–I⁴,K²=38 leaves, 8 vo; (5)iv–vi(1)6–72 ¶ Evans 30208; Pearl 22, Sabin 13884 ¶ CtY; MWA; NN

Contents: half-title, blank, title, blank, Preface [iii]–vi; The Gros Mousqueton Diplomatique [5]–72; pp. [5]–11, Note of Adet,

French Minister, to Pickering, Secretary of State, dated Oct. 27, 1796, with copy of French decree on neutral trade, taken from Aurora of Oct. 31, 1796; pp. 11–16, Pickering to Adet Nov. 1, 1796 in reply; pp. 17,18 'Cockade Proclamation' [caption] Adet to the French citizens Nov. 2, 1796, from the Aurora of Nov. 5, 1796; pp. 19,20, Adet to the French citizens Nov. 15, 1796, from the Aurora of Nov. 16, 1796; pp. 20–46, Adet to Pickering, Nov. 15, 1796, from the Aurora of Nov. 21, 1796; pp. 46–72, notes in support of the preceding item. Running title pp. iv–vi. P. 64, figure missing at beginning of last line. Dated in Porcupine's Works (No. 59) 'October 1796'. Gazette of the United States, November 28, 1796: 'This day is published....' Account Book Sale Date November 25, 1796. The Book records sales of 400 copies at 25¢.

The preface justifies the use of the word 'blunderbuss' to characterize Adet's communications: 'such a gasconading, impudent bluff....' p. [iii].

24a   Playfair, William 1759–1823.

The | History of Jacobinism, | its crimes, cruelties and perfidies: | comprising | an enquiry | into the manner of disseminating, under the appearance of | philosophy and virtue, | principles | which are equally subversive of | order, virtue, religion, | liberty and happiness. | [rule] | By William Playfair. | [rule] | with an appendix, | by Peter Porcupine, | containing a history of the American Jacobins, commonly | denominated Democrats. | [rule] | Vol. I [II] | [rule] | [three lines from] | Burke. | [rule] | Philadelphia: | printed for William Cobbett, North Second | Street, opposite Christ Church. | 1796. Third Title: History | of the | American Jacobins, | commonly denominated | Democrats. | [rule] | By Peter Porcupine. | [rule] | [three lines from] | Burke. | [rule] | Philadelphia: | Printed for William Cobbett, North Second | Street, opposite Christ Church. | [rule] | Nov. 1796.

[a]–d⁴,A–U⁴X–Uu⁴,Xx⁴;[a]⁴,A–U⁴,X–Oo⁴;[A]–F⁴=192; 152; 24 leaves, 8 vo; (5)6–11(8)20–30(3)36–385(1);(9)10–250(1)252–301 (3);(5)8–48(2). Signature Oo and following pages on wove paper watermarked 1796 ¶ Evans 31016, Pearl 23 ¶ cty

Contents: half-title, blank, title, blank, 'To the Public' [5]–11, dated p.11 'June 4th, 1795', blank, 'Contents' [13]–[17], blank, 'Preface' [19]–30, blank leaf, 'History' [35]–385, blank. [Vol. II] half-title, blank, title, blank, 'Contents' [5]–[7], blank, 'History' [9]–250, 'Notes' [251]–301, blank. 'Appendix', blank, title, blank, 'Dedica-

tion to William Playfair' [5],[6] dated on p.[6] 'Philadelphia 10th
Nov. 1796', 'History' [7]–48, blank leaf. 'END' on p. 48. Running
titles and catchwords in Vols. I and II. Vol I, p. '12' for p. '125';
Vol. II, p.'6' for p. '61'. In appendix, p.30, l.12 'recal'; p.45, l.20
'groupes'. The 'Appendix' page is part of the last gathering of Vol.
II. It accounts for the paging of the third title. This title also ap-
peared separately (see No. 24d). Printed by Samuel Sansom, Jr. of
Philadelphia. See Cobbett's Account Book, appendix, at page 000.
Account Book Sale Date November 28, 1796. The Book records
sales of 259 copies at from $2.50 to $3.75. The Life...of Porcupine
(No. 19a) has appended 'Proposals...for publishing by subscription
"The History of Jacobinism...", with an appendix by Peter Porcupine' in 2 volumes at a dollar and a quarter per volume to subscribers, a dollar and a half to others. The proposals were advertised
Gazette of the United States, August 12, 1796. No. 20a, Political
Censor for September, states that 'The History of Jacobinism will
be published in the course of the next month.' Claypoole's American Daily Advertiser, November 29, 1796: 'just published by William Cobbett.'

In the Appendix, Cobbett excoriates all French sympathizers in
the United States, particularly their leaders and the clergy. Much
space is devoted to the activities of the French emissary Genet and
his successor Fauchet, and to the 'Democratic Societies' which supported the French interest. Genet was 'Educated in the subaltern
walks of the most intriguing court in Europe, he was versed in all
the menial offices of corruption; and unencumbered with the family
pride of the French Chevaliers, he could visit a democratic club, and
give the fraternal buss to its shirtless members, with that kind of
cordiality, which gives a zest to flattery, and seldom fails to gain
the affections of the grovelling heart.' (p.10). The Jacobin leaders,
or Democrats (naming as examples, the officers of the Democratic
Society at Philadelphia) were with few exceptions 'Needy, discon-
tented men, too indolent or impatient to advance themselves by fair
and honest means, and too ambitious to remain quiet in obscurity'
(pp.22,23). Attacked are B. F. Bache, rival publisher, 'a grand-son
(whether in a *straight or crooked line*, I know not) of old Doctor
Franklin' (p.32) and members of the clergy with French sympathies,
who 'feared to offend their congregations, on whom they were
totally dependent for support.' (p.41). Several civic celebrations in
the French favor are described, among them a procession of which
Cobbett writes: 'Indeed it was diverting enough to see these great

personages, the good sober-looking, potbellied chiefs of Pennsylvania, come squeezing, and shouldering, and zigzaging along, like so many recruits at drill.' (p.44).

24b ———. A variant in which Volume I correctly has page '125' and signature Oo is on laid paper. ¶ MWA; NN

24c ———. A variant in which Volume I correctly has page '125', signature Oo is on laid paper, and in the Appendix the final leaf has advertisements. The recto: Proposals, | by William Cobbett, opposite Christ Church, | Philadelphia, | for publishing by subscription, | Adams's Defence | of the | American Constitutions. | [rule] | Conditions [3 conditions, including price] [see No. 101, 1797]; the verso: 'Philadelphia. | [rule] | Just published, | by William Cobbett, Opposite Christ Church, | The | History of Jacobinism...'In two volumes octavo....' ¶ ctY

24d History | of the | American Jacobins, | commonly denominated | Democrats. | [rule] | By Peter Porcupine | [rule] | [three lines from] | Burke. | [rule] | Philadelphia: | Printed for William Cobbett, North second | street, opposite Christ Church. | [rule] | Nov. 1796.

[A]–E⁴F³=23 leaves, 8 vo; (5)8–48 ¶ Evans 30209 ¶ NN

Contents: title, blank, Dedication (2), History [7]–48. Dated at end of dedication 'Philadelphia 10th Nov. 1796'. At foot of p.48 'END'. The description of this work is the same as that for the 'Appendix' in No. 24a. It may be noted that the close of the Dedication refers to 'following such a writer as Mr. Playfair' and the final paragraph refers to the text as 'the appendix'. 161st Pennsylvania District copyright issued to William Cobbett, November 24, 1796.

24e History of the American Jacobins, commonly denominated Democrats. | [rule] | By Peter Porcupine | [rule] | [three lines from] | Burke. | [rule] | Philadelphia: | Printed for William Cobbett, North second | street, opposite Christ Church. | [rule] | Dec. 1796.

Conjectural title, based on the fact that the Edinburgh edition of January 1797 (No. 24f) recites that it is taken from a Philadelphia edition 'Printed, Dec. 1796'.

24f History | of the | American Jacobins, | commonly denominated | Democrats. | [rule] | By Peter Porcupine, Philadelphia. | [rule] | being | a supplement | to the | History of Jacobinism | [rule] |

[three lines from] | Burke | [rule] | Philadelphia: Printed Dec. 1796. | [rule] | Edinburgh: | re-printed for J. G. Henderson. | Jan. 1797.

[A]–D⁶=24 leaves, 12 mo; (3)iv(1)6–47(1). Second and third leaves signed except A2 ¶ NN

Contents: title; blank; Dedication [iii], iv; History [5]–47; publisher's advertisement. Dedication dated 'Philadelphia, 10th Dec. 1796'.

Errors noted: p.13, l.3 'Frenau' for 'Freneau'; p.16, l.2 'drunkens' for 'drunkards' and 'snorred' for 'snorted'; p.31, l.6 'revivived'; p.38, l.28 'Piladelphia'; p.43, l.36 'culotts' for 'culotte'.

This is a faithful copy of the first edition except as it refers to a December rather than November 1796 printing, and includes a page of advertising.

25a   Porcupine's | Political Censor, | for November 1796. | [rule] | containing | observations | on | the insolent and seditious notes, | communicated to the people of the | United States | by the late French Minister Adet; | [rule] | Philadelphia: | Printed for, and sold by, William Cobbett, | opposite Christ Church. | [rule] | Nov. 1796.

[A]²B–K⁴L²=40 leaves, 8 vo; (5)6–78(2) ¶ Evans 30226, Sabin 14004 ¶ cty; MWA; NN

Contents: title, blank, 'Advertisement' and 'To Correspondents', blank, caption: 'The | Political Censor, | for November 1796. | [rule] | remarks | on | Citizen Adet's notes to the | Secretary of State.' [5]–78; blank leaf. First two and six or ten of final leaves on wove paper, water-marked '1795' or '1796'.

Two errors noted: p.21, ll.15,16: 'The steps which that of France had taken...'; p.31, l.30: 'Goodwin's' for 'Godwin's'.

There is a careful discussion of treaties, and it will be recalled that in the previous year, Cobbett published his translation of Martens' 'Summary of the Law of Nations...' (No. 8). Account Book Sale Date December 20, 1796. The Book records sales of 2305 copies at 25¢. Dated in Porcupine's Works (No. 59) 'November, 1796.' Claypoole's American Daily Advertiser. December 21, 1796, 'this day is published'.

On page [3] it is stated that 'a double edition' of the present Censor has been printed, and the price reduced to one quarter of a dollar. Some extracts follow: '...hint to those who give me advice... not to do it in too dictatorial a style; for, if I have any good qualities, docility, I am afraid, is not to be numbered amongst them.' (p. 3). As to Adet: *'ne plus ultra* of insolence...' (p.5). '...to unite vices seemingly incompatible is the characteristic of the regenerated French...' (p.14). '...I believe every single sous of it went among the Flour Merchants.—What think you, Mr. Dallas? Come now, d—n it, tell the truth for once in your life...' (p.18). 'After a most piteous and pitiful picture of the distresses of the impressed seamen, drawn by that able painter, the taper-limbed and golden-hued Adonis of New York [Livingston] who has been aptly enough compared to a poplar tree in autumn; after as vigilant and spiteful an enquiry as ever was prosecuted by the spirit of faction, not more than five or six impressed seamen...could be named...' (p.36). In discussing treaties with the French: '...it would seem, that the French Republic looks upon herself in the light of a battered harridan despised by a lusty youth...' (p.43). In summary of the French charges against us by Citizen Adet: 'We may pardon the threats of a simple bully; we may even forgive a sharper or a robber, but when he has the impudence to justify his conduct, and that too with his filthy fist at our mouths, there is no degree of resentment, no mortal means of vengeance, adequate to the insult.' (p.53). On French friendship: 'It appeared something like platonic love; or like the girl that brought a fortune of twenty thousand pounds in the excellence of her disposition...' (p.57). On the presentation by Monroe of the American flag to the French Senate: 'It must have been curious to see the tender tears trickling from the eyes of Robespierre and the rest of those sanguinary villains, who were daily employed in butchering the human species, tearing out their entrails, biting their hearts and lapping their gore. They wept blood instead of brine, I suppose.' (pp.58,9). 'Some imaginations are said to rush forward like a flood, others to flow like a stream, and others to glide like a current; but poor Citizen Adet's neither rushes, flows, nor glides: it trickles...' (p.61). On Thomas Jefferson: 'A man who is a deist by profession, a philosopher by trade, and a Frenchman in politics and morality: a man who has written a passport for Tom Paine's Rights of Man, and would, if necessary, write another for his infamous letter to General Washington: a man, in short, who is at the head of the prostituted party by whose intrigues he has been brought forward and is supported. If this man is elected President, the country is sold to the French; and as plantations are generally sold with the live stock on them, I shall remove my carcass; for I am resolved never to become their property. I do not wish my family vault to be in the guts of cannibals' (pp.68,69). 'Statues and curiosities we have none to stop their [the French] mouths with; unless, indeed, it be the Statue from over the library door. We might also spare them Mr. Jefferson's pivot-chair and his great bull Mammoth; to which they might add Mr. Jefferson himself, for it does not appear that he will be wanted on this side of the water.' (pp.69,70). On a war with France: 'However, though I am certain that the French will not go to war with America, I am as certain that America must soon go to war with them...There is every reason to believe, indeed, with me the fact is certain, that Spain has ceded Louisiana to France. This will put the French in possession of all our Western Frontier, give them the free navigation of the Mississippi, and then, I beg any one to cast his eye over the map of the United States, and see the exposed situation in which they will be placed.' (pp.73,74.)

25b ⸻. A variant in which the collation ends K⁴K² ¶ NJR (Davis)

26a Porcupine's | Political Censor, | for December, 1796. | [rule] | containing, | remarks | on the | debates in Congress, | particularly on the timidity of the | language held towards France. | Also, |A letter |to the infamous | Tom Paine, | in answer to his brutal attack on the Federal Constitution, and on | the conduct and character of General Washington. | [rule] | Philadelphia: | Published by William Cobbett, | opposite Christ Church | [rule] | Price, One Quarter of a Dollar. [1797].

[A]²B–F⁴G²A²BC⁴D²=36 leaves, 8 vo; (5)6–47(2)2–18(6) ¶ Evans 30227, Pearl 15, Sabin 14005 ¶ CtY; MWA; NN

Contents: title; 'N.B.' (referring to the opposite page); title-page for Porcupine's Political Censor Vol. 1; blank; 'Remarks | on the | Debates in Congress' [5]–47; blank; 'A | Letter | to the in-famous |Tom Paine...' [1]–18; 'Proposals, | by William Cobbett, Book-seller of Philadelphia, | for publishing | a News-Paper, | to be entitled, | Porcupine's Gazette | and | Daily Advertiser.' (4); 'Books | published by William Cobbett, | opposite Christ Church'; blank. Type error p.16, l.17 'We— Indies.'; second p.16, col.1, l.15 'carreer'. Dated in Porcupine's Works (No. 59) 'December 1796'. Gazette of the United States, January 24, 1797: 'This day is published...' Account Book Sale Date January 24, 1797. The Book records sales of 1228 copies at 25¢.

This reprints the President's Address to Congress of December 7, 1796 and the answers of Senate and House. The objection to inclusion in the House answer of a compliment to the President was 'accompanied with the consoling reflection, that Mr. Giles was at the head of the opposition. There are certain persons, whose applause we shun with as much solicitude as we seek for that of others...' (p.21). 'The desire to establish harmony [with France] is expressed, as Mr. Ames observed, with little less ardour than the requests of a supplicating lover; and the confidence in the spirit of the country, in case of an appeal to arms, is disguised with as much care [in the House answer] as if it were a crime to be courageous in opposing the violence and resenting the indignities of a horde of base-born grovelling tyrants.' (pp.23,24). 'To what are we to ascribe the immeasurable difference between the daring and insulting tone formerly assumed toward Britain, and the poor, piping, pusillanimous language, that is now held towards France. Is it because one is a monarchy, and the other calls itself a republic? I have heard, or read, of a fellow that was so accustomed to be kicked that he could distinguish, by the feel, the sort of leather that assailed his posteriors. Are our buttocks arrived at this perfection of sensibility?' (p. 38). 'The necessity of a commercial connection between Great Britain and America, is so loudly and unequivocally asserted by the unerring voice of experience...in vain did...citizen Madison speechify the Congress...' (p.39). 'France may deck the heads of our wives and daughters (but by the bye, she shan't those of mine) with ribbons, gauze, and powder...their cheeks with paint...when the rain pours down and washes the rose from the cheek; when the bleak north-wester blows through the gauze, then it is that we know our friends. Great Britain must wrap us up warm...' (pp.41,42). '...nothing could prevent Great Britain from totally cutting off the commerce of America...From the French and their allies, on the contrary, America has little, nay nothing to fear...' (p.44). 'America and Great Britain might bid defiance to the world.' (p.46).

From the 'Letter' to Paine: 'Thus you qualify your tone, kneel, creep and cringe to those who have held you in chains, and brought you to the foot of the scaffold...You are like tame carrion-crows: you flutter in flocks from the presence of the kite, but when he is wounded by the hunter and lies gasping on the earth, you attack his prostrate carcass, and pick out his eyes that are closing in death.' (p.11). 'There is but one thing on earth nearer to the hearts of all true Americans than their constitution, and that is, the spotless character of their chief. Your brutal attempt to blacken this character was all that was wanted to crown his honour and your infamy...' (p.18).

From the proposals for 'Porcupine's Gazette...', designed to answer other lying gazettes: 'Books, or periodical publications in the form of books, may be of some service, but are by no means a match for their flying folios. A falsehood that remains uncontradicted for a month, begins to be looked upon as a truth,.... The only method of opposition, then, is to meet them on their own ground; to set foot to foot; dispute every inch and every hair's breadth; fight them at their own weapons, and return them two blows for one.' He proposed to begin on March 5, 1797 and actually commenced March 4. (See No. 30).

Of the letter to Paine, Washington wrote: 'Making allowances for the asperity of an Englishman, for some of his strong and coarse expressions and a want of official information of many facts, it is not a bad thing'. Letter January 8, 1797 to David Stuart, quoted in Clark, p.79.

The books published were three: 'Adam's Defence...now in the Press'; 'The History of Jacobinism'; and 'The Bloody Buoy'.

26b ———. A variant in which the error noted on page 16 has been corrected. ¶ NN

26c Porcupine's | Political Censor, | for December, 1796. | [rule] | containing, | remarks on the debates in Congress, particu- | larly on the timidity of the language held | towards France. | Also, | a letter to the infamous Tom Paine, in an- | swer to his brutal attack on the Federal Consti- | tution, and on the conduct and character of | General Washington. | [rule] | The Second edition. | [rule] | Philadel- phia: | published by William Cobbett, | opposite Christ's Church. | [rule] | Price, one quarter of a dollar. [1797]

[A]¹B–H⁴,F³=32 leaves, 8 vo; (3)4–45(1)47–64 ¶ Evans 30228 (calls for a plate but none known; his date of 1796 is too early.) ¶ CtY; MWA

Contents: title; blank; | [rule] | 'Remarks | on the | debates in Congress...' [3]–45; blank; | [rule] | 'A | Letter | to the infamous | Thomas Paine...' 47–64. Swelling rule page 18.

Some errors noted: p.9, l.13 'mannners'; p.17, l.10 'occcasion'; p.17, l.16 'atchcievement'; p.39, l.31 'guaze'; p.51, l.3 'poofs'; p.58, l.5 'were' for 'where'.

The text is a new setting of type which faithfully follows the first edition.

26d ———. A variant in that the final signature is 'I' instead of 'F' ¶ NN

26e [rule] | A | Letter | to the infamous | Tom Paine, | in answer to his letter to | General Washington. | [rule] | [Philadelphia, 1797?] [Caption title].

A²B,C⁴=10 leaves, 8 vo; (1)2–18(2) ¶ Pearl 24 ¶ cty; NN

Contents: Letter [1]–18, blank leaf. 'The End' on p.18. This is evidently reprinted from the second part of 26a, but with a final blank leaf instead of the three leaves containing advertisements. It appears to be from the same setting of type. However, p.15, l.2 last word is 'the' and l.3 last word is 'th ey'.

26f A | Letter | to | the infamous | Tom Paine, | in answer | to his | letter | to General Washington. | [rule] | by Peter Porcupine, | author of | The Bone to Gnaw for Democrats, &c. | [rule] | Philadelphia printed: | London reprinted, | for David Ogilvy and son, No. 315, Holborn. | [rule] | 1797. | Price one shilling.

[A]²BC⁴D²=12 leaves, 21.4 cm (trimmed); (5)6–23(1) leaves B2C2 signed ¶ Sabin 13888, Pearl 24 ¶ cty; MWA; NN

Contents: half-title, blank, title, blank, 'A Letter...' [5]–23, blank.

This is a faithful copy of the first edition (No. 26a) with some improvements in punctuation, and some nicety on page 14 where 'Lord Stanhope' has become 'Lord St---pe' and 'Lord Abingdon' has become 'Lord Ab---n'. P.18, l.1 'posey' has become 'poesy.'

26g A | Letter | to the infamous | Tom Paine, | in answer to a letter written by him | to | General Washington, | by | Peter Porcupine, | of Philadelphia. | [ornament] | Glasgow, | printed for James Gillies, bookseller, | Highstreet, | 1797.

[A]⁶B⁶=12 leaves, 17.1 cm; (5)6–24. P. [5] numbered 3 ¶ Pearl 24 ¶ cty

Contents: title, blank, prefatory, blank, A Letter... [5]–24. On p. 24: Finis. On wove paper watermarked 1796.

Lords Stanhope and Abingdon are named (p.14). P.14, last word 'republican' the 'n' is dropped down, second line of note begins 'ave'; p.18, l.16 has 'poesy'; p.24, last word is 'crime' for 'crimes.'

26h   ———. Here the third leaf is signed A3 and p.24 the last line has 'crimes.' ¶ DLC

26i   ———. Pearl 24 notes an Edinburgh edition, 1797. This has not been located.

26j   Observations | on the | debates | of the | American Congress, | on | the addresses | presented to | General Washington, | on his resignation: | with | remarks | on the | timidity of the language held towards France; | the seizures of American vessels by Great Britain | and France; | and, | on the relative situations of those | countries with America. | [rule] | By Peter Porcupine, | Author of the Bone to Gnaw for Democrats,–Letter to Tom Paine. | &c,&c. | [rule] | To which is prefixed, | General Washington's | address to Congress; | and | the answers of the Senate | and House of Representatives. | [rule] | Philadelphia printed: | London reprinted, | for David Ogilvy and Son., No. 315, Holborn. | [rule] | 1797. | Price one shilling.

[A]¹B–E⁴F³=20 leaves; 21 cm; (3)2–38. Second leaves signed, B2–E2 ¶ Sabin 13897, 101860+, Pearl 27 ¶ NN

Contents: title, blank, Observations [1]–38. The preliminary matter is in smaller type and ends on p.11. Page numbers 14 and 38 are enclosed in parentheses instead of brackets.

The text reproduces the first portion, pp.(5)–47, of the Censor for December, No. 26a.

26k   ———. Page number 38 is enclosed by a combination of a bracket and a parenthesis. ¶ cty

27a   Porcupine's | Works. | [rule] | Vol. I. | [rule] | 'The whole tribe of rascals, I made no doubt, would rise | 'to oppose my efforts; but then I was prepared to oppose the | 'whole tribe of rascals. Like a Porcupine, I sat self-collected, | 'with a quill pointed against every opposer.' | [rule] | Philadelphia: | Published by William Cobbett, | opposite Christ Church. [1797].

8 vo ¶ Pearl 26 ¶ cty

Contents: title, blank, contents, blank, and the following pamphlets:

I. Bradford's Fourth edition. Observations...Priestley (No. 2i)

II. A Bone to Gnaw...fourth edition (No. 3e)

III. A Kick for a Bite...second edition (No. 4c)

IV. Part II. A Bone to Gnaw...second edition (No. 6c)

V. A Little Plain English...second edition (No. 7e)

VI. Second edition. A New Year's Gift (No. 10d)

VII. A Prospect from the Congress-Gallery...second edition (No. 11b)

27b ———. A variant in which the first line quoted ends 'rise to'.
¶ cty

28 Porcupine's | Works. | [rule] | Vol. II. | [rule] | [four lines quoted] | [rule] | Philadelphia: |published by William Cobbett, | opposite Christ Church | [rule] | 1796 [i.e. 1797].

8 vo ¶ Evans 30233, similar (see No. 34g) ¶ cty

Contents: title, blank, contents, blank, and the following pamphlets:

I. The Political Censor...[for March] third edition (No. 13c);

II. The Political Censor...[for April] third edition (No. 14f);

III. The Political Censor...[for May] second edition (No. 17c);

IV. The Scare-Crow...Second edition (No. 18c);

V. The Life...of Peter Porcupine...second edition (No. 19c);

VI. The Political Censor...[for September] (No. 20a);

VII. Porcupine's Political Censor, for November 1796 (No. 25a);

VIII. Porcupine's Political Censor, for December 1796 (No. 26a)

29 Porcupine's | Political Censor, | for Jan. 1797. | [rule] | containing, | page | Remarks on the proceedings in Congress, 3 | Mr. Pickering's letter, 4 | Attack on the same by the sans-culotte Bache, 5 | Observations on Citizen Adet's complaints respecting the | French flag and the almanack-makers, 8 | An account of Mr. Adams's election, with remarks on | the conduct of the French emissaries subsequent | thereto, 15 | The Festival of Fools. Their toasts, with remarks, 30 | Mr. Adams's farewel [sic] address to the Senate, with the Se- | nate's answer, 45 | [rule] | Philadelphia: | published by William Cobbett, opposite Christ Church; | where all letters to the publisher are desired to be addressed, post-paid. | [rule] | Price, one quarter of a dollar. [1797].

[A]²B–G⁴[H]²=28 leaves, 8 vo; (5)4–51(3) ¶ Evans 31946 ¶
Cty; MWA; NN

Contents: blank leaf, title, blank, Porcupine's | Political Censor, |
for January, 1797 [3]–51; three blanks. Subtitles on pages 13, 30,
45 and 49. Foot of p. 51 'End of the Censor for January 1797.' P.5,
l.11 'as' for 'has'. Advertised in Porcupine's Gazette, March 4,
1797, 'Just published by William Cobbett.' Dated in Porcupine's
Works, (No. 59) 'January 1797'. Account Book Sale Date March 10,
1797. The Book records sales of 628 copies at 25¢.

Cobbett has great praise for Adams (p.16) but the reverse for
Jefferson (pp.17,18). On Madison he writes (p.20): '...patriot
Madison...was no more than the passive instrument of the then
Secretary of State [Jefferson].... The little man bridled up and assumed a vast deal of self-importance; but we are now told that the
trappings were not his own....' On Jefferson (p.21). 'He did not re-
tire merely to wander through the groves, to listen to the oaten
reed of the smutty swains, nor to solace his limbs in the silver
brooks of his modern Arcadia. He *prudently* retired, to avoid making a figure, *against his inclination....*' On Pennsylvania: '...poor
Pennsylvania, though appearances are against her, though *fourteen*
French votes [for Jefferson as President] to one American one [for
Adams] brand her with ignominy, yet I hope, with the indulgence
of the reader, to prove, that this unfortunate State, this fairest sister
of the family, appears much more culpable than she really is, and
that her transgression has proceeded from her amiable weakness
rather than from any radical vices.' (p.27). 'Hers is precisely that
climate that suits the vagabonds of Europe: here they may bask in
summer, and lay curled up in winter, without fear of scorching in
one season or freezing in the other. Accordingly hither they come
in shoals, just roll themselves a-shore, and begin to swear and poll
away as if they had been bred to the business from their infancy.
She has, too, unhappily acquired a reputation for the mildness, or
rather the feebleness, of her laws. *"There's no gallows in Pennsylvania!"* These glad tidings have rung through all the democratic
club-rooms, all the dark assemblies of traitors, all the dungeons and
cells of England, Scotland and Ireland. Hence it is that we are over-
whelmed with the refuse, the sweepings, of those kingdoms, the
offal of the jail and the gibbet.' (p.28).

'The Festival of Fools' caption designates a dinner on February
6, 1797 attended by, among others, Dr. Priestley, the French Minister Adet and Chief Justice M'Kean of Pennsylvania, to each of whom

Cobbett addresses himself. He also deals with Franklin, Ritten-house and Rush. The work concludes with Vice President Adams's reply to the Senate dated February 23, 1797.

30   Porcupine's Gazette.

This Philadelphia newspaper was a daily of four pages, 50 cm. in height, with five columns, published by Cobbett from March 4, 1797 through August 28, 1799. Because of the yellow fever epidemic, Cobbett then moved to Bustleton, outside Philadelphia, where publication was continued with six weekly numbers, 771 through 776, from September 6 to October 11, 1799, 50 cm., of four pages with five columns. Then followed two pamphlet issues, 777 and 778, October 19 and October 26, 1799. (PPL). The first A¹², 17 cm., [1]2–24; and the second B¹², 16.5 cm., 25–48. Neither carried advertising. A final number was published in New York City, January, 1800 (No. 48). Until April 24, 1797, the paper had four columns only and was known as 'Porcupine's Gazette and United States Daily Advertiser'. Brigham, pp.946,947; Pearl 28. A tri-weekly issue known as 'Country Porcupine' was published March 5, 1798 through August 26, 1799 (No. 36).

Reitzel, p.241, refers to the publication of a Pennsylvania-German version in Reading, Pa. This is evidently 'Der Deutsche Porcupein und Lancaster Anzeigs-Nachrichten', published in Lancaster, Pennsylvania, weekly from January 3, 1798 through December 25, 1799 by Johann Albrecht and Co. (Brigham p.866). Porcupine's Gazette December 4, 1797 advertised that 'The German Porcupine and Pennsylvania Intelligencer' would be published twice a week from January 1, 1798 by John Albright & Co., Lancaster. Cobbett's interest does not appear.

In the issue of the Gazette for April 24, 1797, it is stated: 'Gazette started with about twelve hundred subscribers, this number is now augmented to two thousand and four.'

This paper has been examined but a full study of it has not been made. Advertisements in it and other references are cited herein. Extracts from it occupy large parts of Porcupine's Works, London 1801 (No. 59): all of Vols. V and VI, most of Vols. VII though X and a large part of Vol. XI.

31a   Porcupine's | Political Censor, | for March, 1797. | [rule] | Containing, | page | An interesting letter from a gentleman in Switzer- | land, to his friend in America, describing the situa- | tion

of France, 53 | Noah Webster's attack on Porcupine, 75 | Porcu-
pine's Answer. Letter I, 79 | Letter II, 81 | Porcupine's last will and
testament, 107 | Index to the Gazette for March, 1797, 117 | [rule] |
[hand pointing] | There is no Censor for February, this year. |
[rule] | Philadelphia: | Published by William Cobbett, opposite
Christ's Church, | Where all letters to the publisher are desired to
be addressed, post paid. | [broken rule] | Price, one quarter of a
dollar. [April 1797].

[π]²A–H⁴[I]⁴=38 leaves, 8 vo; (4)53–73(1)75–80(1)82–106(1)
108–115(9) ¶ Evans 31947, semble ¶ cty; mwa

Contents: half-title, blank, title, blank; 'A | Letter | from a Gen-
tleman in Switzerland...' 53–73; blank; 'Mr. Noah Webster's |
attack on Porcupine | [rule] | From the Minerva, | of New-York,
March 21, 1797.' 75–79; 'Porcupine's Answer. 'Letter I' 79,
80; 'Letter II' [81]–106; 'Will and Testament' [107]–115; blank.
'Index to Porcupine's Gazette, for March 1797.' (7); blank. At end
of Index 'End of the Censor for March, 1797.' Running title in
Index.

The word 'March' appears to the left of signatures A and C in
capitals and of signatures D–G in small italics. To the right of signature F, two asterisks; catchword 'IN' on page [107]. Some errors
noted: p.54, l.11 'preceived'; p.54, ll.28,29 'of of'; p.55, note 'seper-
intendance'; p.56, l.16 'he he'; p. 57, l.13 'Yurd' for 'Jura'; p.[81],
5 lines from foot 'two' for 'too'; p.98, last line, an extra 'a'; p.111,
l.4 'tittle' for 'title.' Dated in Porcupine's Works (No. 59) 'March
1797'. Account Book Sale Date April 24, 1797. The Book records
sales of 1160 copies at 25¢. Advertised in Porcupine's Gazette for
April 22, 1797, 'This day is published...'

The opening letter discusses the situation in France in 1794 in
an unflattering light. Cobbett gives a sharp reply to Noah Webster
'a man, the greatest extent of whose travels has been from Connecticut to New York, and the utmost exertion of whose talents is to
be sought for in the compilation of a school-book' (p.97). To Webster he writes on the Minerva charges: 'You best know what stock
of stupidity the readers of the Minerva are blessed with, but this I
am certain of; that the clumsiest and most impudent vagabond
jugler never ventured to play off so barefaced a deception to the
gaping clowns at a country fair' (p.99). 'Are you sure, that the 150
Porcupine's Gazettes daily sent to your city, together with those
which may probably have supplanted your's round your neighbor-

hood, thro' New England, and the Jerseys: consult your heart and tell me, if you are sure, that it is not the spread of these innocent papers, and not anything which they contain, that has roused your lethargic patriotism' (p.100).

The 'Will and Testament' is highly readable. Since he has 'received about forty threatening letters', he is publishing his will 'in order that my dear friends, the Legatees, may, if they think themselves injured or neglected, have an opportunity of complaining before it be too late'. (p.107). The legatees include Dr. Michael Leib, Thomas Jefferson, Benjamin Rush, Noah Webster, F. A. Muhlenberg, 'Tom the Tinker' (Governor Mifflin of Pennsylvania), Tench Coxe, Thomas Bradford, Edmund Randolph, A. J. Dallas, John Swanwick, B. F. Bache, James Monroe, J. T. Callender, Thomas Paine and 'the Political Sinner' (Albert Gallatin).

The bequest to 'Tom the Tinker' (Governor Mifflin) will give the flavor: 'a liberty cap, a tricolored cockade, a wheel-barrow full of oysters, and a hogshead of grog: I also leave him three blank checks on the Bank of Pennsylvania, leaving to him the task of filling them up; requesting him, however, to be rather more merciful than he has shown himself heretofore.' (p.111).

Republished in Porcupine's Works London 1801 (No. 59), Vol. V, as 'Gazette Selections' pp.143–169,177–196,198–205, under date of March, 1797.

In Porcupine's Gazette for June 1, 1797 it is stated that a Censor for April would be 'published next week.' I find no record of it.

31b ———. A variant in that the Index is numbered (1)118–123; 'March' opposite signature D is in capitals instead of italics; and p. 115, l.3 'such' is misaligned. The errors noted have not been corrected. ¶ cty; mwa

31c ———. A variant in which page 107 is numbered, the index is numbered (1)118–123, and there are no asterisks opposite signature F. The errors noted have not been corrected. ¶ mwa

31d ———. Same transcription as preceding three entries, except the last rule is unbroken. Same collation and pagination as 31a, except pp.53 and 77 are not numbered and p.107 is numbered. A new setting of type, but a faithful copy. The word 'march' is in small italics on signatures A–G. No asterisks opposite F. Page [53] has

'February 24th' instead of 'Feb. 24th'; page 55, in note 1.5, 'o' for 'of'; page [81] next to last, 't' for 'it'. The errors noted under 31a have been corrected. There are textual changes, as for examples; p. 64, four lines from the foot, the word 'spectacle' is added; p.69 a new note; on the final page there is no note 'End of the Censor...' ¶ cty

32a Erskine, Thomas. 1750–1823.

A | View | of the | causes and consequences | of the present | war with France, | in answer to Mr. Burke's regicide peace. | [rule] | By the Honourable Thomas Erskine | [rule] | With a dedication to the author, | by P. Porcupine; | and | an appendix, | containing the correspondence between Miles and the infamous Le | Brun, Minister of War, at the time when war was declared | against Great Britain; which develops the real causes of that de- | claration, all the secret steps which the French took previous to it, | and clearly unravels the thread of their ambitious projects. | [rule] | Philadelphia | printed by William Cobbett, opposite Christ | Church. 1797.

[A]²B–K⁴;*A*–*C*⁴=50 leaves, 8 vo; (3)iv(1)6–73(3);(2)3–7 (1)9–24. ¶ Evans 32097, Pearl 29. ¶ cty

Contents: title; blank; Dedication [iii]iv; A View [5]–73; three blanks; Introduction; Appendix [2]–7; Correspondence, &c. [8]–24. Small type, with 48 or more lines to a page. Page [iii] catchword 'his'; p.iv running title; dedication dated at end 'Philadelphia, May, 16. 1797.' On page 73 'The end'. One of two works represented to have been printed by Cobbett in the United States (the other is No. 107).

Errors noted: p.[iii] next to last line, 'euloguim'; p.21, first word 'stating' repeats; p.33, l.8 'altimately'; p.51, l.7 'anopening'; p.59, l.40 'curisy' for 'curity'; p.62, l.28 'ar' for or'; p.70, last 'reseve'; p. 72, l.9 'ef'; p.72, l.37 'impoatant'; p.19, next last 'w' for 'was'; p.19 last 'as' for 'do'. Account Book Sale Date May 18,1797. The Book records sales of 528 copies at 37½¢. Advertised in Porcupine's Gazette May 19, 1797 as 'Just published by William Cobbett...'

The 'View' is a criticism of the British Ministry for beginning and continuing the war with France. In his 'Dedication. To the Author', Cobbett writes in part (p.iv): As to yourself, you come of honest kin at least...but you have had the misfortune to be engaged in very dirty work ever since your talents rendered you conspicuous ...with this knowledge of the author...the perusal of your crafty performance may be entered on without much danger of deception.' In the Introduction to the Appendix, p.[1], Cobbett asserts the matter therein constitutes 'an ample and satisfactory refutation of Mr. Erskine's charges against the British Ministry, relative to the origin of the war with France'.

32b ———. A variant in that the errors noted on page 72 (second) and 19 (both) have been corrected. ¶ MWA

32c ———. In this variant, the transcription is the same through the last rule and then concludes : 'Philadelphia: | printed by William Cobbett, opposite | Christ Church. | 1797'. (It was not seemly to be opposed to Christ). The same setting of type is used. One more error has been corrected: that on p. 51. ¶ CtY

32d ———. Transcription as in 32c. One more error is corrected, that on page 59. ¶ CtY

33 Porcupine's | Political tracts, | of 1794 and 1795. | [rule] | Contents.[in two columns] 1. Observations on the emigration | of Dr. JosephPriestley, com- | monly called the fire-brand | philosopher. | 2. A Bone to Gnaw for the Demo- | crats. Part I. | 3. A Bone to Gnaw for the Demo- | crats. Part II. | 4. A Kick for a Bite. | 5. A Little Plain English; or a | defence of the British Treaty | against the attack of Franklin. | 6. A New-Year's Gift for the De- | mocrats; or observations on | poor Mr. Randolph's precious | confessions. | 7. A Prospect from the Congress | Gallery. | [rule] | Philadelphia: | Published by William Cobbett, | opposite Christ Church. | [rule] | 1797.

8 vo ¶ CtY

Contents: title, blank, and the following pamphlets:

   I. Bradford's Fourth edition. Observations...Priestley...(same as No. 2i, but lacking the final eight pages.)
   II. A Bone to Gnaw...fourth edition. (No. 3e)
   III. A Kick for a Bite...second edition. (No. 4c)
   IV. Part II, A Bone to Gnaw...second edition (No. 6d)
   V. A Little Plain English. (No. 7a)
   VI. Second edition. A New Year's Gift. (No. 10d)
   VII. A Prospect from the Congress Gallery...second edition. (No. 11b)

The contents answer to the title page except that III and IV are transposed. They are the same as No. 27a except a later printing of IV and an earlier of V.

34a Porcupine's | Works. | [rule] | Vol. 1 | [rule] | "The whole tribe of rascals, I made no doubt, would rise | "to oppose my efforts; but then I was prepared to oppose the | "whole tribe of rascals. Like a Porcupine, I sat self-collected, | "with a quill pointed against every opposer" | [rule] | Philadelphia: | Published by William Cobbett, | Opposite Christ Church. [1797].

8 vo ¶ Pearl 26 ¶ cty

Contents: title, blank, contents, blank, and the following pamphlets:

> I. Bradford's Fourth edition. Observations on the emigration ...Priestley...1796 (No. 2i)
> II. A Bone to Gnaw...third edition...1797 (No. 3g)
> III. A Kick for a Bite...second edition (No. 4c)
> IV. Part II. A Bone to Gnaw (No. 6f)
> V. A Little Plain English...second edition (No. 7e)
> VI. A New Year's Gift (No. 10a)
> VII. A Prospect from the Congress-gallery...second edition (No. 11b)

34b ———. Here VI is the second edition, No. 10d ¶ cty

34c ———. Here I is the [1797] edition, with 'Vol. 1' on the signature pages, No. 2k; II is the third edition, No. 3f; and VI is the second edition, No. 10d ¶ Evans 31948 ¶ NN

34d ———. Same as 34c except that the transcription ends: 'Christ Church | [short rule] | 1796 [i.e. 1797]'. ¶ cty

34e ———. Here II is the second edition, No. 3c ¶ NjR

34f Porcupine's | Works. | [rule] | Vol. II. | [rule] | [four lines quoted from Porcupine] | [rule] | Philadelphia: | Published by William Cobbett, | opposite Christ Church. | [rule] | 1796. [i.e. 1797]

8 vo ¶ Evans 30233 similar ¶ cty

Contents: title, blank, contents, blank, and the following pamphlets:

  I. The Political Censor...[for March 1796]...second edition
   (No. 13b)
  II. The Political Censor...[for April 1796]...third edition (No.
   14f)
  III. The Political Censor...[for May 1796]...third edition (No.
   17d)
  IV. The Scare-Crow...second edition (No. 18c)
  V. The Life...Peter Porcupine...second edition (No. 19c)
  VI. The Political Censor...[for September 1796] (No. 20a)
  VII. Porcupine's Political Censor for November, 1796 (No. 25a)
  VIII. Porcupine's Political Censor, for December, 1796...second
   edition (No. 26c)

34g ———. Evans 30233, in which I is the third edition (No.
13c). Evans 30233 assigns 1796 as the publication date. However
VIII is definitely 1797. See No. 28 Vol. II of Porcupine's Works,
with earlier editions of III and VIII ¶ NN

34h ———. The same as the preceding except that VIII is the
variant, No. 26d ¶ cty

34i ———. Evans 31948, in which I is the third edition, No. 13c;
II is 'for April 1797', No. 14g; and VI is No. 20c. The transcription
ends 'Christ Church'. ¶ NN

35 [Cut of a Porcupine, 3.2 x 4.3 cm.] | The | Carriers | of | Porcu-
pine's Gazette | to it's friends, on the commencement of the year
1798 [Philadelphia, 1797]. [caption title].
  Broadside. 36.6 x 27 cm. ¶ Evans 34400 ¶ MWA

Text in two columns, the whole surrounded by a border of type
ornaments. In left column, 44 lines of verse, in right column, 45
lines. The poem begins:

   'Since I the news-boy's toilsome trade profest,
   I've brought you, master, many a pleasant jest;
   Full many a sober truth have spread abroad,
   Of foreign insults, and domestic fraud.'

The content is largely political, with an attack on the French faction and [Benjamin Franklin] Bache and praise of President Adams.

36   [The] Country Porcupine.

A newspaper published by Cobbett at Philadelphia triweekly March 5, 1798 through August 26, 1799, consisting of extracts from Porcupine's Gazette (No. 30). Cobbett announced the project in the Gazette February 14, 1798, stating that readers outside specified nearby areas would receive the Country Porcupine instead of the Gazette, at a lower price and postal charge. He promised that all news would be included, and in fact some advertising was also carried, notably Cobbett's own. As stated in the first issue, all Gazette subscribers would receive it who did not live in New York City, Lancaster, or Baltimore or on the road from Philadelphia to one of those places (in February Lancaster had not been mentioned). The paper was in four pages, 51.5 x 34.5 cm. with five columns to the page.

Evans 33576; Brigham p.898 ¶ MWA

The 'The' was dropped from the title April 30, 1798.

37a   The | Democratic Judge: | or the | equal liberty of the Press, | as | exhibited, explained, and exposed, | in the prosecution of | William Cobbett, | for a pretended libel against | the King of Spain and his Embassador, | before | Thomas M'Kean, | Chief Justice of the State of Pennsylvania. | [rule] | By Peter Porcupine. | [rule] | Philadelphia: | published by William Cobbett, opposite Christ-Church | [rule] | March, 1798.

[A]²B–N⁴[O]²=52 leaves, 8 vo; (4)5–19(1)21–102(2) ¶ Evans 33523, Pearl 31, Sabin 13880 ¶ CtY

Contents: title; blank; Advertisement, dated 'Philadelphia, March 9th, 1798'; blank; Introduction 5–19; blank; American | Liberty of the Press 21–102; blank leaf. Catchwords. Usually 36 lines; reprinted matter, 56 lines.

Some errors noted: p.14, l.25 'reeounting'; p.15, l.4 'autrage'; p. 17, l.22 'leaned' for 'learned'; p.23, l.25 'Honourble'; p.28, l.31 'abscene harpers' for 'obscene harpies'; p.54, l.9 'commo'; p.101, l.1 'whit' for 'with'.

Edition of 4000 copies (see No. 39a.) Account Book Sale Date March 22, 1798. The Book records sales of 1618 copies at 50¢. Advertised in Porcupine's Gazette March 22, 1798 'This day is published by William Cobbett...' The issue of March 29 states more than 700 copies have been 'sold in this city in seven days'.

In the advertisement p.[3] Cobbett speaks of the 'just resentment' which led to the publication. He develops his thesis to the effect that liberty of the press is no longer a reality in America because threats upon it are countenanced by the authorities. He describes the threats against him (p.14): 'The written threats, which I have now by me, to assassinate or poison me, or fire my house, amount to some hundreds.' Reprinted are the Pennsylvania writ against him of Nov. 18, 1797, the bill of indictment which the grand jury did not sustain and the publications complained of from Porcupine's Gazette (which Cobbett did not write.) Also quoted is Chief Justice M'Kean's charge to the grand jury, highly prejudicial to Cobbett. Many selections from other writers are cited to show that they wrote objectionable things unchallenged. As to the French, he writes (p.69): 'Their rascals spend their breath for half an hour in noisy volubility, to produce a faint idea of what ours can express in one short grind of the teeth.'

37b ———. A variant in that the error noted on p. 54, line 9 has been corrected ¶ cty; MWA; NN

38a Detection | of a | Conspiracy, | formed by the | United Irishmen, | with the evident intention | of aiding the tyrants of France | in | subverting the government | of the | United States of America. | [rule] | By Peter Porcupine. | [rule] | Philadelphia: | Published by William Cobbett. | [rule] | May 6, 1798.

[A]⁴B,C⁴[D]⁵=17 leaves, 8 vo; (3)4–24(10). Catchwords [3]–24. (cropping may have cut off some page numbers, catchwords and signatures). ¶ S. T. Evans p.157, Col.1; Evans Supp. B10264, Pearl 34; Sabin 13881 ¶ PPL

Contents: title, blank, 'Detection of a Conspiracy...'[3]–[25], blank, [27], blank, [29] blank, [31], blank, [33], blank.

Some errors noted: p.8, l.16, 'remak'; p.15, l.34 'subect'; p.18, l.20 'committe'; p.20, l.25 'inveig'; p.[27] l.32 'we' for 'well'.

The work largely consists of a reprint of 'Declaration and Constitution of the American Society of United Irishmen.–Philadelphia; printed for the Society, August 8, 1797.' (Evans 32676, no copy located), with commentary by Cobbett intended to show that the Society is subsidized by the French and, though purporting to work for the freedom of Ireland, has as its real aim an insurrection against the government of the United States. His case is tenuous.

38b   Detection | of | a conspiracy | formed by | the United Irish-men: | with the evident intention of | aiding the tyrants of France | in subverting the government of the | United States of America. | [rule] | By Peter Porcupine. | [rule] | London: | printed for J. Wright, opposite Old Bond-Street, | Piccadilly. | [rule] | 1799.

[A]¹,B,C⁸=17 leaves, 8 vo; (3)2–32. Second, third and fourth leaves signed. ¶ Pearl 34 ¶ PPL

Contents: title, blank, 'Detection of a Conspiracy...' [1]–32. On p.32 'The end.' Press numbers.

Some errors noted: p.4, l.1 'he' for 'the'; p.13, l.2 'oftner'; p.14, l.11, extra 'shall'; p.19, l.22, 'award' for 'avoid'.

Dated in Porcupine's Works (No. 59) 'May, 1798'.

The work includes, with slight alterations, the material contained in the Philadelphia edition of the previous year. Added are seven footnotes and new matter beginning in the middle of page 28. These additions do not much change the general effect of the whole.

38c   Detection | of | a conspiracy | formed by the | United Irish-men: | with the evident intention of | aiding the tyrants of France | in subverting the government of the | United States of America. | [rule] | by Peter Porcupine. | [rule] | Dublin. | [rule] | printed by J. Milliken, No. 32, Grafton-Street. | [rule] | 1799.

[A]¹B,C⁸=17 leaves, 21.1 cm; (3)2–32 ¶ DLC (Davis—copy now missing.)

39a   The | Republican Judge: | or the | American liberty of the press, | as | exhibited, explained, and exposed, | in the base and partial prosecution | of | William Cobbett, | for a pretended libel against | the King of Spain and his Embassador, | before | the Su-preme Court of Pennsylvania. | with | an address to the | People of England | [rule] | By Peter Porcupine. | [rule] | London: | Printed for J. Wright, opposite Old Bond Street, Piccadilly. | 1798.

[A]²B–G⁸=50 leaves, 8 vo; (3)iv(1)iv,v(2)8–19(1)21–96(1)2. ¶ Sabin 14053, Pearl 32 ¶ CtY (without the final leaf); RPJCB

Second, third and fourth leaves signed B–G. B larger type.

Contents: title, blank, advertisement [iii]–iv, subscribed 'The Publisher London May 24, 1798'; Address [iii]–v, subscribed 'Peter Porcupine, Philadelphia, April 10th, 1798; blank; introduction [7]–19; American | Liberty of the Press [20]–96, new publications [1]2.

In the Advertisement, the publisher says the work was published in America 'some few days before the last packet sailed; and in that short space of time, the whole edition, of four thousand copies, was nearly sold.' Press numbers. P.23, line 7 'Fouquies' for 'Fouquier'; p.41, line 1 'the'; p.42, line 2 'remaiming'; p. 90, line 9 'courtss'.

Dated in Porcupine's Works (No. 59) 'November 1797'—a large error. This edition contains virtually all of the Philadelphia edition (see No. 37a) with many additions. The address states the purpose: 'To prove to you, that you are happier and more free than the people of America...' (p.v.) New notes are added on pp.12 (on Benjamin Rush 'the sneaking, trimming doctor'), 16, 18, (the note p.18 begins 'In this second edition, I shall add one more instance...of Feb. 19, 1798'); 22 (a long description of Judge M'Kean; 'pettifogger'; 'persecutor'; 'beats his wife'; 'notorious drunkard'; 'Spanish Minister, a most contemptible animal, is to be married to his daughter.') 29,32,36,57,71,78,80,82,85(2) and 87. Other changes: on p.15, the asterisks are replaced by 'The Chief Judge'; p.19, two lines added; p.30, the Jury are listed as 'For the Bill' or 'Against it'; p.47 note, two sentences added; p.61, changed reference to Washington; and p.95, the final paragraph is rewritten for Britons.

39b ———. Same transcription and collation. The first two leaves consist of half-title, blank, title, blank, and the paging is (5) iv,v(2)8–19(1)21–27,29,30,30–96(1)2 ¶ RPJCB

39c ———. Same transcription, etc. The paging is corrected to 21–96 and there is no final leaf ¶ CtY; MWA

39d ———. The title just above 'London' has the addition: Third Edition. | [rule]. |

[A]²B–G⁸=50 leaves, 8 vo; (5)iv,v(2)8–19(1)21–96(2). ¶ RPJCB

Contents: half-title, blank, title, blank, Address [iii]–v, blank, introduction [7]–19; American Liberty of the Press [20]–96; blank leaf.

39e ———. Same transcription as 39d

[A]¹B–F⁸G⁷=48 leaves, 8 vo; (3)iv(3)8–19(1)21–27,29,30,30–96. Second, third and fourth leaves signed. Signature B in larger type. Press number ¶ Pearl 32 ¶ NN

Contents: title, blank, Address [iii]–[v]; blank; Introduction [7]–19; American Liberty of the Press [20]–96.

40   French arrogance; | or, | "The cat let out of the bag;" | a po-
etical dialogue | between the | envoys of America, | and | X.Y.Z.
and the lady. | [rule] | Philadelphia: | Published by Peter Porcupine,
opposite Christ- | Church, and sold by the principal booksellers. |
1798. | [Price 25 cents.] | [Copy-right secured according to Law.]

[A]–D⁴=16 leaves, 8 vo; (5)6–31(1) ¶ Evans 33526, Sabin
13883, Pearl 35 ¶ cty; mwa; nn

Contents: title, blank, Advertisement, blank, French Arrogance
&c. [5]–31, blank.

Error noted: p.28, l.8 'schollars'.

Account Book Sale Date May 25, 1798. The Book records sales
of 90 copies at 25¢. Advertised in Porcupine's Gazette Saturday
May 26, 1798: 'on Monday next will be published...'

The text is in ridicule of the French demand to the American
envoys for a 'douceur', or bribe, in the form of a dialogue between
America and France in Hudibrastic verse. In a somewhat extreme
example (p.24, ll. 1,2) France intones:

'Witness, you know, the fate of Venice,
Who were to us like balls at Tennis;'

41   Remarks | on the insidious letter | of the | Gallic despots, | By
Peter Porcupine. [Philadelphia, 1798] [Caption title] | The hireling
Bache has published a | letter from the French Minister of Foreign |
Affairs to our envoys at Paris, dated the | 18th of March last.

Broadside, 43.8 x 26.5 cm. Text in four columns. At the foot:
[rule] | price, one cent. ¶ Evans 33529; Pearl 36 ¶ mwa

This is reprinted from Porcupine's Gazette of June 16, 1798.
Second column line 4 'pupt'.

The work is intended as an answer to Bache and Talleyrand.
Cobbett writes (final paragraph): Bache has received the letter for
'the express purpose of drawing off the people from the Government...' (See next entry.)

42   The | Detection of Bache; | or | French diplomatic skill de-
veloped. | very necessary to be kept in all families in town and
country. [Philadelphia, 1798] [caption title].

Broadside, 32.5 x 21 cm. Text in two columns. At the foot:
[rule] | price, one cent. ¶ Evans 33524; Pearl 37 ¶ phi (ppl)

This is reprinted from Porcupine's Gazette of June 20, 1798 and
was advertised in the Gazette of June 21, 1798, 'Just published.

Price only one cent...' It deals further (see preceding entry) with a letter from Talleyrand published in B.F. Bache's Aurora June 16, 1798, the object of which, Cobbett says, was to persuade the people of America erroneously to consider France as friendly to them. Quoted is a letter from John Riddle June 18, 1798 that he innocently bore the letter to Bache. This Cobbett says proves Bache 'in close correspondence' with the French.

43a Democratic principles | illustrated | by | example. | [rule] | By Peter Porcupine. | [rule] | Part the first. | [rule] | London: | printed for J. Wright, opposite old Bond- | Street, Piccadilly |[rule] | 1798. (Price 3d. Twelve for 2s, 6d, or one guinea per hundred.)
[A]¹²=12 leaves, 12 mo; (5)6–23(1). Leaves signed A3–A6 ¶ Pearl 38 similar ¶ cty

Contents: title; blank; Address to the Reader; 'The following facts are faithfully extracted'; Democratic Principles... [5]–23; advertisement for Part the Second. On page 23 'the end'. Catchwords except in preliminaries and on p.18. Page 21 last letter 'd' is pied.

The work consists almost entirely of a description of the revenge of the National Convention of France on the citizens of Lyons, taken from 'Part II, A Bone to Gnaw, for the Democrats...1795'. (No. 6a). Compiler has an eighteenth edition, 1798. In the later editions the final paragraph is revised and largely capitalized.

43b Democratic principles | illustrated | by | example. | [rule] | By Peter Porcupine. | [rule] | Part the first. | [rule] | London: | Printed for J. Wright, opposite Old Bond-Street, Pic- | cadilly; and sold by Mundell and Son, Edinburgh; | and J. Mundell, Glasgow. | [rule] | 1798. | (Price 3d. Twelve for 2s.6d. or 18s. per hundred.)
[A]¹²=12 leaves, 12 mo; (5)6–21(3). Leaves signed A2–A6 ¶ Pearl 38 ¶ cty; mwa

Contents: title; blank; address to the Reader; 'The following facts are faithfully extracted...'; Democratic Principles, | illustrated by example [5]–21; advertisements (2); blank. On page 21 'The end.' On page 9, the first note is marked by †, instead of * as in text. On page [22] the advertisement begins: 'Speedily will be published, Part the Second...'

43c ———. A variant in which the final leaf is misplaced and follows the title page. ¶ nn

43d　Democratic Principles, | illustrated | by | example. | [rule] | By Peter Porcupine. | [rule] | Part the first, | [rule] | Dublin: | Printed for J. Milliken, No. 32, Grafton-street. | [rule] | 1798.

[A]⁴[B]⁴C⁴=12 leaves, 20.8 cm; (5)6–23(1). Second leaves signed A2, C2 ¶ Pearl 38 ¶ cty

Contents: title, blank, address to the Reader; 'The following facts are faithfully extracted...'; Democratic Principles [5]–23, blank. On page 23 'the end'. Catchwords except in preliminaries.

43e　Read and reflect! | [rule] | One pennyworth of useful wisdom; | most earnestly recommended to the serious attention of every man in | Britain, whether called Jacobin or Loyalist, who has a heart | capable of feeling for the sorrows and sufferings of others, and a | soul that cannot but shudder with abhorrance at the atrocious | and unheard of cruelties in the following pamphlet. | [rule] | A faint picture of the horrors and calamities, | which have proceeded from | The French Revolution; | In which, as in a glass, every man and woman of common | sense in England, may see too clearly what is to be expected | if ever the French land in this envied Island. | By a friend to humanity, | (commonly called Peter Porcupine.) | Birmingham: printed and sold by E. Piercy, in Bull-street; and by all the | booksellers in all the neighbouring towns. | Price one penny, or eight for sixpence. | [rule] [1798 ?] [Caption title].

[A]⁴=4 leaves; (1)2–8 ¶ Pearl 38 ¶ Reference Library, Birmingham (repro).

Contents: caption title and text pp. [1]–8. The text omits about 95 lines of the original and the footnotes. It is taken from a later edition of the original, since the final paragraph is in the revised form, with the extensive capitalization.

43f　Democratic | principles | illustrated by example | [rule] | By Peter Porcupine | [rule] | [rule] | part the first | [rule] | Aberdeen: | printed for A. Brown, Homer's head, Broad- | Street | [rule] | | 1798. | Price 2d.--12 for 1s. 8d.--or 100 for 12s.6d.

[B]⁶C⁶=12 leaves; (2)3(1)5–22(1)24. ¶ Not located (Davis)

Contents: title, blank, address 3, explanatory, [4], text 5–22, blank, Advertisement 24.

43g　Democratic principles | illustrated | by | example | [rule] | By Peter Porcupine | [rule] | Part the first | [rule] | sixteenth edition. |

Quebec: | printed at the new-printing-office, |Garden Street |
[rule] | | 1799. | Price 6d. twelve for 5s6d or 45s per hundred.

(2)iii–v(1)2–25(1) ¶ Bibliotheque Saint-Sulpice, Montreal
(Davis)

44a Democratic Principles | illustrated. | Part the second. | [rule] |
containing | an | instructive essay. | tracing | all the horrors | of | the
French Revolution | to their real causes; | the licentious politics, and
infidel | philosophy of the present age. | [rule] | By Peter Porcu-
pine. | [rule] | London: | Printed for J. Wright, opposite old Bond- |
Street Piccadilly; | [rule] | 1798. | (Price 4d. or twelve for 3s6d.)

[A]¹B¹¹C¹²D²=26 leaves, 12 mo; (3)4–52. Leaves signed B2-B6,
C2–C6 ¶ Pearl 38 ¶ cu (Davis)

Contents: title, Address to the Reader, An | Instructive Essay,
&c. [3]–52. On p.52 following the text an advertisement: 'In a few
days will be published...The Bloody Buoy, abridged...'.

This is extracted, somewhat abridged, from 'The Bloody Buoy',
probably the 1798 'Fourth Edition' (No. 12j). On p.49 is retained
an inapplicable reference to page 52, found on p.215 of the larger
work. After the second paragraph, the lines of verse and paragraph
following are omitted. French extracts are omitted on pages 7 and
12. Seven paragraphs on Rousseau, p.16; footnotes pp.19,34,37,42
and 44; a sentence after Des Moulins, p.46; 4 paragraphs at p.51,
all are omitted. The conclusion is altered and shortened. The note
on p.51 is revised to attack the English 'opposition' papers.

Compiler has a 'Twelfth Edition' of this, still dated 1798. The
edition numbers of the later editions appear at the top of the title
page.

44b Democratic Principles | illustrated | Part II. | Containing an |
instructive essay | tracing | all the horrors | of the | French revolu-
tion | to their | real causes, | the licentious politics, and infidel philo-
sophy of the present age. | [rule] | By Peter Porcupine | [rule] |
London: | printed for J. Wright, Piccadilly; for Mundell and son, |
Edinburgh, and J. Mundell, College, Glasgow. | [rule] | 1798. |
[rule] | (Price 4d. or twelve for 3s.6d).

[A]¹²B¹²=24 leaves, 12 mo; (3)4–48. Leaves signed A2–A6,
B2–B6 ¶ NN

Contents: title, address to the reader, An instructive essay, &c.
[3]–48. P.46, l.4 has an inapplicable reference to p.52.

44c   Democratic principles | illustrated, | part the second | [rule] | containing | an | instructive essay, | tracing | all the horrors | of | the French Revolution | to their real causes; | the licentious politics, and infidel | philosophy of the present age. | [rule] | By Peter Porcupine. | [rule] | Dublin: | printed by John Exshaw, 98, Grafton-Street. | [rule] | 1798.

[A]¹B¹¹C¹²D²=26 leaves, 19 cm; (3)4–52. Leaves signed B2–B4, C2–C6 ¶ NN

Contents: title, address to the reader, an instructive essay [3]–52. P.49, l.10 has the inapplicable reference to p. 52.

44d   Fifth edition. | [rule] | Democratic principles | illustrated. | [rule] | Part the Second. | containing | an | instructive essay, | tracing | all the horrors | of | the French Revolution | to their real causes; | the licentious politics, and infidel | philosophy of the present age. | [rule] | By Peter Porcupine | [rule] | Dublin: | Printed for J. Milliken, No. 32, Grafton-Street. | [rule] | 1798.

[A]–C⁸D⁴=28 leaves, 20.8 cm; (5)4–52(2). Second leaves signed B2 etc. Third leaf of B signed B3 ¶ Pearl 38 ¶ CtY

Contents: half-title, blank, title, Address, An Instructive Essay &c. [3]–52, blank leaf. On p.52 'Finis'. Press numbers.

44e   Democratic Principles | Illustrated. | [rule] | part the second | [rule] | containing | an | instructive essay, | tracing | all the horrors of the French revolution to their real | causes, the licentious politics, and infidel philosophy of the | present age. | [rule] | By Peter Porcupine. | [rule] | [rule] | seventh edition | [rule] | Aberdeen: | printed for and sold by A. Brown, Bookseller. | [rule] | MDCCXCVIII. | [rule] | (Price 4d. or twelve for 3s.6d.)

[A]–D⁶E³=27 leaves, 12 mo; (3)4–54. Second and third leaves signed A2A3–D2D3 ¶ NN

Contents: title, Address to the Reader, an instructive essay [3]–54. P.54 'FINIS'. Catchwords.

45a   [rule] | By William Cobbett, | of the City of Philadelphia. | [rule] | proposals | for publishing by subscription, | a | new, entire, and neat edition | of | Porcupine's Works. | [rule]. [Philadelphia 1799]. [caption title].

Two conjugate leaves, unsigned and unpaged, 36.2 x 25.4 cm. ¶ Pearl 43. (Evans 35316 is actually 45b.) ¶ MiU–C (Repro.)

Contents: text on first leaf, dated verso: Philadelphia, Jan. | 1st, 1799. Second leaf blank. English watermark dated 1794. To justify his undertaking, Cobbett speaks of the reception of his works, p. [1]: 'Of each pamphlet, published under my assumed name of Peter Porcupine, about six thousand copies, upon an average, have been printed and sold in America. The sale of those, which have been honoured by a re-publication in England, has, probably, been much greater. All of them, I believe, have passed through three or four, and some, in an abridged state, have attained to ten, twelve, and even seventeen editions. On Porcupine's Gazette no observation of this sort is required, as its superiority, in point of extensive circulation, over all others, in this country, has long been universally known and acknowledged.'

The proposals were reprinted in 45b. and in Porcupine's Gazette and the Country Porcupine during 1799. A large part of the proposed edition apparently was printed, but all was junked as waste paper to help satisfy the judgment against Cobbett rendered in favor of Benjamin Rush in December 1799 in his action for libel. (See No. 49 and see the Rush-Light, 15th Feb. 1800, No. 51). The collected works were published in London in 1801 (No. 59).

The Clements Library copy has on page [3] a transmittal letter by Cobbett dated 'Philadelphia, 5 Jany. 1799.' to John Hodgson, Baltimore, asking his assistance.

45b [rule] | By | William Cobbett, | of the City of Philadelphia. | [rule] | Proposals | for publishing by subscription, | a new, entire, and neat edition | of | Porcupine's Works. | [rule] [London 1799]. [caption title].

[A]⁴=4 leaves, 8 vo; (1)2–6(2) ¶ Pearl 43. ¶ cty; RPJCB

Catchwords. Press number p.3. Dated, p.[7]: 'Philadelphia, | Feb. 5th, 1799.', followed by spaces for subscriber's names on that and the succeeding page. Subscriptions to be received by named persons in London, Edinburgh, Glasgow and Dublin. Error noted, p.3 ll.28, 29: 'recolcection'.

In general, the text follows 45a with, however, eight new lines at the foot of page 4, an added paragraph making up page 6 and conditions revised for Great Britain giving English prices, etc.

46 Remarks | on the | explanation, | lately published by | **Dr. Priestley,** | respecting the | intercepted letters of his friend and |

disciple, | John H. Stone. | To which is added, | a certificate of civism | for | Joseph Priestley. Jun. | [rule] | By Peter Porcupine. | [rule] | London: | printed for J. Wright, opposite Old Bond Street, | Piccadilly. | [rule] | 1799.

[A]¹B–D⁸[E]¹=26 leaves, 8 vo; (3)4,5(1)7–50,52(1). Second, third and fourth leaves signed. ¶ Sabin 14012, Pearl 40 ¶ cty; nn; rpjcb

Contents: title; blank; introductory address[3]–5; Remarks [6]–47; Certificate of Civism 48–50,52; blank. Three press numbers. The address is dated on p.5 'Philadelphia, | January 30th, 1799.'; The certificate is dated on p. 48 'Philadelphia, Jan. 15th, 1799' with a postscript dated on p. 52 'Feb. 5th.' Error noted p. 35 l. 15 'bible' for 'bribe'. Dated in Porcupine's Works (No. 59) 'October 1798.'

The work is a bitter attack on Dr. Priestley, on his son, on John H. Stone and on the ultimate addressee of the intercepted letters, Benjamin Vaughan.

It has been suggested that Cobbett was the editor of Evans 34606: 'Copies of original letters recently written by persons in Paris to Dr. Priestley in America...Philadelphia printed, from the second London Edition, by James Humphreys...[1798]. (There were at least three London editions in 1798, one in French—see rpjcb). However, this seems unlikely. The footnotes appear to be English, not American, viz: 'here' page iv and 'us' page 8, referring to England. In his 'Remarks' *supra*, page 11, Cobbett refers to 'The Preface and notes of the English publisher' in the English edition, which are also those in the Philadelphia edition.

47   The | Trial of Republicanism: | or, | a series of political papers, | proving | the injurious and debasing consequences | of | republican government, and written constitutions. | with an introductory address | to | the Hon. Thomas Erskine, Esq. | [rule] | By Peter Porcupine. | [rule] | London: | printed for Cobbett and Morgan, at the Crown and | Mitre, Pall-Mall. | April, 1801.

Colophon p. [64]: Printed by T. Rickaby, Peterborough Court, Fleet-Street.

[A]–H⁴=32 leaves, 21 cm; (3)4–63(1). Second leaves signed B2, C2 ¶ Sabin 64166, 96805+; Pearl 42. ¶ cty; mwa; nn

Contents: title; 'Printed by T. Rickaby, Peterborough-Court, Fleet-Street'; The Trial...[3]–63, advertisement.

Errors: p. 5, 5 lines from foot 'repulican'; p. 8, ll. 26 and 35, 'Priestly'.

Pp. 15–62 contain a discussion of and quotations from 'Eumenes', by William Griffiths [i.e. Griffith] (Evans 35570) concerning the government of the State of New Jersey.

Dated in Porcupine's Works (No. 59) 'June 1799'. Pearl suggests there was a Philadelphia edition 1799 but does not locate a copy.

48 [rule] | Porcupine's Gazette, No. 779. | [rule] | New-York—Published by Wm. Cobbett.—Jan. 13, 1800. | [rule] | To the | subscribers to this Gazette | [rule] | Gentlemen, | agreeably to my notification, made by | advertisement, on the 11th ultimo, I now ad | dress to you the farewell number of Porcupine's | Gazette. [Caption title.]

C^{12}=12 leaves, 12 mo., 18 cm; 49–72. A single folded sheet ¶ Evans 38303 ¶ cty

Errors noted: p. 51, l. 2 'adventerous'; p. 67, l. 12 'Philapelphians.' Dated in Porcupine's Works (No. 59) 'January 1800.'

Cobbett's paper had been suspended since October 26th, (p. 49). It had never been profitable, he wrote, and events had ended its utility. Adams had 'suddenly tacked about, and I could follow him no longer.' (p. 50). Benjamin Rush, his suit, his doctor friends and the treatment Cobbett intends for him occupy most of the work. Cobbett notes the death of Washington on December 14 and quotes the report of the attending physicians to show the treatment 'was in precise conformity to the practice of Rush...'

A Cobbett phrase (p. 72): 'The delicate son-in-law of [Governor] Mifflin [Joseph Hopkinson, of counsel to Rush]...when he hears that another number of the Porcupine is arrived in Philadelphia, he'll tremble like a dog upon a wet sack.'

49a A | Report | of an | action for a libel, | brought by | Dr. Benjamin Rush, | against | William Cobbett, | in the Supreme Court of Pennsylvania, December term, | 1799, for certain defamatory publications in a | newspaper, entitled Porcupine's Gazette, | of which the said | William Cobbett was editor. | [rule] | [taken in shorthand, by T. Carpenter.] | [ornament] | Philadelphia: | Printed by W. W. Woodward, No. 17, Chesnut Street. | [rule] | 1800.

[A]^{2}B–E^{4}F^1; Aa–Dd^4=35 leaves, 8 vo. Not paged ¶ Evans 37103, Sabin 14030 ¶ mwa; nn

Contents: title, blank, charge by Judge Shippen (2), Trial, including the publications, openings by counsel, testimony and addresses to the jury. Catchwords. Running titles. Verso of C, catchword is 'to' for 'too'; verso of F is blank.

From the judge's biassed charge page [4] 'Every one must know that offences of this kind have for some time past too much abounded in this city; it seems high time to restrain them—that task is with you, Gentlemen. To suppress so great an evil, it will not only be proper to give compensatory, but exemplary damages; thus stopping the growing progress of this daring crime—at the same time, the damages should not be so enormous as absolutely to ruin the offender.' At the foot of page [4] 'The jury, after an absence of two hours, brought in a verdict in favor of the Plaintiff of Five Thousand Dollars.'

49b   ————. Here there is no catchword on E2 verso ¶ PU (Davis)

50   Anthing, Johann Friedrich. 1753–1805.

History | of the | campaigns | of | Prince Alexander Suworow | Rymnikski, | Field-Marshal-General in the service of | His Imperial Majesty, the Emperor | of all the Russias, | with | a preliminary sketch of his private | life and character. | [rule] | Translated from the German of Frederic Anthing. | [rule] | to which is added, | a concise and comprehensive history | of his | Italian campaign. | [rule] | Vol. I. [Vol. II] | [rule] | New-York: | Printed by G. and R. Waite, for Wm. Cobbett. | 1800.

Third title: A | Concise and comprehensive | history | of | Prince Suworow's | Campaign in Italy. | in the year 1799. | [rule] | By William Cobbett. | [rule] | New-York: | printed for the author, by G. and R. Waite. | 1800.

[A]–A2⁴;[A]–X⁴;[π]¹Y³Z–Dd⁴Ee²=96,84,26 leaves, 8 vo;(3)iv (1)vi–xvii(1)19–26(1)28–192;(3)4–154(1)156–167(1);(3)172–219(1). Vol. I to left of signatures B–A2. ¶ Evans 36845 ¶ CtY; MWA; NN

Frontispiece: portrait of the Prince, by T. Clarke 'Published by W. Cobbett, New York, 1800'.

Contents: title, blank, To the Reader [iii]iv, Contents [v]–xvii, Life [18]–26, Campaigns [27]–192; title, blank, Campaigns [3]–154; supplement [155]–167, blank; title, blank, History [171]–219, blank. Running titles in text. Top of page xii: 'CAAP. XI'. The index does not give page references. The index shows Chapters X–XV in Vol. I, whereas they are in Vol. II, and has Chapters X–XVII misnumbered for XVI–XXIII. In the text Chapters I–VI, XIII and XIV have chapter headings.

Account Book Sale Date February 10, 1800. The Book records sales of 428 copies at $2.50. Dated in Porcupine's Works (No. 59) 'January 1800.' On January 20, 1800 Cobbett wrote Thornton: 'I shall have Suworow out this week' (Cole-Thornton p. 36).

Aside from some passing shots at the French, Cobbett tells his 'History' straight on.

51a The | Rush-Light. | 15th Feb. 1800. | containing [in two columns] page | An Introduction to the Rush | Light, 1 | Rush and his supporters, | Part I. containing a sketch | of the birth, and of the | moral and literary charac- | ter of Doctor Benjamin | Rush; interspersed with | various entertaining and | instructive anecdotes, –4 | page. | Rushite frankness and grati- | tude, exemplified in the | conduct of Doctor | Mease, the pupil and | friend of Rush, and one | of his witnesses,--42 | A letter from Dr. Mease to | William Cobbett, --45 | a paragraph by the same, | with remarks,---45 | [rule] | By Peter Porcupine. | [rule] | New York: | Published by William Cobbett, No. 141, Water-Street, | Where all communications to the editor are requested | to be addressed, post paid.

[π]^{1}A^3,B,C^4[D]^{4}E,F^4=24 leaves, 8 vo; (2)1–46 ¶ Evans 37198, Pearl 44 ¶ cty; MWA

Contents: title, blank, 'The Rush-Light. | 15th Feb. 1800 | [rule] | Being the first number of Volume 1. | [rule]' 1–46. Catchwords. Subtitles pp. 1,3,4,6,42. P. 46: '[End of No. I–15th Feb. 1800]'.

Printed by John Furman, New York, for $33.75. (Cobbett's Account Book, appendix p. 242).

Some errors noted: p. 3, l. 7, 'dischaage'; p. 25, l. 2 'ann' for 'and'; p. 26, l. 2 'retrain' for 'restrain'; p. 29, sixth from last 'amidgst'; p. 34, l. 1, 'obolquy'; p. 44, l. 11 'out' for 'ought'.

Account Book Sale Date February 25, 1800. The Book records sales of 1618 copies at 25¢. Cobbett wrote Thornton that 2500 copies were printed (Cole-Thornton, letter of April 17, 1800).

P. 1: Cobbett writes he had determined to discontinue Porcupine's Gazette before the $5000 judgment against him in favor of Dr. Benjamin Rush. P. 2: As a result of the latter 'a great number of books in sheets, (among which was a part of the new edition of Porcupine's Works) were sold, or rather given away, as waste paper; so that, the total of what has been, and will be, wrested from me by Rush, will fall little short of *eight thousand dollars.*' P. 4: 'Yesterday I finished the *History of the Italian Campaign*' (No. 50). p. 28: Dr. Rush's son John assaulted Dr. Andrew Ross, over 60 years of age and infirm, but for the same remarks and more he refrained from attacking Cobbett, 'a stout man of thirty years of age.' (Cobbett became 37 on March 9, 1800).

51b ———. The title page has a border of double rules, and 'New York' has become 'NEW YOKK'.

[π]¹A–E⁴[F]³=24 leaves, 8 vo; (2)1–46 ¶ cty; nn; mwa

A new setting of type. On page 1 in the sub-title 'Rush-Light' is 7.4 cm. long and the second and third rules have two lines. The errors noted in the previous entry have been corrected. Catchwords. Some of the pages have a bluish cast. In blue wrappers: The first recto begins: No. I | [rule] | The | Rush-Light. | 15th Feb. 1800. | [rule] | By Peter Porcupine. | [rule] | New-York: | Published by William Cobbett, No. 141, Water-Street. | Price 25 cents. It continues that 'Rush will occupy a considerable portion of the first three numbers...' A number to be published on the 15th and on the last day of every month.... Each number will contain 48 octavo pages. Printing by G. and R. Waite, of New-York. The verso lists seven titles for sale by Cobbett. The backwrapper recto lists four more titles and the verso six more.

51c ———. The wrapper front recto omits the first paragraph in 51b, referring to Rush, and adds the first two titles for sale; the verso adds eleven titles, some not the same. The back wrapper recto has five titles and verso six more. A new setting of type throughout. Examples of many variations: p. 4., the rule is broken; note, p. 7., line 3 ends 'specimen of' instead of 'speci-'; p. 10, second catchword 'and' instead of 'tyrant'; p. 11, no second catchword; p. 13, the note is five lines instead of six; p. 25., note is fourteen lines instead of seventeen; p. 34., note four lines instead of six; p. 41, catchword is 'RUHSITE' instead of 'this'. ¶ nn; mwa

52a The | Rush-Light. | 28th Feb. 1800. | Containing | [28 line index with 25 page references] | [rule] | By Peter Porcupine. | [rule] | New York: | Published by William Cobbett, No. 141, Water-Street, | Where all communications to the editor are requested | to be addressed, post paid.

Cobbett Works 99

[A]–H⁴I¹²=34 leaves, 8 vo; (2)47–112. Catchwords except pp. 110,111 ¶ cty; MWA

Contents: title, blank, [rule] | The Rush-Light. | 28th Feb. 1800 | [rule] | Being the second number of volume 1. | [rule] | [three lines quoted] | [rule] | pp. 47–112. At the foot of p. 112: 'End of No. II.– March 10, 1800'. Subtitles pp. 47,49,81,85,87,88,92,103,104,109, 111.

Some errors noted: p. 51, n. l. l. 4 'farcial' for farcical'; p. 61, l. 13 'rnin' for 'ruin'; p. 67, l. 16 'thursting'; p. 90, l. 12 'evacutions'; p. 92, l. 18 'bs';

Account Book Sale Date March 10, 1800. The Book records sales of 1742 copies at 25¢. Cobbett wrote Thornton that 2500 copies were printed (Cole-Thornton, letter of April 17, 1800).

On p. 47 is an announcement that advertising pages will be added; on pp. 50, 51 a note on Noah Webster 'that pestilential writer'. The main thrust is of course against Dr. Rush. An instance, p. 60, involves the charge Rush's medicine loosened teeth and his reply that there were only two cases involving a loss of teeth: 'But my dear "Hippocrates" there is some little difference between *loosening* and *losing* one's teeth. You think it is nothing I suppose, unless your patient's teeth drop into his porridge?' Governor M'Kean is dealt with pp. 92–95 and former Governor Mifflin pp. 95–101. On p. 111 is a letter to the Secretary at War, reporting that Capt. Still 'came to my house, to call me to account, on the part of Lieut. Rush, about a passage in the first number of the Rush-Light. He was armed "a la mode de Rush", to wit: with a bludgeon cane, which, as it had an iron poker to encounter, remained quiet in his hand; and so the noble captain marched off without beat of drum.' P. 112 Cobbett reports that the first two numbers of the Rush-Light goes [sic] to Wright in London to republish; Also that Porcupine's Works will be published in London and part of the copy has gone forward.

52b ———. The title page has a border of two-line rules. The caption title on p. 49: [rule] | The | Rush-Light. | 28th Feb. 1800. | [rule] | Being the second number of volume 1. | [rule] | [three lines quoted] | [rule].

[F]¹G–O⁴[P]¹=34 leaves, 8 vo; (2)47–112 ¶ cty; NN

Contents: title, blank, The Rush-Light, 47–112. Catchwords.

The text is the same as the preceding entry, but the type is a complete new setting. The type itself is more advanced, using the modern 's' and 'ss' throughout. Subtitles pp. 47,49,81,85,87,88,92, 103,104,109,111. On page 75 l. 10, 1796 is corrected to 1797. Some errors noted: p. 49, l. 23 'Mecurial'; p. 53n, l. 13, 'Repbulick'; p. 70 catchword lacks final s; p. 75, l. 1 last word, type out of line; p. 81, l. 9 same; p. 93, l. 5 'Pennylsvania'; p. 96 catchword is '5th' for '4th'; p. 103, l. 4 'lierty' for 'liberty'.

In blue wrappers printed as in 51c.

52c ———. A variant in which the error noted on page 96 has been corrected ¶ cty; nn

52d ———. A variant in which the errors noted on pages 81 and 96 have been corrected. ¶ nn

52e ———. A variant in which two leaves of advertisements are added and signature N has been altered slightly. The catchword on p. 96 is corrected to 4th; the misaligned type on p. 98 beginning l. 1 and 2 is lined up; p. 100, l. 2, 'ciscumstances'. ¶ cty

Advertisements: 1st leaf recto, 'The Swiftsure Line of Stages', with cut of a stage drawn by four horses; verso, 'A Sketch...Yellow Fever in the year 1799...' by William Currie; 'The Pursuits of Literature....'; Porcupines Works, repeating the last paragraph on p. 112 and adding that applications should be made before May 1. At the foot of the page a catchword 'Notifications'; 2nd leaf recto, 'Notifications to the Publick'; verso: 'List of the 5,000 Jury' and solicitation of orders for English publications.

53a [rule] | The | Rush-Light | 15th March, 1800. | [rule] | Being the third number of Volume I. | [rule] | Rush and his supporters... [caption title].

Q–X⁴,[Y]²=26 leaves, 8 vo; 113–160(4). Catchwords, except pp. 126–128,152 ¶ cty; mwa; nn

Contents: The Rush-Light, 113–160; Advertisements (4) At foot of p. 160: 'End of No. III. March 24, 1800.' Advertisements as in previous entry. This and succeeding two numbers of the Rush-Light use the modern 's' and double 'ss'. 'Rush-Light' is 7.4 cm. The pamphlet is enclosed in a thin blue printed wrapper with the caption: No. III. [rule] | The | Rush-Light. | 15th March, 1800 | [rule] | By Peter Porcupine | [rule] | New-York: | published by William Cobbett, No. 141, Water-Street. | Price 25 cents. | [rule]. The wrappers continue as in 51c. MWA copy lacks advertising pages and wrappers.

Account Book Sale Date March 24, 1800. The Book records sales of 1269 copies at 25¢. Cobbett wrote Thornton that 3000 copies were printed (Cole-Thornton, letter of April 17, 1800).

Some errors noted: p. 113, last line 'pamhplets'; p. 117, l. 19 'council' for 'counsel'; p. 122, l. 17 'ou' for 'our'; p. 129, l. 1 last word 't' out of line; p. 131, last, 'expresions'; p. 137 catchword 'inten' for 'intent'; p. 141, l. 1 'ands' for 'sands'; p. 144, note l. 13 'o e' for 'one'; p. 148, l. 12 'taloons'; p. 160, l. 3 'intregity'.

The number discusses in detail the action of Rush against Cobbett, the charges, the evidence, the hostile witnesses, counsel and matters of defence. Extracts: p. 143: As to the charge that Cobbett said about Rush 'that he would persecute his memory after death, the thing is absolutely incredible: he might as reasonably have threatened to persecute the memory of a butterfly or a maggot'. P. 151n: Mr. Robert G. Harper, of Cobbett's counsel, had said with respect to Rush's Eulogium on Rittenhouse that it was 'very impertinent' of Cobbett to express his disapprobation. 'Let Mr. Harper... enjoy all the popularity he deserves for his zealous, his great, and efficacious endeavours, in support of the government; but, let me conjure him, to resolve, before he undertakes another cause, never to seek to preserve that popularity by traducing the character of his client, even though that client should have the misfortune to be the subject of a king.'

53b ———. A variant in which the errors noted on pp. 113, 137, 141 and 144 are corrected except that in line one on p. 141 in the last word 'the' the 'e' is still out of line. ¶ CtY

53c ———. A variant in which the errors noted on pp. 122, 137, 141, 144 are corrected except that on p. 122, l. 17 'which', out of line, is substituted for 'that'. ¶ NN

53d ———. A variant in which the errors noted on pp. 113, 122, 137, 141 and 144 have been corrected. ¶ CtY; NN

The NN copy has one leaf of advertisements before the title and one leaf at the end.

54a [rule] | The | Rush-Light. | 31st March, 1800. | [rule] | Being the fourth number of volume I. | [rule] | A peep into a Pennsylvanian | Court of Justice. | [rule] | [six lines quoted from] | Reeve's Thoughts, &c. Let. I. | [rule] [caption title].

Y–Dd⁴=24 leaves, 8 vo; 161–208 ¶ cty; MWA

Contents: The Rush-Light 161–198; Porcupine's Revenge, 199; A Tragedy Scene, 200; A Portrait of a Governor, 201–208. Catchwords.

Account Book Sale Date April 14, 1800. The Book records sales of 1659 copies at 25¢. Cobbett wrote Thornton that 3000 copies were printed (Cole-Thornton, letter of April 17, 1800).

Some errors noted: p. 167, last, 'inevetibly'; in p. 169, the 1 is smaller type; p. 196, last letters a and e misaligned; p. 197, l. 15 'huzzars'; p. 200, last line 'the' for 'thee'; p. 202, l. 1 'vigilent;' p. 203, l. 22 'collission'.

Discussed are the prejudicial Judge's charge and other legal matters in the suit of Rush against Cobbett. 'Revenge' and 'Tragedy', in verse, concern Rush. 'A Portrait' is an attack on Governor M'Kean. On p. 208 is an advertisement by Cobbett's Philadelphia Agent, John Morgan. At the foot of the page: '[End of No. IV— April 14, 1800.]'

54b ———. A variant in which the error noted on p. 197 is corrected. In blue wrappers: front recto-caption: 'No. IV. | [rule] | The | Rush-Light. | 31st March, 1800....' Advertisement, shortened to two paragraphs, proposals for importing four titles, continued on verso. Rear wrapper, recto six books for sale and verso four more. ¶ NN

54c ———. Two leaves are added, one in the front (with advertisements same as in previous 2 numbers) and one at the end containing an appeal on behalf of Rev'd. Mr. Glasse, Rector of Hanwell, Middlesex, dated at end 'New-York 30th March 1800'. The error noted on page 197 is corrected. In blue wrappers as 54b ¶ NN

55 [rule] | The | Rush-Light. | 30th April, 1800. | [rule] | Being the fifth number of volume I. | [rule] | Letters from P. Porcupine | to | Dr. Priestley, and Thomas Cooper. | [rule] | [two lines from] Samuel | [rule] [caption title].

Ee–Kk⁴Ll²=26 leaves, 8 vo; 209–258(2) ¶ cty; MWA; NN

Contents: Rush-Light 209–258; Advertisements (2). Catchwords.

On page 258 is a note with a pointing hand: 'The letter to Mr. Cooper will appear in the next | number of the Rush-Light | [rule] | [End of No. V.–30th April, 1800]'. The final leaf contains advertisements by Cobbett: 'Just published, by William Cobbett, The Unsexed Females...' (No. 126); 'Just received, and for Sale by William Cobbett...Yellow-Fever...by William Currie.' (Evans 37294); '...subscription proposal...'The Lay Preacher...' two volumes; 'will contain many unpublished numbers in addition to those...in the Farmer's Museum...' There is a list of those receiving subscriptions, including the publisher, John Ward Fenno [Philadelphia], William Cobbett in New York, and 16 others. (The 'Lay Preacher' was Joseph Dennie. Apparently the venture never went forward).

The NN copy is in blue wrappers; the front recto has the caption: 'No. V. | [rule] | The | Rush-Light | 30th April, 1800...and continuing as in 54a recto and verso. The rear wrapper recto has four books for sale and the verso seven more. Included in Porcupine's Works (No. 59) Vol. XI, pp. [395]–434.

Account Book Sale Date May 21, 1800. The Book records sales of 551 copies at 25¢. Cobbett wrote Thornton publication would be on May 17, 1800 (Cole-Thornton, letter of May 15, 1800).

Some errors noted: P. 214, l. 19 'apppointment'; p. 234, next to last l. 'tremely' for 'extremely'; p. 249, l. 28 'fnrnished'; p. 250, l. 13 'perfetly'; p. 252, l. 7 'invonvenience'; p. 252, l. 8 'seheme'; p. 254, l. 3 'mong-headed'.

56a [rule] | The | Rush-Light. | 30th August, 1800. | [rule] | being the sixth number of volume I. | [rule] | An Address | to the people of England.[London 1800] [caption title].

Mm–Rr⁴Ss²=26 leaves, 8 vo; (1)260–295(1)297–309(1). Second leaves signed Nn2–Rr2 ¶ cty; NN

Contents: the 'Address' [259]–295; 'To the People of the United States of America.' [296]–309; blank. On p. 309 'William Cobbett. | London, August 30, 1800.' Catchwords except pp. 292, 295. Uses old-style letter 's'.

Errors noted: P. 264 next last 'Northumbra–'; p. 268, l. 30 and 308, l. 1, 2 'downfal'; p. 289, l. 11 'successfuly'. The catchword 'or' on p. 300 is missing on p. 301.

This sixth number of the Rush-Light appeared after Cobbett's return to England from America. In the address, Cobbett deals pretty harshly with Americans generally and with some Americans he names. On Adams and Jefferson, he writes (p. 277): '...we all know that as long as a King of England has a million of secret service money, a president of America will never be found who could find in his heart to disagree from so amiable a monarch. Some people are indeed of opinion that should Jefferson succeed to that office he would be above a br–be, and I myself have some reason to believe it; but of such an event there is not the smallest probability.' He regards Alexander Hamilton as 'one of our warmest friends' (p. 281). In the remarks 'To the People of the United States...' Cobbett advises a strong executive, avoidance of the French and a joinder with Great Britain.

56b ———. The description is generally the same as 56a, but this is a reprint [New York?] ¶ cty; NN

Page numbers 260–290 larger than 291–309. Some errors noted: p. 264, l. 16 'furtune'; p. 264, l. 32 'Northumbra–'; p. 269, next to last 'poject'; p. 270, l. 16 'villian'; p. 274 l. 1 'nich'; p. 278, l. 13 't' inverted; p. 281, l. 28 'spcaking'; p. 289, l. 24 'cocades'; p. 268, l. 30 and p. 308, l. 1,2 downfal.

There are many small variations from the previous entry. Notable are the last 5 lines on p. 283, with the catchword 'carrying' instead of 'of', and the first 5 lines on p. 284. Also on p. 277, l. 29 and p. 278, l. 5 the word 'bribe' is used instead of 'br–be'; The NN copy is noted to the effect this is an American reprint.

56c [Supplement to the democratic press.] | An | address | to the | people of England, | By William Cobbett. | [rule] | Philadelphia: | printed by John Binns, No. 70, Chesnut-street. | [two rows of dots] | 1812.

[A]⁸=8 leaves, 20.8 cm. (cropped); (2)3–16. Second leaf signed A2 ¶ Sabin 14021; A.B. 25104 ¶ MWA; NN

Contents: title, Address [2]–16, subscribed on p. 16 'William Cobbett', with a concluding sentence below: '[lend this to your neighbor as the confession of a Tory]' The address is preceded by a note that it was published under Cobbett's signature on the 30th of August 1800, an 'account of his nefarious mission and of his aiders, abettors and supporters.'

The Address is taken from the August Rush-Light with, however, five omissions (at pp. 275, 280–1, 283–4, 292 and 293) totaling about two pages of the original 37 page Address. The first three omissions concern material which might be considered derogatory of George Washington. The last two concern Dr. Benjamin Rush. There are fourteen notes to the text, which are new. Emphasis is supplied by capitalization and italics. Pages 9 and 10, 'bribe' is spelled out.

Errors noted: p. 4, 6 lines from the foot, in 'their' the 'he' is at a right angle; p. 10, l. 24 'agrinst.'

57a   The American | Rush-light; | by the help of which, | wayward and disaffected Britons | may see | a complete specimen | of the | baseness, dishonesty, ingratitude, and perfidy | of | Republicans, | and of the | profligacy, injustice, and tyranny | of | Republican governments. | [rule] | By Peter Porcupine. | [rule] | [four lines quoted from] | Speech of K. Geo. III–1782. | [rule] | London: | published for the author by J. Wright, | Piccadilly. | 1800.

Colophon: Printed by S. Gosnell, | Little Queen Street, Holborn [p. 192].

$[\pi]^1[A]$–E^4F^2G–M^4N^3O–T^4V^1X–BB^4CC^2=97 leaves, 22 cm; (5) iv–vi(1)8–43(2)46–98(1)100–147(2)150–192. Second leaves signed beginning A2 except F and CC. 'No. I' lower left margin of p. 7 and signature pages B–F; 'No. II' same, signatures G–N; 'No. III' same, signatures O–V; and 'No. IV' same, signatures X–CC. ¶ Sabin 13872, Pearl 45 ¶ ctY; MWA; NN

Contents: title; 'S. Gosnell, Printer | Little Queen Street, Holborn' Advertisement to the English edition, dated London, Nov. 10, 1800; blank; Advertisement [iii]–vi; The Rush-Light No. I [7]–43; blank; The Rush-Light No. II [45]–98; The Rush-Light No. III [99]–147; blank. The Rush-Light No. IV [149]–190; Postscript by Peter Porcupine 191, 192. Running title pp. iv–vi, catchwords, press numbers.

Some errors noted in catchwords: p. 87 '4th' for '14th'; p. 89 's' and 'p' in 'supply' broken; p. 105 'not'; p. 134 'o serving'.

There are many changes, mostly minor, from the first editions. Some of them follow: No. I. Notes revised pp. 10, 13 (third paragraph omitted), 15, 29 and 34; new notes on pp. 16, 27 (two) and 31; several changes on p. 10; last paragraph revised substantially. On p. 13 l. 9 'though a native Philadelphian' the 'though' is new.

No. II Advertisement omitted, and final page. New notes on pp. 81, 82 (two) and 89.

No. III. New notes on pp. [99], 110, 115; note p. 131 two lines added; new matter pp. 139–147, beginning 'Postscript to the second edition.' and including 'To the Liverymen of London' and 'Republican morality', with a letter from Halifax dated November 7, 1800 signed 'E'.

No. IV. New notes on pp. 156, 161, 162, 163, 168, 172, 179 and 181; 2 lines omitted from note p. 180; note p. 190 enlarged; the Postscript by Peter Porcupine, pp. 191, 192, is new.

Reprinted in Porcupine's Works (No. 59), Vol. XI, pp. [209]–394.

57b   ———. A variant in which the catchword on p. 89 is corrected ¶ NN

58a   By William Cobbett. Prospectus of a new daily paper to be entitled the Porcupine [London 1800].

Colophon: Printed by J. F. Dove, 178, Piccadilly, opposite Burlington House.

Broad sheet, 32 x 25.4 cm. (Davis) ¶ Pearl 46. (Copy not seen).

Pearl notes the broad sheet was issued Sept. 9, 1800.

58b   By William Cobbett. | [rule] | Prospectus | of a new daily paper, | to be entitled | The Porcupine | [rule] [London 1800] [caption title]

Colophon: Printed by S. Gosnell, Little Queen Street, Holborn.

A⁴=4 leaves, 19.8 cm; (1)2–8. Second leaf signed A2 ¶ Pearl 47 ¶ NN

Dated at the foot of p. 7: 'Pall Mall, 29th Sept. 1800.'

Catchwords. Final leaf blank.

Cobbett cites the examples of America and France against the 'Republican Faction' in England: 'Having, in America, witnessed the fatal effects of revolution: having seen piety give place to a contempt of religion, plain-dealing exchanged for shuffling and fraud... a country...torn to pieces by faction, plunged, by intriguing demagogues, into never-ceasing hatred and strife...' (p. 1).

Reprinted as an addendum of six pages to the two London editions (1808) of 'The British Treaty', by Gouverneur Morris or Charles Brockden Brown (See Jacob Blanck, compiler, Bibliography of American Literature, 1511), with a ½ page foreword by the publisher, John Joseph Stockdale, entitled 'Cobbett against Himself.'

'The Porcupine' was published (London) in 183 numbers, October 30, 1800 to May 30, 1801.

58c   Cobbett's Advice | [rule] [1808 ?] [Caption title].

Colophon: Printed by B. M'Millan, Bow-street, Covent Garden.

One leaf, 8 vo; numbered on verso '2' ¶ NJR

The text begins: 'Having, in America, witnessed the fatal effects of Revolu- |'.

59   Porcupine's | Works; | containing various | writings and selections, | exhibiting a faithful picture | of the | United States of America; | of their | governments, laws, politics and resources; | of the characters of their | presidents, governors, legislators, magis- | trates, and military men; | and of the | customs, manners, morals, religion, virtues | and vices | of the people: | comprising also | a complete series of historical documents | and remarks, | from the end of the war, in 1783, | to the | election of the President, in March, 1801 | [rule] | By William Cobbett. | [rule] | In twelve volumes. | (a volume to be added annually.) | Vol. I. [–XII] | [rule] | London: | Printed for Cobbett and Morgan, at the Crown | and Mitre, Pall Mall. | [rule] | May, 1801.

Colophon: S. Gosnell, printer, Little Queen Street, Holborn, London.

¶ Pearl 49 ¶ cty; MWA

Volume I (b)–cc^8=200 leaves, 22 cm; (3)4–400. 2nd, 3rd and 4th leaves signed.

Contents: title; blank; Dedication [3] 4; List of the Subscribers [5]–13; blank; Preface [15]–26, dated 29th May 1801; General Contents [27]–32; Title: A |summary view | of the | politics of the United States, | from the | close of the war | to the | year 1794; blank; a summary view... 35–120; Addresses to Doctor Priestley 121–144; Title: Observations | on | Priestley's emigration. | to which is added, | A story | of | a farmer's bull; blank; Introductory address... 147–149; blank; Observations... 151–220; Title: Account | of the | insurrection | in the | Western counties | of | Pennsylvania, | in 1794.; blank; Account... 223–341; blank; Dispute between America and Great Britain, 343–400. Running titles; catchwords; p. 620 for 260, 71 for 271.

The subscriber list includes 181 in the United Kingdom, headed by the Prince of Wales, four dukes and two princes, 288 in the United States, and residents of Jamaica, Canada, New Brunswick and Nova Scotia.

The material in Volume I is new to Cobbett except the 'Observations on Priestley's Emigration,' taken from the third edition, Philadelphia 1795, with the addition of new notes on pp. 169, 172, 173, 189 (2d par.) 195, 198 and 220. The 'Account of the insurrection' consists largely of extracts from Alexander Hamilton's report of August 16, 1794; presidential proclamations; newspaper accounts; report of Alexander J. Dallas; Fauchet's intercepted letter No. 10; Edmund Randolph's letter to the President August 5, 1794; and James T. Callender, 'Sketches of the History of America,' Philadelphia 1798 (Evans 33485) pp. 115–155, with omissions at 118–9, 122–6, 133–4 and 146–7. Similarly the 'Dispute' is mainly quotations, including on pp. 346–358 extracts from (Smith, Wm. Loughton) 'The Pretensions of Thomas Jefferson to the Presidency Examined...Part II', 1796 (See No. 103) pp. 10–22, with some omissions. (See Volume XII pp. 192–217 for further excerpts).

In his preface, Cobbett declares his object to be to correct the falsehoods concerning America which have circulated in England. He says his pamphlets, down to the time of his Gazette, are placed according to their dates, with intermediate new matter as required to render the whole intelligible. With the Gazette he includes extracts therefrom, still maintaining a general chronological order. At page 24 he writes: '...I harbour not the least resentment toward America or her inhabitants in general...but I also wish to convince the world, that their prosperity and happiness have not been augmented by a rebellion, though a successful one, against the mildest, most just, and most virtuous of Sovereigns.' On page 25: 'I have spent my best days in America; I have contracted friendships there, which never can cease but with my life...' On page 26: 'I have never acted, in any instance, under the influence, direct or indirect, of his Majesty's Ministers;...I have never received at their hands, or at the hands of any other person whatever, any reward for anything I have ever written.'

Volumes II–XII are very similar to Volume I and will not be analyzed as to form except to point out that three printers were used: S. Gosnell, Little Queen Street, Holborn, London, Vols. I, III, V, VI, VII, VIII and XII (Index); T. Baylis, Greville Street, Hatton Garden, Vols. II, IV, IX, XI, and XII (text); and T. Rickaby, Peterborough-Court, Fleet-street, Vol. X. Each printer set up his own title page. Baylis is distinguishable from Gosnell in that the final rule is ornamental. Rickaby added the word 'octavo' after 'volumes.' The twelve volumes comprise slightly over fifty-two hundred pages. The equivalent of about five volumes is made up of selections from Porcupine's Gazette. The summaries which follow differentiate matter printed by Cobbett for the first time.

Volume II. The reprinted matter consists of: (a) A Bone to Gnaw for the Democrats, pp. [1]–64. There are minor changes throughout and notes new or enlarged on pp. [5,] 19, 22, 24, 26, 37, 38, 41, 44, 54, 56 and 60.

(b) A Kick for a Bite pp. [65]–93. Follows original, with new introductory page; on p. 80 B**** has become Brown; p. 86 new note.

(c) A Bone to Gnaw for the Democrats. Part II. pp. [95]–153. Omits the 6 page preface, the introductory verse pp. [97], 114, three minor notes, and the concluding sentence. On p. 104 a new note added; G----es and Ma----ns become Gileses and Madisons.

(d) A Little Plain English...pp. [279]–366. Omits the 4 page preface and the 8 page supplement; also 6 lines on p. 292 and a note p. 309. A note is altered p. 300 and two notes added p. 355.

(e) A New Year's Gift to the Democrats...pp. [403]–472. Omits note on p. iv and final paragraph.

Matter new to Cobbett (1). Summary of the Proceedings of Congress...Session commenced Nov. 4, 1794. pp. [155]–230, including the President's Speech of Nov. 19, the Answers of the Senate and House, debates, especially the speech of Fisher Ames, and consideration of an act on Naturalization.

(2) Popular Proceedings relative to the British Treaty [231]–277. A copy of the Treaty is printed pp. 245–271.

(3) An Analysis of Randolph's Vindication. pp. [367]–402. Extracts from the 'Vindication' (Evans 29384) occupy pp. 374–393, 394–402.

Volume III. Reprinted matter: (a) Political Censor, No. I [i.e. The Prospect from the Congress Gallery] pp. [1]–78. Omits preface; includes introduction to March Censor except first and last paragraphs; omits paragraphs of remarks p. 14, p. 42; p. 54, 4 pars.; p. 55. New note p. 55; p. 66 note reduced.

(b) The Bloody Buoy pp. [79]–243. From the third London edition of 1797. P. 158, 4 pars. omitted.

(c) Political Censor. No. II [i.e. Censor for March 1796] pp. [245]–307. Introduction omitted (see (a) above). Material on Washington cut down by omissions on p. 267, 3 pars.; p. 268 1 par.;

p. 269, 1 par. except 1st sentence; p. 270 6 pars., p. 268 last par., last sentence shortened. Pp. 297–302 L----- becomes Livingston and S----- becomes Swanwick. P. 304 G---t becomes Genet.

(d) Political Censor No. III [i.e. Censor for April 1796] pp. 309–367. At p. 314 the debate on the call for the treaty papers, pp. 76–112 of original is omitted and the President's message in reply inserted; p. 319 par. omitted; p. 324 2 par. omitted, l. 3–5 altered; p. 328 poetry omitted; p. 356 second speech of Grenville altered.

(e) Political Censor No. IV. [i.e. Censor for May 1796]. pp. 369–425 P. 396 a new note, 10 pars. omitted. P. 401 1st par. re. Pitt altered.

New matter pp. 426–440: (1) Letter from Gov. Shelby [of Kentucky] to Oliver Wolcott, Secretary of the Treasury. 426–428. (2) Reply by A. B. to Shelby 428–432. (3) The author's complaint, 432–4. (4) Misc. 434–440.

Volume IV. Reprinted matter: (a) The Scare-Crow. pp. [1]–21. Pp. [3], 4 a new introduction describing the opening of his bookshop in July 1796. P. 19 the note is abbreviated.

(b) The Life and Adventures of Peter Porcupine. pp. [23]–70. P. [31] 1st. par., last line revised; p. 38 name Berkley omitted.

(c) The Political Censor. No. V. [i.e., the Censor for September, 1796] pp. [71]–136. At p. 120 four pars. omitted on his marriage.

(d) The Gros Mousqueton Diplomatique. pp. [137]–206.

(e) The Political Censor No. VI. [i.e., the Censor for November 1796], pp. [207]–275.

(f) The Political Censor No. VII. [i.e., the Censor for December 1796]. pp. [277]–332.

On p. 292 one par. omitted; p. 329 one par. substituted for two pars.; final five pages advertising omitted.

(g) The Political Censor No. VIII. [i.e., the Censor for January 1797] [333]–370.

Omissions: p. 336, one par.; p. 346, 3 pars.; p. 369, last par. in part; p. 370, second half of final par. and 7 pages containing Adams' farewell addresses to the Senate and the Senate's reply.

New matter, pp. [371]–444: (1) Report of Secretary of State Pickering Feb. 27, 1797. Pp. [371]–377. (2) Washington's retiring: the farewell address, pp. 378–398; publications, 'Valerius' [On Washington] 10/21/95, pp. 399–403; 'Calm Observer' [J. J. Beckley] 10/23/95, pp. 403–408; Oliv. Wolcott 10/24/95 and others, pp. 409–426, remarks on the above 426–428; further similar publications, 428–444.

Volume V. Selections from Porcupine's Gazette 4th March 1797 through 31st May 1797, pp. [1]–432. Included in 'Gazette Selections' is Porcupine's Political Censor for March 1797; pp. 143–169, 177–196 and 198–205, with a new note p. 188 and names for blanks on pp. 199, 201, 203.

Volume VI. Selections from Porcupine's Gazette 1st June 1797 through 15 August 1797, pp. [1]–432. Papers on the Session of Congress ended July 10, 1797 are collected pp. 104–238.

Volume VII. (a) Selections from Porcupine's Gazette. 16th August 1797 through 29th November 1797, pp. [1]–311.

(b) The Republican Judge, pp. [313]–407. P. 335 new connective sentence; p. 348 note, the author of the second libel charged to Cobbett is given: John Sitgreaves.

(c) Gazette selections 1st December through 30th December 1797, pp. 408–430.

Volume VIII. (a) Selections from Porcupine's Gazette January 1798 through May 1798, pp. [1]–196.

(b) Detection of a Conspiracy formed by the United Irishmen, pp. [197]–229, copied from the London edition of 1799. (No. 38b).

(c) Gazette Selections June 1798, pp. 231–257.

(d) The Cannibal's Progress...abridged from the Translation of Anthony Aufrère, pp. [259]–320. Copied from the edition published by Cobbett, Philadelphia, 1798. (No. 118).

(e) Gazette Selections, pp. [321]–480. Report of the Secretary of State respecting the depredations committed on the commerce of the United States, June 21, 1797, and documents, pp. [321]–476.

Volume IX. (a) Selections from Porcupine's Gazette for July 1798 pp. [1]–135. Pp. 66–124 contain the instructions to the envoys to France, Pinckney, Marshall and Gerry, and related papers. Cobbett had published the instructions in a pamphlet, Philadelphia, 1798 (No. 113); (b) Gazette selections August, September 1798, pp. 180–224; (c) Remarks on the Explanation...Dr. Priestley...letters of...Stone, pp. 245–278, published London 1799 (No. 46); and (d) Gazette selections October 1798, pp. 278–304.

New Matter: (1) Papers on the Blount Conspiracy, pp. 135–180; (2) Letters of Stone to Dr. Priestley, pp. 224–245; (3) Anecdotes, pp. [305]–388; (4) 'Priestley's Charity Sermon for Poor Emigrants'

[February 19, 1797, Evans 32714] with a two page foreword and long notes by Cobbett written in May 1801, pp. [389]–410; and (5) Letter to the people of Wales, pp. 410–412.

Volume X. (a) Selections from Porcupine's Gazette November 1798 through June 1799, pp. [1]–230. Includes, pp. 116–143, Report of Pickering on France 18th January 1799, Evans 36548.

(b) The Trial of Republicanism, pp. [387]–449; published London 1801 (No. 47).

New Matter: (1) Appendix to Jedidiah Morse's Sermon preached November 29, 1798, Evans 34151, on France, pp. 231–275. The notes are also by Morse.

(2) Galloway's Exposure of Sir William Howe, pp. 275–386; evidently taken from the work by Joseph Galloway reprinted Philadelphia 1787, Evans 20382.

(3) Puff for (b) above, 30th April 1801, pp. [450]–[452].

Volume XI. (a) Selections from Porcupine's Gazette July 1799 through November 1799, pp. [1]–119.

(b) 'Some account of a manuscript...entitled Talleyrand's Descent into Hell' [by William Cliffton], from the Gazette, pp. 120–136.

(c) Porcupine's Gazette, 'farewell number' January 1800, pp. 137–160, (No. 48.)

(d) A concise and comprehensive History of Prince Suworow's Campaign in Italy, pp. [161]–207 (No. 50).

(e) The American Rush-Light...Wayward and disaffected Britons may see...the baseness...of Republicans..., consisting of a title-page and advertisement, pp. [209]–213 (the advertisement is from Rush-Light No. 1), and the first five numbers of the Rush-Light. The first four numbers are from the 'American Rush-Light' London 1800. (No. 57). There are many changes throughout as is indicated in the description of the last-named work. In No. 1, as an extreme example, the note is new on page 235 that Rush's wife was illegitimate.

Volume XII. Pp. [3]–252 contain fifteen miscellaneous selections, followed by the Index of 82 unnumbered pages. A brief description:

The Trial of [Thomas] Cooper. Pp. [3]–16.

Address of the Emigration Society of Philadelphia pp. 16–20.

Washington's Death, papers pp. 20–29.

Congress Session beginning third December, 1799. Pp. 29–53. (Notes by Cobbett, pp. 30, 33, attack President Adams).

An account of the British Commissioners under the Jay Treaty pp. 53–89. Pp. 64–89 contain an article from the Anti-Jacobin Review on the pamphlet [by Thomas MacDonald] 'A brief Statement of Opinions, given in the Board of Commissioners...' (No. 169).

Defence of the Quakers of Pennsylvania, pp. 89–108. By Cobbett, taken from the Anti-Jacobin Review.

Farewell advertisements [of May 31, 1800] pp. 108–111 (extracts and comment).

Prison Eclogue [by Joseph Dennie] pp. 112–118 (from the Porcupine, London).

Republican Morality. pp. 118–129 (from the same). Pp. 123–9 is the same letter as Volume XI, pp. 347–50 with corrections, as 'Cadiz' for 'Charleston'.

Jefferson's Election. pp. 130–150 and 174–192 (from London Porcupine).

Review of the pamphlet 'Letter from Alexander Hamilton concerning the public conduct and character of John Adams', pp. 150–174 (Evans 37556) from the Anti-Jacobin Review, with extensive extracts from the pamphlet.

Jefferson's Character pp. 192–217. Extracts from Evans 31212, 31213 [Smith, Wm. Loughton] 'The Pretensions of Thomas Jefferson to the Presidency Examined...', pp. 14–43, with omissions, not all of which are noted, and same, Part the Second...pp. [3]–5 and 39. (Cobbett also excerpted from this pamphlet in Volume I. pp. 346–358; and see no. 103.)

Convention concluded between America and France in 1800, pp. 218–239.

Proceedings in Congress—Session which ended in March 1801, pp. 239–252.

60   A | Collection | of | facts and observations, | relative to the | peace with Bonaparte, | chiefly extracted from | the Porcupine, | and including | Mr. Cobbett's letters to Lord Hawkesbury. | To which is added, | an appendix, | containing | the divers conventions, treaties, state papers, and dispatches, con- | nected with the subject; together with extracts from the | speeches of Mr. Pitt, Mr. Fox, and Lord Hawkesbury, | respecting Bonaparte, and a peace with France. | [rule] | By William Cobbett. | [rule] | [four lines from] Ezekiel, vii, 25 | [sixteen dots] | Philadelphia: | printed for John Morgan, | and sold by Benjamin Davies, No. 39 Chesnut-Street. | [six dots] | 1802.

[A]–X⁴Y²;A–G⁴[H]²=116 leaves, 23.4 cm.; (3)4–172;(1)ii–lvii (3) ¶ A.B. 2044 ¶ MWA

Contents: title, blank; a | collection | of | facts and observations, &c. [3]–172; appendix [i]–lvii; blank; proposals for publishing (2).

The collection includes extracts from the [London] Porcupine of scattered issues 15th June to 27th October 1801 and beginning at page 117 eight letters to Lord Hawkesbury. The text answers to the title page. Running titles. Page no. xlvii is at top left instead of right.

61   The | ninth letter | to | Lord Hawkesbury, | relative to the | peace with Bonaparte. | [rule] | By William Cobbett. | [rule] | [three lines from] | Letter to Lord Hawkesbury. | [rule] | Philadelphia: | printed for B. Davies, No. 39 Chesnut Street. | [fourteen dots] | 1802.

[π]⁴Aa⁴=8 leaves, 8 vo; (2)175–187(1). ¶ A.B. 2045 ¶ NjR

Contents: title, blank, Letter IX 175–187, blank. Running titles: 'Facts and Observations' and 'Relative to the Peace'. Subscribed page 187 Wm. Cobbett. This is excerpted from a longer work containing all nine letters (No. 60 has eight), with a new title page.

62a   Forsyth, William 1737–1804.

A | Treatise | on | the culture and management | of | fruit trees; | in which | a new method of pruning and training | is fully described. | together with | observations | on | the diseases, defects, and injuries, in all kinds of fruit and | forest trees; | as also, | an account of a particular method of cure, | made public by order of the British government. | [rule] | By William Forsyth, F.A.S. & F.S.A. | gardener to his Majesty at Kensington and St. James's. | [rule] | To which are added, | an introduction and notes, | adapting the rules of the treatise to the | climates and seasons of the United States of America. | [12 dots] | By William Cobbett. | [rule] | Philadelphia: | Printed for J. Morgan, 51 South Second Street. | [12 dots] | 1802.

[A]–Ll⁴=136 leaves, 8 vo; (5)vi–viii(1)x–xii(1)2–190(3)194–204(3)208–220(3)224–233(3)237–250(1)252–259(1). 13 plates, 11 folding ¶ Pearl 54, A.B. 2236 ¶ CtY; MWA

Contents: half-title, blank, title, blank, introduction [v]–viii, preface [ix]–xii, a treatise [1]–190; second title, blank, introduction [193]–204; appendix, blank, appendix [207]–220; supplement, blank, supplement [223]–233, blank; Explanations, blank, explanation 237–250; Index [251]–259, blank. The plates are interleaved between the explanation pages. There are more than 100 footnotes by Cobbett, who also wrote the introduction.

Error: p. 324 for p. 224. There are running titles.

This is a pioneering work. See U. P. Hedrick, A History of Horticulture in America to 1860, New York 1950, page 473.

62b ———. A new title page has been tipped in to replace the Philadelphia title-page, transcribing as follows: A | Treatise | on | the culture and management | of | fruit trees; | in which | a new method of pruning and training | is fully described, | together with | observations | on | the diseases, defects, and injuries, in all kinds of fruit | and forest trees; | as also, | an account of a particular method of cure, | made public by order of the British Government. | [rule] | By William Forsyth, F.A.S. & F.S.A. | gardener to his Majesty at Kensington and St. James' | [rule] | to which are added, | an intro- duction and notes, | adapting the rules of the treatise to the | cli- mates and seasons of the United States of America. | [rule] | By William Cobbett. | [rule] | New York: | published by Ezra Sargeant & Co. | No. 129, Water Street | [rule] | 1802.

A.B. 2235 ¶ MWA

This collaboration between publishers in 62a and b is not sur- prising, as Morgan was Cobbett's Philadelphia agent and Sargeant a former employee.

62c ———. A | Treatise | on | the culture and management | of | fruit trees, | in which | a new method of pruning and training | is fully described. | together with | observations | on | the diseases, de- fects and injuries, in all | kinds of fruit and forest trees; | as also, | an account of a particular method of cure, | made public by order of the British Government. | [rule] | by William Forsyth, F.A.S. & F.S.A. | gardener to his Majesty at Kensington and St. James'. | [rule] | to which are added, | an introduction and notes, | adapting the rules of the treatise to the | climates and seasons of the United States of America. | [22 dots] | By William Cobbett. | [22 dots] | Albany: | printed for and sold by D. & S. Whiting, | at the Albany book-store, No. 45, state-street. | Sold also by Thomas & Andrews, Boston; A. & A. Stansbury, N. | York; O. Penniman & Co. Troy; S. P. Good- rich, Utica; J. | Glover & Co. Oxford, and H. Chapin, Canandai- gua. | 1803.

[A]–U⁴,W–C2⁴,E2–M2⁴=140 leaves, 8 vo; (5)vi–viii(1)x–xii (1)14–202(3)206–216(3)220–232(3)236–245(3)249–262(1)264–271(2)274–280. 13 plates, 11 folding, grouped before p. 249 ¶ A. B. 4218 ¶ cty; mwa

Contents: half-title, blank, title, blank, introduction [v]–viii, preface [ix]–xii, A Treatise [13]–202, second title, blank, introduction [205]–216, appendix, blank, appendix [219]–232, supplement, blank, supplement [235]–245, blank, explanations, plates, explanation 249–262, index [263]–271, blank, the editors...[273]–280.

Text and plates as in Philadelphia edition 1802, with the addition of an eight page letter, pp. [273]–280, from Peter W. Yates dated 'Albany, September, 1803.'

63a   An | epitome | of | Mr. Forsyth's treatise | on the | culture and management | of | fruit-trees. | Also, | notes on American gardening and fruits: | with designs for promoting the ripen- | ing of fruits, and securing them | as family comforts: | and further, | of economical principles in building | farmers' habitations. | [rule] | By an American farmer | [rule] | Philadelphia: | printed by T. L. Plowman, | for John Morgan, No. 26 South Third- | street. | [seven dots] | 1803.

[A]²,B–V⁴X–Aa⁴=98 leaves, 8 vo; (5)2–121(4)126–163(3)167–186(6) ¶ Pearl 54, Sabin 25154, A.B. 4217 (under Forsyth) ¶ cty; mwa

15 plates following p. 184, the last two being new in this work.

Contents: title, blank, advertisement (2), A Treatise [1]–121, blank, subtitle: 'Notes on Fruits and American Gardening...by an American Farmer.', blank, Notes, &c [125]–163, blank, subtitle: 'Explanations of the engravings'; blank, explanation 167–186; Index (6).

Forsyth's Treatise (No. 62) is much abbreviated, with a number of subtitles omitted altogether, such as cherries, apples, etc., and substantially rewritten. The notes include much new material, in particular that relating to country habitations, usefulness of birds, etc.

Attributed to Cobbett by Pearl and Sabin, and by Melville, William Cobbett, 2:278. The publisher John Morgan was Cobbett's Philadelphia agent.

63b   An epitome | of | Mr. Forsyth's treatise | on | the culture and management | of | fruit-trees. | Also | notes on American gardening and fruits; | with designs for promoting the ripening | of fruits, and securing them as family | comforts: | and further | of economical principles in building | farmers' habitations | [rule] | By an American farmer | [rule] | Philadelphia: | published by Wm. Poyntell & Co. | proprietors of the | Class Press | [14 dots] | 1804.

¶ Pearl 54; A.B. 6318 (under Forsyth) ¶ CTY; MWA

Except for the title page, this is from the same setting of type as the previous entry. The title page is on wove paper and the rest on laid, suggesting that the new publisher took over a remainder.

64   Elements of Reform, | or | an account of | the motives and intentions | of the | advocates | for | parliamentary reformation | [rule] | By William Cobbett, | proprietor of the Political Register. | [rule] | "Englishmen read, mark, learn and inwardly digest." | [rule] | London: | printed and published by T. Gillet, No. 7, Crown Court, | Fleet-street, and to be had of all booksellers and newsmen | in town and country. | [rule] | 1809. | Price two shillings.

Colophon p. 37: T. Gillet, printer, 7, Crown-court, Fleet-street, London.

[A]²B–E⁴F²=20 leaves, 20.3 cm; (5)4–37(1) ¶ Pearl 68 ¶ CTY

Contents: title, blank, dedication, blank, Elements of Reform [3]–37, blank. Running titles.

Pearl notes this represents extracts from Cobbett's works tending to discredit him. It begins with an extract from the prospectus of 1800 (No. 58) and includes various extracts from Porcupine's Works, London 1801 (No. 59).

65   The | trial | of | Messrs. Lambert & Perry. | To which also is added, | the trial | of | William Cobbet, [sic] | for | libelling | his present majesty, George III. | King of England, | and | his government. | [rule] | [6 lines quoted from] T. | [rule] | The first American edition. | [rule] | New-York: | published by D.C. & P. Burkloe, | No. 24, William-street. | J. Seymour, print. | [rule] | 1810.

[A]–H⁴=32 leaves, 21.6 cm; (5)6–43(1)45–64 ¶ A.B. 21519 ¶ NN; MWA

Contents: title, blank, preface, blank, King vs. Lambert [5]–43; Trial of Mr. W. Cobbet [sic] [44]–64.

Cobbett was convicted of a libel in that in July 1809 he had published an attack on the ministry for using German cavalry to suppress a supposed 'mutiny' among some local militia, and for flogging the leaders. Cobbett was sentenced to pay a £1000 fine, be imprisoned in Newgate for two years, and furnish a £5000 bond to keep the peace.

66　Porcupine revived, | or | an old thing made new; | being | 1. an argument against the expediency of a war | with England. | 2. an exposition of the absurdity of sending Al- | bert Gallatin to treat with the British. | [rule] | by William Cobbet. [sic] | [rule] | with additional notes and comments. | [rule] | [one line of Latin] | [rule] | New-York: | printed for the publisher. | 1813.

[A]–C⁴=12 leaves, 21 cm; (7)8–16(1)18–24 ¶ A.B. 28167; S. 64165 ¶ MWA

Contents: title, blank, dedication, blank, preface, blank, 'Arguments.' [7]–13; 'An Exposure...' 13–16, Remarks...by the Editor [17]–24. Subscribed page 24 'An American' and dated July 24, 1813. At foot of page 24 four lines of errata. Running titles in the body of the work. The 'Arguments' and 'Exposure' are taken from Cobbett. The sources are not given except to say they were '17 years ago' [page 18]. Actually both excerpts come from 'The Political Censor...[for April 1796]...' (No. 14a), pp. 155–158 and pp. 158–165, with small omissions. Included are the portions quoted under No. 14a from pp. 156, 158, 164, 165. The 'Exposure' relates to Albert Gallatin, whose nomination (the editor writes p. 20) as commissioner to treat with the British had just been rejected by the Senate. Cobbett's name is misspelled throughout.

67　Public documents...No. 1 | [rule] | New-Haven | remonstrance. | together with an | exposition of the remonstrants; | or | a curiosity for the curious. | [rule] | [three lines quoted from] | Holy Writ | [rule] | [rule] | [two lines quoted] | [rule] | Printed for Peter Porcupine, on the King's Birth Day. | [rule] | 1814 [London?]

[π]²A⁴B⁶=12 leaves, 20 cm; (3)4–24. Third leaf of B signed B2 ¶ CTY

Contents: title, page of verse, New-Haven Remonstrance, [3]–6; The President's reply, 6–10; From the Sun of Liberty of Sept. 9, 1801 [letter of Abraham Bishop], 11–23; To the Public...Peter Porcupine | London August 11, 1814...Catalogue of Books...p.24.

Just before retirement President Adams appointed a strong federalist to be Collector at New Haven. President Jefferson removed him and appointed a republican, Samuel Bishop, father of Abraham

Bishop. A number of New Haven merchants sent to Jefferson a 'Remonstrance' (said to have been drawn by Noah Webster, Jr.— See Skeel, a Bibliography of the Writings of Noah Webster, p. 522, note 4) protesting the removal and alleging Bishop's incompetence due to age and infirmity.

68a Letters | on | the late war | between the | United States and Great Britain: | together with | other miscellaneous writings, | on | the same subject. | [rule] | By William Cobbett, Esq. | [rule] | New-York: | published by J. Belden and Co. | Van Winkle & Wiley, Printers. | [eleven dots] | 1815.

[1]–51⁴=204 leaves, 23 cm; (3)iv–vii(2)10–407(1) ¶ Pearl 78; A.B. 34378; Sabin 13889 ¶ CtY; MWA; NN

Contents: title, copyright, Preface [iii]–vii, dated p. vii New-York, November, 1815; blank; Letters [9]–407; blank. Running titles.

The preface is full of praise for Cobbett, though declining to defend his writings in this country as Peter Porcupine. There are approximately 50 miscellaneous compositions in the 'Letters', written from 1811 through July 1815, including 11 addressed to the Prince Regent, 8 to the Earl of Liverpool, English Premier, and 11 entitled 'American War.' Pearl notes these are mainly reprinted from Cobbett's 'Political Register'.

Cobbett is very outspoken in defense of American rights, particularly in letters to the Prince Regent, the earliest dated from Newgate Prison in 1811 and 1812. His treatment is most sympathetic to the United States. Examples (p. 131): '...In America, where the government [is] chosen by, and resting upon, the free and unbought voice of the people...'; (p. 136): '...upon trial, it has been found that our frigates are not a match for those of America....' He discounts the burning of Washington (p. 178): 'Why did our army not *remain* at Washington?' He emphasizes the losses of the British on Lake Erie and Lake Champlain (pp. 183–193); etc., etc. He dwells on the growth of the British debt and tax burden, and her killed, wounded and missing soldiers.

Pp. 259–273 contain an article addressed 'To the cossack priesthood of the State of Massachusetts', reprinted also in Boston the same year (Nos. 69a and 69b). On pp. 281–6 he attacks as hypocritical the federalists, the members of the Hartford Convention and the Washington Benevolent Societies.

68b ———. The transcription is the same as preceding entry down through 'New-York:' and continues: Published by J. Belden and Co. and sold by Van Winkle | and Wiley, No. 3 Wall-street. | [sixteen dots] | 1815. On page [ii] at the foot: [rule] | Van Winkle and Wiley, Print. | [rule]. Otherwise this appears to be the same setting of type as the preceding entry. Priority between them has not been determined ¶ cty

69a An | address | to the | clergy of Massachusetts. | written in England, Nov. 13, 1814. | [rule] | By William Cobbett, | [rule] | With | a prefatory epistle, | to certain priests, | by Jonathan, | one of the people called Christians. | Ye shall know them by their fruits. | New Testament. | [rule] | Boston: | printed at the Yankee-office | [12 dots] | 1815. [By Rowe & Hooper?]

[1],2⁶=12 leaves, 19 cm; (3)4–8(1)10–24; third leaves signed 1* and 2* ¶ Pearl 79, A.B. 34376, Sabin 13870 ¶ cty; mwa

Contents: title; blank; To the Clergy of Massachusetts [3]–8, signed p. 8 Jonathan. Boston May 8th, 1815; To the Cossack Priesthood | of the State of Massachusetts | [rule] | Botley, (Eng.) Nov. 29, 1815 [i.e.1814] pp. [9]–24. Signed p. 24, William Cobbett. Quotation pp. 17–19 is in small type. The preface attacks the Massachusetts clergy who 'fight the battles of party, with the weapons of religion', especially Drs. [David] Osgood and [Elijah] Parish. Cobbett objects to the thanksgivings celebrated by the clergy in Massachusetts on the entrance of the Cossacks into Paris and the downfall of Napoleon. The reason for this hatred of Napoleon by the clergy is stated p. 23: 'They begun [sic] to fear, that, if Religion became out of fashion in Europe, it might become out of fashion in Massachusetts, and leave them in a situation like that of the buckle-makers, when shoe strings came in vogue.'

Pearl notes that the work was published in Cobbett's Political Register, London, December 10, 1814. He quotes from the Register of July 22, 1815 that: 'five thousand copies had in several editions been sold.'

69b ———. Here the transcription includes before 'Boston' the following: 'Second edition | [rule] |' ¶ A.B. 34377 ¶ mwa; nn

70a The | pride of Britannia humbled; | or, | the queen of the ocean unqueen'd, | by | "The American Cock Boats," | and | "The fir built things, with bits of striped | bunting at their mast heads." |

(as the Rt H. Mr. Canning, in the British parliament, called our frigates.) | Illustrated and demonstrated | by four letters addressed to Lord Liverpool, | on the late American war. | By William Cobbett, Esq. | To which is added, | a glimpse of the American victories, | on land, on the lakes and on the ocean. | with a persuasive to political moderation. | Most respectfully addressed to the persons composing the two great | parties in the United States, in general, and to | the politicians of Connecticut and Mas- | sachusetts, in particular | [rule] | Published by T. Boyle, of New-York; Wm. Reynolds, of | Philadelphia; and J. Campbell of Baltimore. | [12 dots] | 1815.

[A]–S⁶=108 leaves, 19.5 cm; (3)4–216; third leaves signed A2 etc. Page numbers omitted: 20,30,40,59,82,88,119,138, 145 and 194. Frontispiece, 'Naval Hero s' [sic], portrait of 4 Naval Heroes, engr. by 'J O Lweis' [i.e. Lewis] ¶ Pearl 80; A.B. 34379 ¶ cty; NN

Contents: title, advertisement, Letter I [3]–216. There are numerous subtitles. The material on pp. [145]–210, 'A Glimpse, &c', appears to be by Thomas Branagan. Most of the rest of the work appeared also in 'Letters on the late War...' (no. 68) but was not taken from it but rather from Cobbett's Political Register. In three instances matter is omitted as obliterated which appears in the 'Letters'. On p. 38 the names 'Pickerings' and 'Otises' are inserted and the words omitted: 'I really believe to be traitors to their country; or, at least, that they would sell themselves, if you and your master were not too honest to buy them.' ('Letters' p. 308). There are notes by the compiler (Thomas Branagan—Pearl) who writes (p. 188) that he presented to Cobbett for publication the first piece he wrote for the press, seventeen years before (1798).

The covers are paper over boards. The front cover within a border of type ornaments has a title substantially following the title page, with the imprint, however, 'Philadelphia: | published by Wm. Reynolds, T. Boyle and J. | Campbell. | 1815.' The back cover advertises 'A Glimpse of the American Victories...' etc.

DLC has the publishers' proposals for publishing this work, n. p. n. d., 2 leaves, fol. 34 cm., printed only on the front recto, with spaces for subscribers' names. The work is to be 'Between 2 and 300 pages', priced in boards at 87½ cents.

70b The | pride | of Britannia humbled; | or, the | queen of the ocean unqueen'd, | "By the American Cock Boats," | or, "the fir built

things, with bits of striped bunting at their mast heads."—(as the |
Right Hon. Mr. Canning, in the British parliament, called our
American frigates.) | Illustrated and demonstrated | by four letters
addressed to Lord Liverpool, | on the late American War | [rule] |
by Wm. Cobbett, Esq. | [rule] | Including a number of his other
most important letters, and arguments, in defence of | the American
Republic | To which is added | [text as in first edition] A new edi-
tion. | [rule, broken] | Philadelphia: | published by William Rey-
nolds,—Daniel Griffin, New York;–J. Campbell, Baltimore,– | and
P. Boyle, New Jersey | [rule] | 1815. | A Griggs & K. Dickinson,—
Printers, Whitehall.

[A]–L⁶[M]–S⁶=108 leaves, 18 cm; (3)4–215(1). Third leaves
signed A2 etc. Frontispiece as in No. 70a, much worn ¶ Pearl 80;
A.B. 34380. ¶ cty; mwa

A new setting of type, in the same kind of binding, and with contents substantially the same as the first edition. The material on pp.
59–[144] is rearranged into chronological sequence, resulting in a
blank p. [144]. The advertisement is dated Philadelphia, May 8,
1815 and a new paragraph added dated Philadelphia, July 18, 1815
that: 'The last edition of 2000 copies selling off with great rapidity,
the Editor, after a lapse of two weeks, puts to press a new edition of
4000 copies.' Lines 6 to 8 on page 172 and the last six lines on p.
[216] are new. The printed covers are substantially the same, with
the addition of 'Second Edition.'

Errors noted: Parenthesis not closed around page number 109;
question mark omitted at foot of page 71.

70c ———. A variant from the preceding entry in which signature M is printed ¶ cty; nn

70d The | pride of Britannia humbled; | or, | The queen of the
ocean unqueened, | by | "The American Cock Boats", | and | "The fir
built things, with bits of striped | bunting at thier [sic] mast heads." |
(As the Rt. Hon. Mr. Canning, in the British Parliament, | called
our frigates.) | illustrated and demonstrated | by letters addressed to
Lord Liverpool, | on the late American war. | [rule] | By William
Cobbett, Esq. | [rule] | to which is added, | a glimpse of the Ameri-
can victories | on land, on the lakes, and on the ocean. | with a per-
suasive to political moderation, | most respectfully addressed to the
persons composing | the two great parties in the United States. |

[rule] Cincinnati: | published by John R. Fletcher, William Pouns-ford, and | Williams and Mason; | Williams and Mason, printers. | 1817.

[A]–F⁶[G]–S⁶=108 leaves, 20.2 cm.; (3)4–19(1)21–29(1)31–39 (1) 41–58(1)60–80(1)82–86(1)88–107(1)109–117(1)119–129(1) 131–137(1)139–144(1)146–178(1)180–192(1)194–209(1)211–216. Third leaves signed A2–R2 ¶ A.B.40499; Pearl 80 ¶ NjR

Contents: title; advertisement; To the Earl...[3]–19; To the Earl ...[20]–29; To the Earl... [30]–39;To the Earl...[40]–58 dated page 58 Botley, 28th December, 1814; To the Cossack priesthood...[59]–80; from Cobbett's Weekly Register...[81]–86; From Cobbett's Register...[87]–107; From Cobbett's Weekly Register...[108]–117; From Cobbett's Register of January 21, 1815 [118]–129; From Cobbett's Register...[130]–137; From Cobbett's Register [138]–144; A Glimpse [145]–178; Victory...[179]–192; Official accounts [193]–209; Conclusion [210]–216.

In boards with printed covers. On the front cover the title page is reproduced (with 'thier' corrected) in a border of type ornaments. On the rear are advertisements dated 'December 1817'.

70e ———. Here the imprint includes, after the first 'Williams and Mason', '; and John Hellings, Chillicothe.' ¶ A. B. 40500 [?] ¶ MWA; NjR

71a Cobbett's Weekly Political Register—New York volumes.

[*Vol. I*] Title page: Cobbett's | American | Political Register | [rule] | Volume XXX. | from January to June, 1816, | inclusive | [rule] | copy right secured according to law. | [rule] | New=York: | published by H. Cobbett and G. S. Oldfield, No. 19 Wall-street. | Van Winkle & Wiley, printers | [thirteen dots] | 1816. ¶ Pearl 83; Mott, Frank L. A History of American Magazines 1741–1850, pp. 131, 795; A.B. 37283 ¶ DLC; MWA; CtY [lacking five numbers].

Contents: title, departments of the U.S. Government, letters No. 1–No. 26, index of...persons [813]–816; index...of places [817] 818; contents, two leaves. The letters are entitled 'Cobbett's Week-ly Political Register,' in eight leaves, 23.7 cm., two columns to a page, columns numbered 1–812. Final number 26 has three pages of text, indices in three columns to a page. No. 1 is noted 'written in England Jan 6—published at New York May 21, 1816.' In No. 26 the dates are June 29 and Sept. 24, 1816.

Henry Cobbett was Cobbett's nephew. Not a great deal of the content is of United States interest. No. 1 has an address to the people of the United States; No. 2 is on a national bank; there are three sections entitled 'The American Packet', cols. 436–48, 469–72 and 594–608; an address to Commodore David Porter, cols. 528–544; and addresses to correspondents, cols. 609–11 and 705–8.

[*Vol. II*] Title page: Cobbett's | political register. | [rule] | Volume II. American, | or | Volume XXXII. English. | from | May to October 1817, | inclusive. | [rule] | Copy right secured according to law. | [rule] | New=York: | published by H. Cobbett, No. 19 Wall-Street | [twelve dots] | 1817.

Colophons: Published by H. Cobbett at Cobbett's Register Office, No. 19 Wall Street ¶ DLC

Contents: title, blank, contents (2) and twenty six numbers of eight leaves each, two columns to a page, except the last two pages of No. 25 contain a notice to subscribers not numbered, and that No. 26 is in six leaves (no doubt because it also included the title and contents leaves.) Columns numbered 1–820. The 26 numbers are entitled Cobbett's Weekly Political Register. | [rule] | Vol. 33 No. 1 [–26] New York. Thursday, May 15, 1817–[November 6, 1817.] | [Price $5 per ann. or 12½c. per no. | [rule] Running titles. No. 1 announces Cobbett's resumption of publication in America. The other numbers are on English subjects.

[*Vol. III*] DLC has five numbers of Vol. 34, Nos. 1 to 4 and 7, without a title page. These are in eight leaves, in two numbered columns per page. The title is: Cobbett's Weekly Political Register. | [rule] | Vol. 34 No. 1 [–4, 7] New-York Thursday, November 13, 1817 [November 20, December 13, December 20, 1817, January 10, 1818] | Price 5 dolls. per ann. or 12½c. per no. | [rule].

Colophon nos. 1–3: Published by H. Cobbett, at Cobbett's Register Office, No. 19 Wall-street; Nos. 4, 7: Published by H. Cobbett, corner of John and Cliff Streets. The content is of English interest. There is no indication that the publication expired with No. 7.

71b   Cobbett's Weekly Political Register—London volumes.

[*Vol. XXXII*]. Title page: Cobbett's | weekly | political register | [rule] | Vol. XXXII. | [rule] | of which the former part was written in England, | and | the latter in America. | [rule] | in the whole thirty-eight numbers, being all that | were published in the year 1817 | [rule] | London: | printed and published by and for William

Jackson, | 11, Newcastle street, and 192, Strand. | [rule] | entered at Stationers' Hall. ¶ MBAt

Contents: title, blank, Table of Contents [vi]vii and vol. 32 No. 1–No. 38, in eight leaves with two numbered columns per page. With No. 7 the title for the rest of the year became 'Cobbett's weekly political pamphlet.' In lieu of No. 14 is 'Mr. Cobbett's | taking leave of his countrymen' [caption], dated Liverpool, March 28, 1817, eight leaves. No. 15 published July 12, 1817 has the date Long Island, May 3, 1817. No. 38 published December 27, 1817 is dated Long Island October 17, 1817. Numbers [14]–38 first appeared in the New York Volume II, except nos. 25, 31 and 38.

[*Vol. XXXIII*]. Title page: Cobbett's | weekly | political register...[rule] | Vol. XXXIII. | [rule] | From January to June, 1818. | [rule] | written in America. | [rule] | London: | printed and published by and for William Jackson, | 11, Newcastle street; 192, Strand; and 34, Wardour | Street, Soho. | [rule] | entered at Stationers' Hall ¶ MBAt

Contents: title, blank, Table of Contents [iii]iv and Vol. 33 No. 1–No. 23, weekly from January 3 through June 20, except March 21 and May 2, in eight leaves (except No. 12, 6 leaves), numbered columns, dated Long Island October 17, 1817 through April 9, 1818. The first three numbers appeared in the New York Volume II. The later numbers may have appeared in the New York Volume III except nos. 5 and 11. Some numbers are variously dated Lancaster, Bustleton, 'near Harrisburgh', etc.

[*Vol. XXXIV*]. Title page: Cobbett's | weekly | political register. | [rule] | Vol. XXXIV. | [rule] | From August 1818, to August 1819. | [rule] | written in America. | [rule] | London: | printed for, and published by Thomas Dolby, | 34, Wardour-Street, Soho. | [rule] | entered at Stationers' Hall. ¶ MBAt

Contents: title, blank, Index [iii]iv, and Vol. 34 No. 1–No. 36. Weekly from August 22, 1818 through May 22, 1819, except October 14, and a concluding number August 21, 1819, in eight leaves (except Nos. 2 and 36 in 6 leaves), numbered columns, dated North Hampstead [sic] L.I. April 30, 1818 through March 1, 1819. Nos. 1–19 printed by W. Molineux...for W. Jackson; Nos. 20–24...for T. Dolby; Nos. 25–36 printed by Hay and Turner...for T. Dolby.

[*Vol. XXXV*]. Title page: Cobbett's | Political Register. | [rule] | Volume XXXV. | including the time between | August 14, 1819, and January 27, 1820. | [rule] | London: | printed and sold by William Benbow 269, Strand. | [rule] | 1820 ¶ MBAt

Contents: title, table of contents, Index of persons (2) and Vol. 35 No. 1–No. 21. Printed by Hay and Turner ...for T. Dolby. Weekly from August 14, 1819, excluding August 21, in eight leaves, numbered columns. Nos. 1–12 dated from North Hampstead [sic] June 30–Sept. 24, 1819. No. 12 has communications dated Sept. 29 and October 4, just before Cobbett sailed for England for the last time.

72   Price Three Halfpence | [rule] | Cobbett's | address | to the | Americans. | [rule] | Jamaica, Long Island, May 9, 1817. | To the People of America. [caption title] [London 1817]

Colophon p. [8]: Printed by Hay & Turner, 11, Newcastle-Street, Strand, and published by J. Duncombe, 19, Little Queen-Street, Lincoln's-inn-Fields, and may be had of all booksellers and newsmen, in town and country.

[A]⁴=4 leaves, 20.6 cm; (1)2,3(1)5–7(1) ¶ Pearl 90 ¶ NN

Contents: Address [1]–3; Cobbett's | American Register [4]–7; advertisement. [8.] Catchwords.

Cobbett replies to insinuations in the New York Evening Post that he fled England because of debts. He then announces the revival of the American Register (see No. 71), which had been published by Cobbett's nephew, Henry Cobbett, and G. S. Oldfield, but had been stopped because Cobbett's communications had been intercepted. The advertisement is for The Black Dwarf.

73   Price two pence. | [rule] | Mr. Cobbett's | address to his countrymen, | on his future | political works; and on | the state of their political affairs. | [lozenge] [1817] [caption title].

Colophon: Printed by R. Carlile, 183, Fleet-street, London.

[A]⁴=4 leaves, not paged. Text in two columns, numbered (2)3–14. ¶ Pearl 91 ¶ CU (Davis)

Contents: text, cols. [1]–12, headed 'Jamaica, Long Island | May 11th, 1817.' signed: William Cobbett; Cols. 13, 14 advertisements. Final page blank.

74a   Our | Anti-Neutral condunct [sic] | reviewed. | [line from] | Franklin; | [two lines from] | Burns [caption title] [New York? 1818?]

[A]⁸=8 leaves, 18.7 cm. (trimmed); (1)2,3(1)5–16 ¶ Pearl 83; A.B. 40498 ¶ DLC

Contents: Introductory Remarks by 'Montgomery' [1]–3; [caption] 'From Cobbett's Political Register, | printed at New York. | [Price 5 dolls per ann, or 12½ cents per no.] | To Major Cartwright. | Letter III. | On the measures of the United States, and on the conduct of the boroughmon- | gers, with regard to Spanish America. | North-Hampstead [sic], Long-Island, December 8, 1817.' [4]–16; subscribed p. 16 William Cobbett. Pp. [4]–16 in small type. Running titles.

Montgomery, 'A Republican Citizen of the United States', recommends to the Congress the views of a 'celebrated foreign reformer now in the United States' (p. [1]). The Act of March 7, 1817 which purports to reinforce United States neutrality is in fact discriminatory against the Spanish colonies in South America, is much too broad and unnecessarily operates to the prejudice of this country in favor of England.

Errors noted: p. 2, l. 4 'enterpizes'; l. 28 'interprize'. Reprinted from Cobbett's Weekly Political Register, Vol. 34, No. 3, New York, December 13, 1817.

74b ———. The title is corrected to 'conduct'. 22 cm. ¶ CtY; MWA

75a The trial | of | Miss Mary Ann Tocker, | for an alleged libel on R. Gurney, jun. vice-warden of the | Stannary Court, in the County of Devon; which trial took | place before Mr. Justice Borrough [sic], one of the judges of the | Court of King's Bench, on Wednesday, the 5th of August, | 1818, at the town of Bodmin, in the County of Cornwall. | to which | is prefixed a letter to Miss Tocker, and to which is added | an address to jury-men on their duties as jurors, and | especially on trials for criminal libel. By William | Cobbett. | [rule] | New-York: | printed, for William Cobbett, by Clayton & Kingsland. | 1818.

[1]–4⁶=24 leaves; 19.5 cm.; (3)iv,v(2)8–23(2)26–48. Third leaves signed 1*–4* ¶ A.B. 43652; Pearl 99 ¶ CtY; MWA

Contents: title; blank; To | Miss Tocker. | North Hempstead, Long-Island, 2d Nov. 1818. | Madam,... [iii]–v, subscribed page v Wm. Cobbett; blank; The Trial [7]–23; blank; To | English Jurymen...North Hempstead, Long Island, 5th Nov. 1818. [25]–48, subscribed page 48 Wm. Cobbett. Running titles.

In the introduction Cobbett writes he is publishing the Trial to make Miss Tocker's virtuous conduct more widely known. The lady had been acquitted by a jury of the charge of libeling a public official by accusations of bribery and corruption in office, on showing the truth of the accusations. Cobbett appended notes on ten pages of the trial. His address commends the jury and asserts the correctness of the verdict. He illustrates by a simulated trial between the King and John Bull.

75b   The triumph of Virtue, | [rule] | The trial | of | Miss Mary Ann Tocker, | who plead her own cause. | for an alledged libel on R. Gurney, Jun. Vice-War- | den of the Stannary Court, in the County of Devon; | which trial took place before Mr. Justice Borrough [sic], | one of the judges of the Court of King's Bench, on | Wednesday, the 5th of August, 1818, at the town | of Bodmin, in the County of Cornwall. | to which | is prefixed a letter to Miss Tocker, and to which is | added an address to jury-men on their duties as | jurors, and especially on trials for criminal libel. | by William Cobbett. | from the third New-York edition. | [rule] | Boston. | printed, for N. Coverly, 16 Milk-street. | 1818.

[1]–4⁶=24 leaves, 19.5 cm; (3)4,5(1)7–25(1)27–48. Third leaves signed 1*–4* (1* is on the verso) ¶ A.B. 43653; Pearl 99 ¶ MH

Contents: title, blank, To | Miss Tocker | North Hempstead, Long-Island, 2d Nov. 1818. [3]–5; the Trial [6]–25; To English Jurymen [26]–48, subscribed p. 48 'Wm. Cobbett'.

Errors noted: p. [3] l. 6 'freee'; p. 5 l. 11 'republicaion'; p. 6 final sentence incomplete; p. 7 l. 27 'judicicial' etc.

Davis notes an issue with page number 20 for 21.

76   List | of | field seeds and garden seeds, | contained in one of the boxes, | sold for five dollars. | also, | hints respecting the sowing of each sort | of seed, and the cultivation | of the plants. | [rule] | By William Cobbett. | [rule] | sold at W. Cobbett's seed and book | store, No. 63 Fulton-Street, | New York; | and by Mr. John Morgan, Philadelphia. | [rule] | printed by Clayton & Kingsland, | No. 15 Cedar-Street. [New York] | [eleven dots] | 1819.

[1],2⁶3⁴=16 leaves, 12 mo; (3)4–30(2). Third leaves signed 1* 2* ¶ A.B. 47651 ¶ MWA

Contents: title; copyright notice by William Cobbett, New York; Lists and Hints [3]–30; blank leaf. Errata slip pasted on page [31].

The errata slip notes omission of No. 72, 'Beet, Red,' and three errata: on page 15 line 2 Fall for Tall, page 20 line 9 Charille for Cherville and page 30 line 20 Top for Tap. Repeated is the advertisement for boxes of seeds imported March 1819 and to be ready for sale April 5, 1819 ('The Third Part of Cobbett's Year's Residence will be published...the same day.') Page 6: The 'Hints' are abridged from a book 'Kitchen Gardening and Cattle-Feeding' not yet ready for the press (such a book is not known). 72 kinds of seeds are described briefly.

77a   A | Year's Residence | in the | United States of America; | treating of the face of the country, the climate, the | soil, the products, the mode of cultivating the land, | the prices of land, of labour, of food, of raiment; of | the expenses of house-keeping and of the usual man- | ner of living; of the manners and customs of the peo- | ple; and, of the institutions of the country, civil, | political and religious. | In three parts. | [rule] | By William Cobbett | [rule] | Part I. | Containing I. A description of the face of the country, | the climate, the seasons and the soil; the facts | being taken from the author's daily notes during a | whole year. II. An account of the author's agricul- | tural experiments in the cultivation of the Ruta | Baga, or Russia, or Swedish, turnip, which afford | proof of what the climate and soil are. | [rule] | New-York: | printed for the author by Clayton and Kingsland | No. 15 Cedar-Street. | [sixteen dots] | 1818.

[1]–11⁶12²=68 leaves, 19 cm; (5)6–9(2)12–45(1)47–69(1)71–134(2). Third leaves signed 2*–11* ¶ Pearl 94, Sabin 14021, A.B. 43654 ¶ ctY; MWA

Contents: title; copyright notice; contents; blank; general preface [5]–9 dated on p. 9, North Hempstead, Long Island, 21 April, 1818; blank; A Year's Residence &c. [11]–134, blank leaf. Paragraphs numbered 1–156, except in the journal, pp. 15–66. Running titles. In a brown wrapper, printed on front recto with the contents of the title page within a border of printer's ornaments.

Errors noted: p. 24, l. 21, 'tramples' for 'trample'; p. 27, next to last, 'head-achs'; p. 57, l. 2, 'Surry' for 'Surrey'; p. 72, l. 11, 'mangle wurtzle' for 'mangle wurzle'. The following errors are pointed out in Part II (at pp. 145,6): p. 27, l. 10 'Peas' for 'Pears'; p. 92, l. 15, 'transplant' for 'translate'.

[Part II.] A | Year's Residence | in the | United States of America; | treating of the face of the country, the climate, the | soil, the products, the mode of cultivating the land, | the prices of land, of labour, of food, of raiment; | of the expenses of housekeeping and of the usual | manner of living; of the manners, customs and cha- | racter of the people; and of the government, laws | and religion. | In three parts. | [rule] | By William Cobbett. | [rule] | Part II. | [rule] | New-York: | Sold at No. 53 Vesey-street, where all orders | will be attended to | Clayton and Kingsland, printers. | [sixteen dots] | 1819.

[13]³14–26⁶27⁴=85 leaves, 19 cm; (3)138(3)142–304. Third leaves signed 14*–26*. Other pages which are not numbered: 147, 165,173,180,191,196,214,224,232,242,255,265,273. ¶ A.B. 47652

Contents: title; copyright notice; dedication dated 15th Nov. 1818 [137] 138; Part II Contents; blank; Preface [141]–146; A Year's Residence, &c. [147]–304. On p. 304: End of Part II. Running titles. Paragraphs numbered 157–453 except in dedication. In plain brown wrappers.

The work contains Chapters III–XIV. As compared to the table of contents, Chapt. VIII adds 'Feeding' and Chapt. XI omits 'state'.

Errors noted: p. [191], l. 7 'Ploudome' for 'Plandome'; [196], next to last line 'li e' for 'live'; p. 281, l. 19 '1815' for '1805'.

P. 142: 'I am now about to send a second edition of the First Part of this work to the press.' P. [191]: 'About the first of June last [1818], I received the First Part of your Year's Residence...' P. 194: Under date of 9th December, 1818 Cobbett writes: 'I shall to-morrow send the second part of my Year's Residence to the Press. I dare say it will be ready in three weeks.'

[Part III] A | Year's Residence | in the | United States of America; | treating of the face of the country, the soil, the cli- | mate, the products, the mode of cultivating the land; | of the prices of land, labour, food, and raiment; | of the expenses of house-keeping and of the usual | manner of living; of the customs, manners, and cha- | racter of the people; and of the institutions of the | country, civil, political, and religious. | In three parts. | [rule] | By William Cobbett. | [rule] | Part III. | [rule] | New-York: | sold at No. 53 Vesey-Street, where all orders | will be attended to. | Clayton and Kingsland, Printers | [sixteen dots] | 1819.

[27]¹[28]–37⁶38⁴=65 leaves, 19 cm; (5)308(1)310(1)312–319(2) 322–365(2)368–395(1)397–426(6). Fourth leaf signed 28*; third leaves signed 29*–37*.

Contents: half-title; copyright notice; title; blank; dedication to Timothy Brown, Esq. dated 10th Dec. 1818 [307], 308; Preface to the Third Part. [309]310; Introduction to the Journal. Philadelphia, 30th Sept. 1818. subscribed Thomas Hulme [311]–319; blank; Journal [321]–365; blank; to Morris Birkbeck, Esq. [367]–419; Fearon's Falsehoods, dated Hyde-Park. Jan. 9th, 1819. 419–426; Index [427]–[432]. At foot of p. 426 note on a mathematical error in paragraph 608. The Index is for all three parts. Beginning in preface, paragraphs numbered 454–663. Running titles. The half-title is between two rules of printer's ornaments. In brown paper wrappers printed on the outer pages within a border of printer's ornaments. Front cover begins: 'A | Year's Residence | in the | United States of America; | [rule] | By William Cobbett. | [rule] | Part III. | [rule] | English seeds, | for the field and for the garden.' It continues that the seeds were imported in March 1819 and 'sold at his seed and book store, No. 63 Fulton-Street, New York' and by John Morgan at Philadelphia. Some of the seeds are described. Boxes will be available of assorted seeds, with a small pamphlet [See No. 76] with hints as to the cultivation of each, [on back cover] to be sold at five dollars. The pamphlet will be sold separately for 25 cents. The boxes will be ready for sale 5th of April. Third Part of Year's Residence will be published the same day. Cobbett's English Grammar [See No. 78] was published in London the 7th of December [1818] in an edition of 5000. A second edition put to press two days afterwards, and a part sold to booksellers in sheets from the Printing-office.

Errors noted: p. 317, l. 33 'there' for 'there–'; p. 337, next to last 'in' for 'in–'; p. 341, note 'vear' for 'year'; p. 389, (an error noted p. 426), par. 608 'three quarters of a cent' for '8 cents'; p. 391, l. 1 'hım' for 'him'; p. 425, l. 9 'whe' for 'whe–'.

The subject matter of the three parts is well indicated in the titles. Pp. 15–66 contain a daily journal from May 5, 1817 through April 24, 1818 (actually Cobbett did not return to England until October 1819); pp. 70–134 is the essay on Ruta Baga. In part III, Mr. Hulme's Journal, from June 3 to August 8, 1818, describes in an interesting and informative manner a trip from Philadelphia to Pittsburgh, down the Ohio to Shippingport, to Evansville, Birkbecks' in Illinois, Harmony and New Albany, Indiana, Frankfort and Lexington, Kentucky, Chillicothe and Zanesville, Ohio, and back to Philadelphia. The Letters to Morris Birkbeck ridicule his claims and discourage English settlers.

'Fearon's Falsehoods' have to do with a visit Fearon made to Cobbett on Long Island. Dated Jan. 9, 1819, this was sent to the New York National Advocate for publication and printed in Cobbett's Weekly Political Register March 6, 1819.

Extracts from the General Preface: 'From my very infancy, from the age of six years, when I climbed up the side of a steep sand rock, and there scooped me out a plot four feet square to make me a garden, and the soil for which I carried up in the bosom of my little blue smock-frock, or hunting-shirt, I have never lost one particle of my passion for these healthy and rational and heart-cheering pursuits, in which every day presents something new, in which the spirits are never suffered to flag, and in which, industry, skill and care are sure to meet with their due reward. I have never, for any eight months together, during my whole life, been without a garden. So sure are we to overcome difficulties where the heart and mind are bent on the thing to be obtained!' [p. 7]. 'As to *farming*, I was bred at the plough-tail, and in the Hop-Gardens of Farnham in Surrey, my native place, and which spot, as it so happened, is the neatest in England, and I believe, in the whole world.' [p. 8]. 'I wish it to be observed, that, in any thing which I may say, during the course of this work, though *truth* will compel me to state facts, which will, doubtless, tend to induce farmers to leave England for America, I *advise* no one so to do...my unchangeable attachment to the people of England, and especially those who have so bravely struggled for our rights: these bind me to England; but I shall leave others to judge and to act for themselves'. [p. 9].

77b ———. Part I. Transcription, l. 7 ends 'raiment'; l. 8 ends 'usual'; l. 9 ends 'of'; l. 10 ends 'country.' The rule is ornamental. The date is 1819. A new issue.

19.2 cm. ¶ NN

On page [3] 'Contents of Part I'. Page 46 is numbered.

The errors noted on pages 27, l. 10; 57; 72 and 92 are corrected. Evidently the sales of Part I published in 1818 induced the printing of larger numbers of Part II and Part III and the reprinting of Part I with a new title page.

77c   A | Year's Residence, | in the | United States of America, | [rule] | treating of the face of the country, the climate, the soil, | the products, the mode of cultivating the land, the prices | of land, of labour, of food, of raiment; of the expenses | of house-keeping, and of the usual manner of living; of | the manners and customs of the people; and of the | institutions of the country, civil, political, and religious. | In three parts | [rule] | By William Cobbett. | [rule] | Part I. | containing—I. a description of the face of the country, | the climate, the seasons, and the soil, the facts being taken | from the author's daily notes during a whole year. II. An | account of the author's agricultural experiments in the | cultivation of the *Ruta Baga*, or Russia, or Swedish turnip, | which afford proof of what the climate and soil are. | [rule] | London: | printed for Sherwood, Neely, and Jones, | Paternoster-row. | [rule] | 1818.

Second title (at p. [187]) A | Year's Residence, [continuing as in Part I] | of housekeeping, and of the usual manner of living; of | the manners, customs, and character of the people; and | of the government, laws, and religion. | In three parts. | [rule] | by William Cobbett. | [rule] | Part II | Containing,–III. Experiments as to cabbages.–IV. Earth- | burning.–V. Transplanting indian corn.–VI. Swedish | Turnips.–VII Potatoes.–VIII. Cows, sheep, hogs, and | poultry.–IX. Prices of land, labour, working cattle, | husbandry implements.–X. Expenses of housekeeping.– |XI. Manners, customs and character of the people.– | XII. Rural sports.–XIII. Paupers and beggars.–XIV. Government, laws, and religion. | [rule] | London: | printed for Sherwood, Neely and Jones, | Paternoster-row | [rule] | 1819.

Third title [at p. [435]] A | Year's Residence, [continuing as in Part II] Part III. | Containing,–Mr. Hulme's Introduction to his Journal– | Mr. Hulme's Journal, made during a tour in the Western | Countries [sic] of America, in which tour he visited Mr. Birk- | beck's settlement–Mr. Cobbett's letters to Mr. Birkbeck, | remonstrating with that gentleman on the numerous delu- | sions, contained in his two publications, entitled "Notes on | a Journey in America" and "Letters from Illinois"–Post- | script, being the detail of an experiment made in the culti- | vation of the Ruta Baga— Second postscript, a refutation | of Fearon's falsehoods | [rule] [concluding as in Part II].

Colophons: p. 186: Printed by J. M'Creery, | Black-Horse-Court, London; p. 434: John M'Creery, Printer, Black Horse Court, London; p. 610: Printed by J. M'Creery, | Black-Horse-Court, Fleet-Street, London.

[A]²B–M⁸N⁴O¹[P]²Q–2G⁸2H²[2I]⁴2K–2T⁸2U⁴=307 leaves, 21 cm; (5)ii–viii(1)10–186;(5)192,3(2)196–201(2)204–434;(4)439–

442(1)444–607(1)609,610. In some copies there is a folded map of
the United States 'Engraved for Cobbett's Years Residence'. In
part I, 'Part I' appears to left of signatures. Second leaves signed beginning B2 except N, [P], 2H, [2I] and 2U ¶ Pearl 94; Sabin 14021
¶ cty; NN

Contents: title; entry notice, J. M'Creery, Printer; Contents of
Part I; blank, general preface [i]–viii dated at end 'North Hempsted' [sic] Long Island, 21st April, 1818.'; A Year's Residence, &c.
[9]–186; second title; entry notice, John M'Creery, Printer; Contents of Part II; blank; dedication dated 'North Hempstead, Long
Island, 15th Nov. 1818' [191]–193; blank; Preface to the second
part [195]–201; blank; A Year's Residence, &c. [203]–434; third
title; entry notice, John M'Creery, Printer; Contents of Part III;
blank; dedication dated 'North Hempstead, Long Island, 10 Dec.
1818', 439–40; Preface to Part III, 441–2; A Year's residence, &c
[443]–607; Index to Part I [608]–610. In Par. 1051 under date of
January 3, 1819 he writes '...the Second Part of my *Year's Residence*, which will be published at New York, in a few days....'

Running titles. The paragraphs are numbered, 1–156 in part I;
157–448 in part 2; and 849–1067 in part 3, except paragraph [11].

Errors: p. 261, l. 28 'burried'; p. 268 'Ploudome' for 'Plandome';
p. 400, par. '116' for '416'; p. 445, l. 17 'thei'; p. 590, last line
'But'.

The text follows the first edition in general. However, the paragraphs do not correspond. Sometimes new paragraphs are created.
Other times two paragraphs are combined. Omitted are pars. 160
(concerning the price); 167 (concerning errors); 251, 3 lines; 269
(English opinion on Ruta Baga); 313 (poultry); 358 last sentence
(his son William); 376, 12 lines (closed season for game); 442 last
paragraph (geography); 551, 6 lines; and 608. Page 332 par. 330
Cheese 'of Cheshire in Massachusetts' changed to 'of the North
River produce.' Page 502 line 6 'Colonel F----r' was 'Colonel
Fletcher'. Paragraphs added are 264 (Long-Island judges); 1004
(manure) and 1049–1055 (Postscript on Ruta Baga). Pars. 287 and
288 'an acre' added to captions; Par. 352, first 2 lines new: page 497
a new note on rate of exchange.

77d   A | Year's Residence | in the | United States of America; |
treating of the face of the country, the climate, the soil, the | prod-
ucts, the mode of cultivating the land, the prices of land, | of labour,

of food, of raiment; of the expenses of house- | keeping and of the usual manner of living; of the manners | and customs of the people; and, of the institutions of the | country, civil, political and religious. | [rule] | By William Cobbett. | [rule] | Belfast: | printed at the Ulster Register Office, | from an American copy. | [rule] | 1818.

[A]–M⁶=72 leaves, 17.2 cm; (5)6–10(1)12–71(1)73–144 ¶ cty; PPL

Contents: title, blank, contents, blank, general preface [5]–10, A year's residence, &c [11]–144. Running titles. Cut of ox-yoke p. 128. Ornament p. 144. Paragraphs numbered 1–156, except in Cobbett's journal. Consists of descriptions of Long Island, the journal and ruta baga culture.

77e   A | Year's Residence, | [continuing as in 77c part I] the expenses | of housekeeping, [continuing as 77c] | By William Cobbett. | [rule] | second edition. | [rule] | Part I. | [continuing as 77c] 1819.

Colophon: John M'Creery, printer, | Black Horse-Court, Fleet-Street.

[A]²B–M⁸N⁴O¹[P]⁴=99 leaves, 22 cm; (5)ii–viii(1)10–186(8). Second leaves signed B2–M2 ¶ MH

Contents: title; entered at Stationers' Hall; Contents of Part I; blank; general preface [i]–viii, dated, North Hempsted [sic], Long Island, 21st April, 1818; A Year's Residence [9]–186; advertisements by Sherwood, Neely & Jones, 8 pages, with a colophon: Coe, printer, Little Carter-lane, St. Paul's; dated March 1, 1818. Running titles. Cut page 165. The text is in 156 numbered paragraphs, not including the journal on pp. 15–93.

77f   A | Year's Residence, | in the | United States of America | [rule] [continuing as in 77c] | [rule] | By William Cobbett | [rule] | Third Edition | [rule] | [continuing as in 77c] London: | Printed for J. M. Cobbett, 183, Fleet Street | [rule] | 1822.

Colophon p. 360: B. Bensley, Bolt Court, Fleet Street. With a folded map of United States 'Engraved for Cobbett's Years Residence.'

[π]¹[A]⁴B–E¹²F¹¹G–Q¹²=184 leaves, 18.5 cm; (5)ii–vi(1)2–100 (3)106–109(2)112–246(2)249–252(1)254–354(1)356–360. Second and fifth leaves signed B–Q except F5 ¶ NN

Running titles. Numbered paragraphs. Catchword 'when' on p. 87.

77g   A | Year's Residence, | in the | United States of America | [continuing as in 77c] | [rule] | By William Cobbett. | [rule] | Third edition. [Continuing as in 77c] | [rule] | Printed by B. Bensley, Andover, | and | Published by the Author, 183, Fleet Street, London. | and sold by all book-sellers. | [rule] | 1828.

Colophon p. 370: B. Bensley, printer, Andover; final p. 12: G. Peirce, printer, 310, Strand.

[A]–P¹²Q⁵[R]⁶=191 leaves, 18.6 cm; (5)vi–x(1)12–110(3)114 (1)116–120(1)122–256(2)259–262(1)264–370;(1)2–12. Second and fifth leaves signed A–Q, except G, 5th leaf is 5G, M 2nd leaf is M3, N 5th leaf not signed and Q 3rd leaf is 3Q, 5th leaf not signed ¶ cty

Contents as in 77c, plus 12 pages of advertisements. A paragraph check indicates the text is the same. Paragraphs numbered. Running titles. The second and third title pages are abbreviated but retain the summary of contents. There are no tables of contents. Indices to all three parts. The advertisements are of books by the Cobbett family published by A[nne] Cobbett, Cobbett's daughter.

Distinguishing errors: Par. 160 for 260; p. 313 for 315; par. 601 not numbered.

77h   ———. In this variant twelve pages advertising Cobbett's works, 'The Cobbett-Library', are bound in first, with the colophon page 12: Mills, Jowett, and Mills, Bolt-Court, Fleet-street ¶ MWA

78a   A | Grammar | of the | English language, | in a series of letters. | Intended for the use of schools and of young persons in gene- | ral; but, more especially for the use of soldiers, sailors, | apprentices, and plough-boys. | [rule] | By William Cobbett. | [rule] | New York: | printed for the author by Clayton and Kingsland, | No. 15 Cedar-Street | [18 dots] | 1818.

[1]–15⁶16²=92 leaves, 17.3 cm; (3)iv(1)6–11(2)14–42(1)44–70 (1)72–171(1)173–184. Third leaves signed 2*–15* ¶ Pearl 96; A. B. 43651 ¶ cty; MWA

Contents: title; copyright notice; dedication to Mr. Benbow [iii], iv, dated on page iv. 'Hyde Park, North Hempstead, Long Island, May 2, 1818'; To Mr. James Paul Cobbett, Letter I. [5]–11; blank; Letter II [–Letter XXIII] [13]–184. On p. 184 'END.' Row of type ornaments beginning each letter. Running titles. First letter dated Dec. 6, 1817. Beginning with Letter II the paragraphs are numbered 1–285 through Letter XX. The Letters are of very unequal length. Letter XXI, beginning on p. 151, is entitled 'Specimens of false grammar, taken from the | writings of Doctor Johnson and from those | of Doctor Watts.'

Pearl notes this is the first edition. It was reprinted London December 7, 1818 in 5000 copies (See No. 77a, Part III). There were many later printings including: London, 1819(2), 1820, 1823, 1824, 1826, 1831, 1833, 1835; Andover (England) 1829; Berlin, 1824; Jena, 1825. Cobbett stated that more than 100,000 copies had been sold by 1834 (See Pearl). Cobbett's son James Paul was born in 1803.

78b   A | Grammar | of the | English language, | in a series of letters. | intended for the use of schools and of young persons | in general; but more especially for the use of | soldiers, sailors, apprentices, and plough-boys. | [rule] | By William Cobbett. | [rule] | to which are added, | six lessons, intended to prevent statesmen from using | false grammar, and from writing in an | awkward manner. | [rule] | New-York: | published by John Doyle, 12 Liberty-Street; | and Thomas Doyle, Market-street, Providence, R.I. | Stereotyped by James Conner, New-York. | [rule] | 1832.

[1]–18⁶=108 leaves, 15 cm; (3)4(1)6(1)8–213,(1)2,3. Third leaves signed 2*–18* ¶ PPL

Contents: title, blank, table of contents [3]4, dedication [5]6, to Mr. James Paul Cobbett [7]–213, works [1]–3. On page 213 'The end.' Running titles. Paragraphs numbered 1–285 in letters II through XX.

78c   ———. Transcription same as preceding entry through 'John Doyle', continuing: 12, Liberty-Street. | stereotyped by Conner & Cooke, New York | [rule] | 1833.

[1]–17⁶18⁵[19]²=109 leaves, 15.5 cm; (3)4(1)6(1)8–213(1)(4). Third leaves signed 1*–18* ¶ PPL

Contents: title, blank, table of contents [3]4, dedication [5]6, to Mr. James Paul Cobbett [7]–213, blank, Books recently published by J. Doyle (4). Last four pages inserted. Running titles, with XIX for XXI on page 153. Paragraphs numbered 1–285 in letters II through XX.

79   Long Island Prophecies. | [rule] | Cobbett's | too long petition, Nov. 1817.–Letter to Tierney, July 1818. | Letter to the Regent on

that wild and visionary project, | Peel's Bill, Sept. 1819. | [rule] | [two lines quoted from] Reg. Sept. 5, 1819 | [rule] | To the Honourable the Commons | ..[London 1819] [caption title].

Colophon: Printed by and for J. M. Cobbett, No. 183, Fleet-street.

[A]¹B⁸C⁵=14 leaves, 22 cm., second leaf of B signed B2. Pages not numbered. 2 columns to a page numbered beginning on page [2]:3–54 ¶ Pearl 93 ¶ MH

Contents: To the Honourable the Commons...The petition of William Cobbett...now residing at North Hempstead, in the State of New York, this 20th day of November 1817...Cols. [1]–17; Letter | to the right Hon. George Tierney, | on his opposition to the Bank Protecting | Act. | North Hampstead [sic], Long Island, | 1st July, 1818. Cols. 18–37; To | the Prince Regent. | on the wild and visionary schemes | of the Borough-Mongers. | New York, Sept. 5, 1819...Cols. 37–54; final page blank, except for colophon. Running titles.

The material in this pamphlet was first published in Cobbett's Weekly Political Register Vols. XXXIII–V.

79A   An | Answer | to the | speech of the Attorney-General, | upon the trial | of | her majesty, | the Queen of England. | [rule] | By William Cobbett. | [rule] | New-York: | published by James P. Cobbett. | Clayton & Kingsland, printers. | [14 dots] | 1820.

[A]⁸=eight leaves, 21.2 cm (trimmed); (3)4–16 ¶ PPL

Contents: title, blank, an answer [3]–16, dated page [3] London, 23d August, 1820; Signed page 16 'Wm Cobbett'. Running titles. The text concerns imputations against the Queen in regard to Baron Bergami.

80a   The | American Gardener; | or, | a treatise | on the situation, soil, fencing and laying-out of | gardens; on the making and managing of hot- | beds and green-houses; and on the propagation | and cultivation of the several sorts of vegetables, | herbs, fruits and flowers. | [rule] | By William Cobbett. | [rule] | [five lines from] | Proverbs: Chap. XXIV. Ver. 30. | [rule] | London: | published by C. Clement, 1, Clement's Inn | [rule] | 1821.

[A]–Y⁶=132 leaves, 18.7 cm. Not paged. Gatherings through F, third leaf signed A2 etc.; gatherings G through Y second and third leaves signed, G2 G3, etc., except O3 ¶ Pearl 114 ¶ CtY

Contents: title, blank, dedication (2) dated 'London, 20th June 1821'; Preface (8), par. 1–11, dated at the end 'North Hampstead [sic] Long Island, 1819'; text (246), par. 12–391; Index (6). Paragraphs numbered except in Dedication, and except one after paragraph 125. Four plates included in gatherings, being on one side of leaves D2, I6, S4 and T4, the other side blank. Running titles.

Cover, paper over boards, paper label on spine.

Cole, *Life*, p. 272 says: 'largely written in the United States.' Pearl notes six editions published in the United States, 1841–1856.

Kress Library of Business and Economics, Harvard, C1632, is Italian translation, Corfu 1826.

80b ———. Same description, except the title page after the quotation from Proverbs: Stereotype edition. | London: | Published by C. Clement, 1, Clement's Inn. | [broken rule] | 1821. 19.2 cm ¶ cty; MWA

The stereotype appears to have been taken from the first edition. While this method gave freedom in meeting demand, it led to indistinct type. Par. 196 begins 'EAN' for 'BEAN'. Leaf G2 not signed.

80c The | American Gardener; | or, | A treatise | on the situation, soil, fencing and laying-out of | gardens; on the making and managing of hot- | beds and green-houses; and on the propa- | gation and cultivation of the several | sorts of vegetables, herbs, fruits | and flowers. | [rule] | By William Cobbett. | [rule] | [six lines from] Proverbs, Chap. xxiv. ver. 30. | [rule] | Baltimore: | Printed and published by | J. Robinson, circulating library, and | J. Robinson & Co., Frederick, Md. | 1823.

[1]–3⁶,[4]–21⁶=126 leaves, 13.8 cm; (3)iv–ix(1)11–40(1)42–247(1)249–252. Third leaves signed 1*–21* ¶ Pearl 114 ¶ MBAT

Contents: title, blank, Preface [iii]–ix; Chapter I[10]–40; Chapter II etc. [41]–247; Index [248]–252.

Running titles. P. 76 has 'American Gardener'. Plates paginated pp. 37, 103, 207, 215.

80d The | American Gardener; | or, | A treatise | on the situation, soil, fencing and laying-out of gardens; | on the making and managing of hot-beds and green- |houses; and on the propagation and culti- vation of the | several sorts of vegetables, herbs, fruits and flowers. |

[rule] | By William Cobbett, Esq. M.P. | for Oldham | [rule] | [five lines from] Proverbs: Chap. XXIV. Ver. 30. | [rule] | New York: | published by John Doyle, No. 12, Liberty Street | [rule] | 1835.

[π]¹[1]–19⁶20¹=116 leaves, 15.3 cm; (5)4–8(1)10–230. Third leaves signed 1*–19* ¶ Pearl 114 ¶ NjR

Contents: title; Scatcherd and Adams, | printers, | 38 Gold Street; dedication, dated London, 20th June 1821; blank; preface [3]–8; text [9]–226; Index 227–230; books published (4). Running titles. Paragraphs numbered 1–391, except the paragraph after 125. Plates pp. 33, 93, 190, 197. Preface dated 1819. The text follows the London edition of 1821. The list of books is an insert.

80e ———. Transcription same through the quotation and continues: [rule] | Claremont, N.H. | Manufacturing Company. | Simeon Ide, Ag't. [1835?].

[1]–19⁶[20]¹=115 leaves, 15.3 cm; (3)4–8(1)10–230 ¶ Pearl 114 ¶ CtY; NN

The contents do not include the dedication or the advertisements. Otherwise it appears to be a stereotype version of the preceding entry with a new title page. Cover in embossed cloth, spine gilt.

Cobbett was elected to Parliament in the Fall of 1832 and continued to his death in 1835. Pearl suggests a publication in 1832, but 1835 or later seems more likely.

81   A Letter | from | the King | to his people. | [rule] | from the twelfth London edition. | [rule] | London: | published by William Sams, bookseller to his royal high- | ness the Duke of York | Philadelphia,-republished by John Conrad, No. 121, | Chesnut Street. | [seventeen dots] | 1821. | [Second Title]: The Queen's answer | to the | letter from the King | to | his people. | [rule] | from Cobbett's Register. | [rule] | Philadelphia | [rule] | 1821. [John Conrad.]

[A]–F⁴;[A]–C⁴[D]²=38 leaves, 23.2 cm; (3)4–47(1);(3)4–27(1). ¶ Pearl 111 ¶ DLC ('Queen's Answer'); MWA

Contents: title; blank; Carlton Palace, Dec. 1, 1820 [3]–45; Apology etc. 46, 47; blank; second title, blank; The Queen's answer, &c. [3]–27; Subscribed page 27 Wm. Cobbett; blank.

The DLC copy of the Queen's Answer is in grey wrappers printed on front recto 'Answer | to the | King's letter' and on the rear verso advertisements beginning: 'published by John Conrad, No. 121

Chesnut Street | A letter | from | the King of Great Britain, to his people.'

On pages 46 and 47 of the letter it is acknowledged that the letter was not in fact written by the King. Cobbett addresses his answer to 'Mr. Parasite' and makes a strong defense of the Queen by attacking the author's credibility and good faith. Cobbett demands justice for the Queen in her marital dispute with the King.

82   Torrey, Jesse, Jun.

American | Slave Trade; | or, | an account of the manner in which the slave dealers | take free people from some of the United States of | America, and carry them away, and sell them as slaves | in other of the States; and of the horrible cruelties | practised in the carrying on of this most infamous | traffic: | with | reflections on the project for forming a colony of | American blacks in Africa, and certain documents | respecting that project. | By Jesse Torrey, Jun. physician | with five plates. | [rule] | London: | reprinted by C. Clement, and published by | J. M. Cobbett, 1., Clement's Inn. | [rule] | 1822.

Colophon p. 119: 'Printed by C. Clement'.

[B]–F^{12}=60 leaves, 18.4 cm; (3)iv–xvi(1)18–119(1). Second and fifth leaves signed ¶ Pearl 118; Sabin 96283 ¶ cty; NN

Contents: title, blank, preface [iii]–xvi; American slave-trade [17]–98; Reflections on the black colony project 99–119, blank. Running titles. Plates: frontispiece and facing pp. 59, 67, 73 and 77.

The preface, subscribed Wm. Cobbett, is dated 'Kensington 18 Sept. 1821.' He notes that the original was published in Philadelphia in 1817. For the English reader, he describes the geography of the United States, its government and the extent of slavery, with comment on the cruelties committed there. The notes are believed also to be by Cobbett.

83a   Cottage economy: | containing | information relative to the brewing of beer, making of bread, | keeping of cows, pigs, bees, ewes, goats, poultry, and | rabbits, and relative to other matters deemed useful in | the conducting of the affairs of a labourer's family; to | which are added, instructions relative to the selecting, | the cutting, and the bleaching of the plants of English | grass and grain, for the purpose of making hats and | bonnets. | [rule] | By William Cobbett. | [rule] | First American from the first London edition. | [rule] | New-York: | published by Stephen Gould and son, | law booksellers, at the old stand, sign of Lord Coke, corner | of Wall and Broad streets, opposite the custom-house, | and Joseph P. Gould, Genesee-street, Utica. | 1824. | [eleven dots] | Printed at the Coke Law Press, Caldwell, N.J.

[1]–11⁶=66 leaves, 21.5 cm; (7)8–125(2)2–4(2). Third leaves signed 1*–10*. Plate of grasses, 15.3 cm., tipped in following title ¶ Pearl 115 ¶ MWA; NN

Contents: title, blank, advertisement, blank, contents, blank, cottage economy [7]–125, blank; advertisement [1]–4; blank leaf. Introduction dated p. 13 Kensington, July 19, 1821. Note added on page 50 referring to 'Now (1823)', making an unnumbered paragraph. Except as noted, paragraphs numbered 1–236. Par. 126 for 129. Par. 220, 222 contain letters, not numbered. Running titles. Page 11 for 111. Table of contents not paged: No. 5 omits pigs and No. 7 omits turnips. Par. 1. refers to an index, not present.

The work was first published in seven parts London 1821, and there were many later editions. An eighth part was added May 31, 1823 and ice-houses added in 1828. There was a seventeenth edition in 1850. (See Muirhead p. 27.)

83b ———. A variant in that page number 111 has been corrected ¶ MWA

83c Cottage economy; | containing | information relative to the brewing of beer, making of bread, | keeping of cows, pigs, bees, ewes, goats, poultry, and rabbits, | and relative to other matters deemed useful in the conduct- | ing of the affairs of a labourer's family; to which are added, | instructions relative to the selecting, the cutting and the | bleaching of the plants of English grass and grain, for the | purpose of making hats and bonnets; and also instructions | for erecting and using ice-houses, after the Virginian manner. | To which is added | the poor man's friend; | a defence of the rights of those who do the work, | and fight the battles. | [rule] | By William Cobbett. | [broken rule] | New York: | published by John Doyle, 12, Liberty-St. | stereotyped by Conner & Cooke. | [rule] | 1833.

[1]–19⁶=114 leaves, 14.8 cm; (5)6–146(1)148–158; (3)4–68(2). 3rd leaves signed 1*–19* ¶ Pearl 115 ¶ MWA

Contents: title, copyright (paste on), contents, blank, Cottage Economy [5]–146(1)148–158; subtitle, blank, Cobbett's Poor Man's

Friend [3]–68, blank leaf. Plate p. [147]. Running titles. Paragraphs numbered 1–265, except on p. 58, and 1–73. Introduction dated Kensington, 19th July 1821; p. 58 an addendum 1823; par. 208 dated May 30, 1823; p. 151 'addition' dated Nov. 14th, 1831; p. 158 the Index. The text follows the London edition of 1831. Cloth binding with red paper label on spine.

Poor Man's Friend is in three numbers, the first dated 22nd August 1826 and the third 13th October, 1826, dealing with the laws applicable to the poor, their food, titheing and care of the aged. Poor Man's Friend was first published at London in 1826 in five parts (Muirhead p. 29).

83d ———. A variant in that the word 'or' is added to the title page centered between 'poor man's friend' and 'a defence'. ¶ cty; nn

Copies 15.5 cm. blue cloth, red label; 14.8 cm. brown cloth, red label.

84a A history | of the | Protestant "Reformation", | in | England and Ireland; | showing how that event has impoverished and de-graded the | main body of the people in those countries. | In a series of letters, | addressed to all sensible and just Englishmen. | [rule] | By William Cobbett | [rule] | Third edition. | Philadelphia: | printed for Bernard Dornin, | No. 189, Lombard Street. | [rule] | 1825.

[1]–28⁶=168 leaves; (3)4–118(2)119–333(1) (not all paged) ¶ Pearl 132 ¶ dcu (Davis)

Blank leaf between pages 118 and 119. Contains the first four-teen letters.

84b Historia | del | Protestantismo | ó | pretendida reforma reli-gioso...Neuva-York: | publicada por James Cunningham. | 1825.

[1],2⁶=12 leaves, 12 mo.; (5)6–23(1) ¶ mb (Davis)

84c A | History | of the | Protestant "Reformation," | in | England and Ireland; | showing how that event has impoverished and de-graded the | main body of the people in those countries. | in a series of letters, | addressed to all sensible and just Englishmen. | [rule] | By William Cobbett. | [rule] | Third American edition. | [rule] | Pittsburgh: | printed and sold by Eichbaum and Johnston. | [dia-mond] | 1825.

[1]–8⁴=32 leaves, 21.3 cm; (3)4–64 ¶ njr

Contents: title, blank, A History [3]–64. FINIS in ornamental scroll page 64. Paragraphs numbered 1–135. Contains only four letters, the last dated 28th February 1825.

84d   A History | of the | Protestant "Reformation," | in |England and Ireland; | showing how that event has impoverished and degraded the | main body of the people in those countries. | in a series of letters, | addressed to all sensible and just Englishmen. | [rule] | By William Cobbett. | [rule] | Philadelphia: | printed by Joseph R. A. Skerrett. | [eleven dots] | 1825. [i.e. 1826?]

Colophon page 382: Skerrett-Ninth street, | Philadelphia.

[1]–9⁶10⁵11–32⁶=191 leaves, 18 cm.; (3)4–285(2)288–333(2) 336–382, except that the page beginning each letter is not numbered. Third leaves signed 1*–32* ¶ PPL

Contents: title, blank, history [3]–285, blank, history [287]–333, blank, history [335]–382. In sixteen letters, the last dated 31st March 1826. Running titles. Paragraphs numbered 1 to 478, except 319 for 219, and except subparagraphs in 379 and 425 not numbered.

84e   ———. After 'Cobbett' continues | [rule] | Second American edition | [rule], | printed for J. Mortimer, | No. 74, South Second Street, Philadelphia, | and sold by T. W. Clarke, | No. 5, Chatham row, N. York. | [rule] | 1825 [i.e. 1826?]

Colophon: Skerrett--Ninth Street, | Philadelphia.

[1]–9⁶10⁵11–32⁶=191 leaves; (3)4–382 [not all paged] ¶ PU (Davis)

Has sixteen letters, the last two dated 1826.

84f   ———. [rule] | by William Cobbett | [rule] | to which is added, his letter to the Earl of RODAN [sic], | on the subject of religion. | [rule] | Fourth edition | rule | Baltimore: | published by James Myres, | at the cathedral | 1826. | [rule] | Matchett, printer.

[π]²1–32⁶=194 leaves; (3)ii(3)4–364(1)366–383(1) ¶ ICU (Davis)

Contains letter XVII pp. 342–64 and Letter | to the | Earl of Roden...pp. [365]–383. Page 17 for 177.

84g   A history | of | the Reformation | in | England and Ireland; | in a series of letters. | [rule] | By William Cobbett. | [rule] | Philadelphia: | published by P. O. Connolly. | [rule] | 1826. Collates etc. with 84f ¶ M (Davis)

84h ———. Philadelphia: | published by M. Fithian. | 61 North Second Street. [n.d.] ¶ MOSW (Davis)
   Page 17 for 177, 1 for 193, 399 for 339.

84i   History | of the | Protestant "Reformation", | in | England and Ireland. | containing a refutation of Hume and Smollett's histories of the | reformation, and showing how that event has impoverished and | degraded the main body of the people of those countries. | in a series of letters; | [rule] | By William Cobbett. | [rule] | New-York: | re-printed from the London edition, and published at | G. Pardow and W. Denman, at the office of the | truth-teller, No. 95 Maiden-lane. | [rule] | stereotyped by T. Seward, 10 Fifth-street | [rule] | 1826. Collates as 84k ¶ MMET (Davis)

84j   A History | of | the Reformation, | in | England and Ireland; | in a series of letters. | [rule] | By William Cobbett. | [rule] | Balti-more: | published by Fielding Lucas, jun'r. | No. 138 Market Street. [n.d.]
   [A]–Ee⁶Ff²=170 leaves, 17.2 cm.; (3)iv–xxiii(2)26–41(1)43–174 (1)176–231(1)233–266(1)268–322(1)324–339(1). Third leaves signed A2–Ee2 ¶ MH
   Contents: title; blank; An Introduction [iii]–xxiii, dated Kensing-ton, 15th April 1824; A History [25]–322, in sixteen letters dated Kensington 29th November 1824 through 31st March, 1826; To the Earl of Roden [323]–339 dated Bagshot, June 10, 1824; blank. Running titles, with p. 197 ix for x and the bracket not closed, and p. 227 x for xi. The letters are in paragraphs numbered 1–284, 284–369, 282, 370–478, except in 379, subparagraphs not num-bered. Page 17 for 177.

84k   A | History | of the | Protestant Reformation, | in | England and Ireland; | showing how that event has impoverished and de-graded | the main body of the people in those countries. | In a series of letters, | addressed to all sensible and just Englishmen. | [rule] | by William Cobbett. | [rule] | New = York. | published by John Doyle, 12 Liberty-Street; | and Thomas Doyle, Market-Street, Providence, R.I. | [rule] | 1832.

[1],2^6[3]^6[4]^6[π]^{6}5–7^6[8]–1$2^6$1$2^6$14–1$9^6$[π]^{1}20,2$1^6$[22]^2=135 leaves, 15.3 cm; (3)4–17(1)19–265(1)267–270. Third leaves signed 1*2*4*6*9*–12*15*–21* ¶ MWA; PU

Contents: title, blank, A history [3]–265, Works of William Cobbett, Esq. [266]–270.

Page numbers 9 and 162 partly obliterated. Out of place signature numbers 8* (p. 102), 16* (p. 211), 19 (p. 231), 19* (p. 235), 20 (p. 243). Running titles: page 69 the T is broken; page 141 five letters broken in 'Reformation'. In sixteen letters 29th Nov. 1824 to 31st March 1826.

84l　A History | of the | Protestant Reformation | in | England and Ireland; | showing how that event has impoverished the main | body of the people in those countries; and con- | taining a list of the abbeys, priories, nunneries, | hospitals, and other religious foundations in Eng- | land, and Wales, and Ireland, confiscated, seized | on, or alienated, by the Protestant "Reformation" | sovereigns and parliaments. | [rule] | By William Cobbett, M.P. | [rule] | in a series of letters, | addressed to all sensible and just Englishmen. | [rule] | Vol. II | [rule] | To which is now added, three letters, by the | same author, never before published | in the United States. | [rule] | New York: | published by John Doyle, No. 12 Liberty-St., 1834. | Stereotyped by Conner & Cooke.

[1]–$30^6$$1^6$=186 leaves, 15.4 cm.; (3)4–40(1)42–185(1)187–276 (1)278–320(1)322–360;(1)2–12. Third leaves signed 1*–27* ¶ Muirhead p. 27 ¶ NN; PU

Contents: title; copyright; Introduction [3]–40; List of abbeys, priories &c [41]–276; To the clergy of the Church of England, Kensington, 15th April, 1824 [277]–301; To the Earl of Roden... June 10, 1824, 301–320; A Letter to his holiness, Pope Pius VIII... 10th Nov. 1828, [321]–348; Extracts from Rural Rides, 348–360; Advertisements [1]–12. Running titles.

84m　A History | of the | Protestant Reformation | in | England and Ireland; | showing how that event has impoverished the main | body of the people in those countries; and con- | taining a list of the abbeys, priories, nunneries, | hospitals, and other religious foundations in Eng- | land, and Wales, and Ireland, confiscated, seized | on, or alienated, by the Protestant "reformation" | sovereigns and parliaments. | [rule] By William Cobbett, M.P. | [rule] | in a series of letters, | addressed to all sensible and just Englishmen. | [rule] | Vol. I [Vol. II] | [rule] | To which is now added, three letters, by the | same author, never before published | in the United States. | New-York: | published by D. & J. Sadlier & Co., | 164 William Street, | Boston:–128 Federal Street. | Montreal:–179 Notre-Dame Street [1834].

Vol. I [1]–22⁶[23]¹=133 leaves, 14.7 cm; (3)4–17(1)19–265(1). Third leaves signed 1*–22*. Page 56 for 66 ¶ MH

Contents: title, copyright notice [1834]; A History [3]–265, blank. In sixteen letters dated Kensington 29th Nov., 1824 through 31st March, 1826. Running titles, with 'Reformation' pied on p. 141. In paragraphs, numbered 1–52,(1),54–93, Section 94, 95–288, 288–479, except subparagraphs in 379 not numbered.

Vol. II [1]–30⁶=180 leaves, 14.7 cm.; (3)4–40(1)42–276(1)278–320(1)322–360. Third leaves signed 1*–30* ¶ Muirhead p. 27 ¶ MH

Contents: title, blank, Introduction [3]–40, dated at foot Kensington 9th July, 1827, in 52 numbered paragraphs; List of Abbeys, Priories, &c [41]–276; To the Clergy..15th April 1824 [277]–301; To the Earl of Roden..June 10, 1824, 301–320; A letter to his holiness, Pope Pius VIII..10th Nov. 1828, in 32 numbered paragraphs [321]–348; Rural Rides 348–360. Running titles, with p. 325 'L' almost gone.

85   American trees and shrubs: | and also, | apple trees, and strawberry, and asparagus, plants. [1827?] [Caption title].

Colophon: Printed and published by William Cobbett, No. 183, Fleet-street.

A⁸=8 leaves, 21.3 cm.; second leaf A2. Not paged ¶ CtY

Text in two columns, each column numbered, beginning with 3 through 32.

Reprinted from Cobbett's Weekly Register of November 25, 1826.

86a   A Treatise | on | Cobbett's Corn, | containing instructions for propagating and cultivating the | plant, and for harvesting and preserving the crop; | and also | an account of the several uses to which the produce is | applied, with minute directions relative to each mode of | application. | [rule] | By William Cobbett. | [rule] | [eleven lines quoted from] Tull's Husbandry | [rule] | London: | Published by William Cobbett, 183, Fleet-Street. | [rule] | 1828.

Colophon: Printed by Mills, Jowett, and Mills, Bolt Court, Fleet Street.

[A]²B–N¹²O²=148 leaves, 18.6 cm. Page number only on iv. Second and fifth leaves signed, B–N. ¶ Sabin 14019, Pearl 154 ¶ cty

Contents: title, printer, table of contents [iii], iv, text.

Paragraphs numbered 1–203. Leaves include three with plates on one side (facing Pars. 11, 117 and 132) and the other side blank. Running titles. As appears from Par. 202, the title page is printed on corn paper and the second leaf is the same. Par. 187, 3rd line 'Politcal'. The heading of Chapter X differs from the table of contents. The cover is paper over boards, with a paper label on the spine.

Much of the text has to do with American agriculture and customs. Par. 137 describes shelling corn with the use of a bayonet, which Cobbett says the Yankees call '*Uncle* George's *toasting-fork.*' In par. 156 he describes Mush—'This is not a word to squall out over a piano-forte; but, it is a very good word, and a real *English* word, though Johnson has left it, as he has many other good words, out of his Dictionary.' In par. 158 Cobbett describes a sea voyage he and his bride of six months took from Havre de Grace (France) to New York in 45 or 6 days September to November 1792. (Note: it probably ended in October. Cobbett wrote to Thomas Jefferson for a position November 2, 1792.)

86b ———. To the transcription is added after 'application': | with | an addition, containing a statement of the result of | experience up to the harvest of 1831. | It concludes: published by William Cobbett, 11, Bolt-Court. | [rule] | 1831. There are three preliminary leaves, the third signed A3, an 'addition' of 25 leaves and 6 leaves of books for sale. ¶ Pearl 154 ¶ njr

The new third leaf contains 'Advertisement to the second edition [v]vi dated at the end 'Kensington, 25th November, 1831.' The addition has paragraphs numbered 204–242.

87   A Letter from | Mr. William Cobbett | to | Mr. Huskisson, | on the subject of the American tariff; | intended as a reply to a speech of the latter, in the British House of Commons. | [rule] | United States and Great Britain. | [from Cobbett's Weekly Political Register, printed at London, | August 2, 1828. | To the readers of the Register. | On Huskisson's schemes, and, particularly, on his recent speech relative | to the American tariff. [1828] [caption title].

Colophon page 16: John Binns, printer [Phila.]

[1],2⁴=8 leaves, 21 cm.; (1)2–16 ¶ Pearl 155, Sabin 13887 ¶ PPL

Contents: text [1]–15; on page 15, 3 lines from foot: I reman. [sic], &c. Wm. Cobbett, followed by a P.\$[sic] carrying over onto page 16.

88a The | Emigrant's Guide; | in | ten letters, | addressed to | the tax-payers of England; | containing | information of every kind, necessary to persons who | are about to emigrate; | including | several authentic and most interesting letters from English emi- | grants, now in America, to their relations in England. | [rule] | By William Cobbett. | [rule] | London: | Printed by Mills, Jowett, and Mills. | Published by the author, at 183, Fleet-Street. | [rule] | DMCCCXXIX.

Colophon p. 153: Mills, Jowett, and Mills, Bolt Court, Fleet Street.

[B]–G¹²H⁵=77 leaves, 17.7 cm.; (5)6–153(1). Second and fifth leaves signed B–G; also H2,H3. ¶ Pearl 158; Sabin 13882 ¶ CtY

Contents: title, blank, Contents, blank, Guide [5]–153, blank. Paragraphs numbered 1–119 (disregarding subparagraphs). Table p. 21. Running titles. Contains 27 letters (pp. 45–84; 90–94) addressed from emigrants in America to England, which arouse the suspicion Cobbett wrote them. The 'Contents' lists ten chapter headings, called 'Letters', without page references and differing from the text captions in all Letters except III and IV, mainly in beginning with 'Of' instead of 'On'. However V omits reference to carrying money, contained in the text caption, which is curious since the information is actually in X. The 'Guide' relates only to emigration to the United States. Muirhead (p. 33) states it is taken from Cobbett's 'Register'.

Some errors noted: p. 11, l. 2 'thehigh', p. 109 running title, 'iv' for 'vi'; p. 113 last line: 'uPon'; p. 118, l. 3 'part' for 'port'.

Extract (p. 139): 'Even at a boarding house at New York, unless of the very lowest description,...not only can no mistress pass for a wife; but no woman will find admission to these houses, if she have had the misfortune to have been connected by *anticipation* with her husband, which I used to think was being starched rather overmuch.'

88b ———. A variant in that p. 113 last line is corrected to 'upon.' Title page measures 18.8 cm. ¶ CtY; NN

88c ———. The transcription begins as in 88a and continues: re-lations in England; and an | account of the prices of house and land, recently obtained from | America by Mr. Cobbett. | A new edition | [rule] | By William Cobbett. | [rule] | London: | printed by Mills, Jowett and Mills. | Published by the author, at 183, Fleet-Street. | [rule] | DMCCCXXX.

Colophon: Mills, Jowett and Mills, Bolt Court, Fleet Street.

[A]⁶[B]–G¹²H⁴I⁴K¹=87 leaves, 18.5 cm.; (1)2–12;(5)6–162. Third leaf signed A2, B fifth leaf B5, second and fifth leaves C–G, H2 H3 and I2 ¶ PHi (PPL)

Contents: List of Mr. Cobbett's Books [1]–12; title, blank, con-tents, blank, Guide [5]–153, Postscript 154–162. The postscript is dated 5th May 1830 and deals with prices and rent of houses. The text follows the first edition. Running titles. Numbered paragraphs. Error noted on page 113 corrected.

88d ———. Same transcription.

[A]–G¹²=84 leaves, 18.5 cm.; (5)6–168. Second and fifth leaves signed ¶ NN; MH (Kress)

Contents: title, blank, contents, blank, guide [5]–153. Postscript 154–162; second postscript 163–168. The second postscript is new, dated 27th June, 1830 and includes a list of sea stores and some advice to farmers.

The text follows the first edition, with the new matter added. Running titles. Numbered paragraphs. The errors noted have been corrected.

89a Advice to young men, | and (incidentally) to | young women. | in the | middle and higher ranks of life. | In a series of letters, ad-dressed to | a youth, a bachelor, a lover, a husband, | a citizen or a subject. | [rule] | By William Cobbett. | [rule] | New = York: | pub-lished by John Doyle, 12 Liberty Street, | and Thomas Doyle, Market Street, Providence, R.I. | Stereotyped by James Conner. | [rule] | 1831.

134 leaves, 15.3 cm. Unpaged. Signatures 3, 4, 11, 15, 16, 19–22 only. Third leaves signed 2* 4* 13* 15* 20* 21* only ¶ Pearl 171 ¶ CtY

Contents: title, blank, Introduction (8), Letter I[–VI] (258). Paragraphs numbered 1–355. Dated at the end: 'Kensington, 25th Aug. 1830.'

The title omits 'a father', contained in original title, but the letter 'To a father' is included. Running titles. Cloth, with green paper label on spine. Original publication in fourteen parts in 1829 (Muirhead p. 29). There are two issues of the London 1829 [1830?] edition which differ, among other things, in that in the latter par. No. 163 and one line are missing.

Particular paragraphs: the introduction gives a resume of Cobbett's life, par. 1–11; New Brunswick and the other girl, par. 142–151; his married life, par. 94, 161, 166–9, 192; rural beauty, par. 288; his children's education, par. 290–3, 98, 99; his term in Newgate prison, par. 301–5.:

Extract: 'When I was a very little boy, I was, in the barley-sowing season, going along by the side of a field, near Waverly Abbey; the primroses and blue-bells bespangling the banks on both sides of me; a thousand linnets singing in a spreading oak over my head; while the jingle of the traces and the whistling of the ploughboys saluted my ear from over the hedge; and, as it were to snatch me from the enchantment, the hounds, at that instant, having started a hare in the hanger on the other side of the field, came up scampering over it in full cry, taking me after them many a mile. I was not more than eight years old; but this particular scene has presented itself to my mind many times every year from that day to this. I always enjoy it over again; and I was resolved to give, if possible, the same enjoyments to my children.' (par. 288).

89b ———. same transcription.

[1]–22⁶23²=134 leaves, 15.7 cm.; (3)4–10(1)12–268. Third leaves signed 1*–22* ¶ MWA

Contents: title; 'Van Norden & Mason, print'; introduction [3]–10; Letter [11]–268, in six letters.

Paragraphs numbered 1–355, except on page 91. Running titles. In cloth with brown paper label.

89c Advice to young men, | and (incidentally) to | young women, | in the | middle and higher ranks of life. | in a series of letters, addressed to | a youth, a bachelor, a lover, a husband, | a citizen or a subject. | [rule] | By William Cobbett. | [rule] | New-York: | Published by John Doyle, 12 Liberty Street, | [rule] | Stereotyped by James Conner. | [rule] | 1833.

[1]–22⁶,23²=134 leaves, 15.4 cm.; (3)4–10(1)12–268. Third leaves signed 1*–22*, except 9* is used for 19*. Page 220 for 229 ¶ Pearl 171 ¶ cty

Contents: title, blank, Introduction [3]–10; Cobbett's advice, in six letters. [11]–268. Dated p. 268, 'Kensington, 25th Aug. 1830'. Paragraphs numbered 1–355. Running titles. Contents same as 89a but a new setting of type. Letter V is 'To a Father', not mentioned in the title. Errors: p. 215 last, 'hich'; p. 237 beginning par. 313 'I' for 'It'; p. 251 in the running title, V for VI; in the caption, 'the citizen' instead of 'a citizen'.

In green cloth with a yellow label on the spine.

90   A full and accurate report | of | the trial | of | William Cobbett, Esq. | (before Lord Tenterden and a special jury,) | on Thursday, July 7, 1831, | in the | Court of King's Bench, London. | [rule] | [four lines quoted from] Dublin Freeman's Journal, July 11, 1831 | [rule] | New-York: | Published by John Doyle, 12, Liberty-Street; | and sold by the principal booksellers in the U. States. | [rule] | 1831.

[A]–F⁴=24 leaves, 22 cm.; (4)5(1)7–47(1). Text in two columns. ¶ Sabin 14030 (confused with the earlier trial in the action by Rush, No. 49) ¶ mwa; nn

Contents: title, blank, advertisement and preface, From Mr. Cobbett's Register [4]5; Court of King's Bench, London [6]–47; Mr. Cobbett (From the Dublin Freeman's Journal) [48]. P. [48] not in columns.

A prosecution for libel, in which Cobbett was charged with a publication intended 'to raise discontent in the minds of the labourers in husbandry, and to incite them to acts of violence...' The prosecution failed, the jury being divided six to six.

91a   A | French Grammar; | or, | plain instructions | for the | learning of French. | in a series of letters. | [rule] | By William Cobbett. | [rule] | New-York: | published by John Doyle, 12 Liberty-Street; | [rule] | Stereotyped by James Conner, New-York [rule] 1832.

[1]–30⁶31⁴=184 leaves; 15.5 cm.; (3)4(1)6–368. Third leaves signed 1*–30*. Two leaves of advertisement tipped in at the back. ¶ nn

Contents: title; 'Henry Mason, Print.'; contents [3]4; A French Grammar [5]–368. Running titles. Paragraphs in general numbered

1–456. In 28 letters, the first dated Kensington, 17th June 1824. The contents are keyed to paragraph numbers. Par. 391 for 393. Page 142 running title TASK for TASKS.

The Grammar was first published London 1824 and there were many later editions (Muirhead p. 33).

91b ――――. After 'Liberty-Street;' is inserted ' | and Thomas Doyle, Market-street, Providence, R.I. |' ¶ cty

The verso of the title leaf is blank. No advertisements. In green cloth with a yellow label on the spine: 'Cobbett's | Grammar | of the | French | language | in a series of | letters.'

92 Gouge, William M., 1796–1863.

The curse | of | paper-money and banking; | or | a short history of banking | in the | United States of America, | with an account of its ruinous effects on landowners, farmers, | traders, and on all the industrious classes of | the community. | [rule] | By Wm. M. Gouge, of Philadelphia, | in 1833. | [rule] | to which is prefixed | an introduction. | [rule] | By William Cobbett, M.P. for Oldham. | [rule] | London: | published at 11, Bolt Court, Fleet Street; | and to be had of all booksellers. | [rule] | July, 1833.

Colophon: Printed by Mills, Jowett, and Mills, | Bolt-court, Fleet-street.

[A]–I¹²K⁴=112 leaves, 18.2 cm.; (3)iv–vii (2)x–xxii(3)2–200 Second and fifth leaves signed A through I; also K2 ¶ Pearl 201 ¶ cty

Contents: title; printer; dedication [iii]–vii, subscribed Wm. Cobbett. Westminster, 14 July, 1833; blank; introduction [ix]–xxii, similarly subscribed; table of contents; blank; The curse of paper-money and banking [1]–200.

Running titles: p. 23 'II' for 'III'; p. 68 '1918' for '1818'; p. 113 'XII' for 'XIII'. Page number '1²⁶'.

The dedication is a note of warning to the Speaker of the House of Commons. In the introduction Cobbett says Gouge is 'exceedingly dull and awkward' but he does have facts. Cobbett comments briefly on U.S. banking. Pearl writes that the preface and introduction were published in the Political Register July 20, 1833. Gouge's 'Short History of Banking in the United States' was published Philadelphia 1833.

93a   Life | of | Andrew Jackson, | President | of | the United States of America. | [rule] | abridged and compiled | by William Cobbett, M.P. for Oldham. | [rule] | with an interesting frontispiece, including a | portrait |[rule]| London: | published at 11, Bolt-Court, Fleet-Street; | and may be had of all booksellers. | [rule] | 1834.

[A]–E¹²F¹¹A⁶ plus leaf tipped in after the title=78 leaves, 12 mo; (5)iv,v(2)viii–x(1)12–142,(1)2–11(1). Second and fifth leaves signed A–F. Frontispiece by Wm. Cobbett, Jr. ¶ Sabin 13891, Pearl 207 ¶ NN

Contents: title; printed by Mills, Jowett and Mills; frontispiece; blank; dedication [iii]–v dated Bolt Court, 27th March, 1834; blank; Preface [vii]–x; The Life [11]–142; Cobbett Library [1]–[12]. Running titles. Paragraphs numbered in the Life 1–212. 117 for 171. Par. 190 contains a long cabinet message Sept. 18, 1833. Postscript 197–212 on Pakenham. On p. x a 'N.B.' states that the Table of Contents and other references will be found at the end of the volume, but they are not present. Instead the contents are given at the head of each chapter.

Pearl points out that the Life was largely from a life by John Henry Eaton (1790–1856) published in Philadelphia, revised edition 1828 (Sabin 21731). Eaton was an American politician and friend and appointee of Jackson. The postscript (par. 197–212), however, is pure Cobbett, and largely an attack on the pretensions of Sir Edward Pakenham, who was killed in the Battle of New Orleans.

93b   Life | of | Andrew Jackson, | President of the | United States of America. | [rule] | By William Cobbett, M.P. | for Oldham | [rule] | New-York; | Harper & Brothers—82 Cliff Street. | [rule] | 1834.

[A]–R⁶[S]⁶=108 leaves, 15.2 cm; (3)iv(1)vi–viii(1)10(3)14–196 (20). Third leaves signed except Q R and [S]. Portrait frontispiece engraved by T. S. Woodcock, Brooklyn, N.Y. ¶ Pearl 207 ¶ CtY; MWA; NN

Contents: title, blank, dedication [iii], iv; preface [v]–viii, contents [9] 10; subtitle, blank, The Life...[13]–196; valuable works 1–8; valuable works [1]–9,[3]. Paragraphs numbered 1–212. The second advertisement includes the titles in the first advertisement. Running titles. Cloth, paper label on spine.

The text follows 93a.

93c ———. This is the same as 93b with the omission of the dedication and the advertisements. ¶ NN

93d Life of Andrew Jackson, | By William Cobbett [1834] [Caption].

Colophon page 16: New York: | printed and published by R. J. Richards, 45 Ann Street. | 1834 ¶ MWA

A single sheet folded into sixteen pages of 34 x 26 cm., with three columns of text to a page, in small type. No table of contents.

93e The | Life | of | Andrew Jackson, | president of the United States | of America. | [rule] | By William Cobbett, M.P. | for Oldham. | [rule] | Baltimore: | printed and published by J. Robinson, | circulating library, No. 2, N. Calvert-street | [rule] | 1834.

[1]–6⁶7⁵=41 leaves, 21 cm.; (4)v(2)8–81(1). Third leaves signed 2*–6* ¶ MWA

Contents: title, blank, dedication, preface [iv]v, contents, The Life [7]–81, blank. Paragraphs in text numbered 1 to 212, except pp. 71–77 and except 22, 23 for 23, 24, and 49 for 46. Running titles: pages 25–35 have 'campaigns' instead of 'campaign.'

93f Life | of | Andrew Jackson, | President of the | United States of America. | [rule] | By William Cobbett M.P. | for Oldham | [rule] | [rule] | 1834. [n.p.]

[1]–17⁶[18]¹=103 leaves, 14.5 cm.; (3)iv(1)vi–viii(1)10(3)14–206. Third leaves signed 2*–17* ¶ Sabin 13891 (has 260 pages). ¶ NJR

Contents: title, blank, dedication [iii]iv, preface [v]–viii, Contents [9] 10, Life, blank, text [13]–206. Paragraphs in text numbered 1–212 except paragraph following 35, paragraph [93], paragraph 91 for 94, no paragraph 196. Running title.

94a Paper against Gold; | or, the | history and mystery | of the | Bank of England, | of the debt, of the stocks, of the sinking fund, | and of all the other tricks and con- | trivances, carried on by the means | of paper money. | [cut of grid-iron] | [rule] | By William Cobbett, M.P. | [rule] | [eight lines quoted from concluding paragraph.] | [rule] | New= York: | Published by John Doyle, |No. 12, Liberty-street. | [rule] | 1834.

[1]–36⁶;1⁶=222 leaves, 15.9 cm.; (3)4–10(1)12–17(2)20–414 (1)416–432;(1)2–12. Third leaves signed 1*, 3*–21*, 23*, 24*, 25, 26*–29*, 30, 31*–36*, 1*. Running titles ¶ Pearl 81 ¶ cty; MWA

Contents: title, blank, Dedication to the Duke of Wellington [3]–10; Introduction [11]–17, with concluding note dated February 20, 1828; blank; Paper Against Gold, in XXIX letters [19]–414; To the Labourers of England...25th June 1831 [415]–426; To the Labourers...Jan. 1, 1832, 426–432; Works of William Cobbett [1]–9; Other Works 9–12. Pearl has a lengthy note on earlier publications of these essays, as a whole or in part, beginning in 1810 in Cobbett's Political Register.

94b ————. There are no added advertisements, the work ending on page 432. Bound in is one-half of a yellow wrapper, printed on both sides with advertisements of ten works by Cobbett published by Doyle; the fifth title: 'COBBBET'S [sic] American Gardener.' 15 cm. ¶ NN

95 GET GOLD! GET GOLD!! | [rule] | My readers know my opinion that, unless this | THING...[Leeds 1834] [caption title].

Colophon: Alice Mann, printer, central-market, Leeds.

[1]⁶=six leaves, 18.6 cm.; (1)2–11(1) ¶ Pearl 208 ¶ Leeds Public Libraries (repro.).

Contents: Text [1]–11, blank. Subscribed page 11 William Cobbett. Colophon foot of page 11. Errors: page 10, third from last, 'bividends'; page 11, line 8, 'know' for 'now.'

Pearl notes this is reprinted from Cobbett's Political Register of August 16, 1834.

The subject is English currency reform. President Jackson is cited as an example to follow in his battle with the central bank and revaluation of the dollar (pages 2, 3 and 7). Mentioned (page 2) is 'a corrupt West Indian of the name of [Alexander J.] Dallas...tool in the hands of a most corrupt and villainous governor of Pennsylvania [evidently Thomas Mifflin].'

96 Thirteen sermons | on | I. hypocrisy and cruelty–II. drunkenness–III. bribery– | IV. the rights of the poor.–V. unjust judges–VI. The | sluggard–VII. murder–VIII. gaming–IX. public rob- | bery–X. The unnatural mother–XI. forbidding marri- | age–XII. parsons

and tithes–XIII. good friday. |To which is added, | an address to the working people, | on the | new dead body bill. | [rule] | by William Cobbett, M.P. | [rule] | New York: | published by John Doyle, No. 12, Liberty Street. | [rule] | 1834.

[1]–24⁶=144 leaves, 14.5 cm.; (3)4–20(1)22–42(1)44–62(1)64–85(1)87–157(1)159–171(1)173–184(1)186–225(1)227–242(1)244–288. Third leaves signed 1*–24* ¶ Muirhead p. 26 ¶ NN

Contents: title, contents, the thirteen sermons [3]–242, Dead-Body Bill [243]–276, Note, and extracts from Rural Rides 277–288.

First published London 1830 under the title 'Good Friday; or, the murder of Jesus Christ by the Jews.'

Running titles. The article on the Dead-Body Bill is dated, p. [243], 24th Jan. 1832.

97   Cobbett's | legacy to parsons, | or | have the clergy of the established church an equitable right to | the tithes, or to any other thing called church property, | greater than the dissenters have to the same? and ought | there, or ought there not, to be a separation of the church | from the state? | [rule] | In six letters, | addressed to | the church-parsons in general, including the cathedral | and college clergy and the bishops | with | a dedication to Blomfield, | Bishop of London. | [rule] | By William Cobbett, Esq. M.P. | for Oldham. | [rule] | New York: | published by John Doyle, No. 12, Liberty-street | [rule] | 1835.

Second title: Cobbett's | legacy to labourers; | or, | what is the right which the lords, baronets, and 'squires, have | to the lands of England? | [rule] | In six letters, | addressed to the working people of England. | with | a dedication to Sir Robert Peel, Bart. | [rule] | By William Cobbett, Esq. M.P. | for Oldham. | [rule] | New York: | Published by John Doyle, No. 12, Liberty-Street. | [rule] | 1835.

[1]–12⁶;[A]–H⁶I⁴=124 leaves, 15.7 cm.; (5)6,7(2)10–143(1); (5)6–33(2)36–104. Third leaves signed 1*–12*; A2–I2 ¶ Pearl 214 ¶ ctY

Contents: title, blank; contents: blank; dedication dated 9th March, 1835 [5]–7; blank; Letters [9]–143; blank. Second title; blank; contents, blank; dedication dated 10 Dec., 1835 [5]–33; blank; Letters [35]–104. Bound in at the back is a 4 p. folder 'Books recently published by J. Doyle...' Running titles. Cloth, lettered on spine: 'Cobbett's Legacies.'

The first title is an attack on the church Establishment in England. The second title argues for the rights of English labourers on the land. First publication of the former was London 1835 and of the latter was London 1834. (Muirhead p. 37).

98   The Life | of | William Cobbett. | dedicated to his sons. | [rule] | Who-What man ever performed a greater quantity of labour than I have | performed? What man ever did so much?–William Cobbett. | [rule] | From the second London edition. | [rule] | Philadelphia: | E. L. Cary & A. Hart | [rule] | 1835.

[1]–18^6=108 leaves, 20 cm.; (5)vi–viii(1)x,xi(2)14–216. Third leaves signed 1*–18* ¶ Pearl 217 ¶ MWA

Contents: title, blank, dedication, blank, contents [v]–viii, preface [ix]–xi, blank, The Life [13]–216. Running titles.

A sympathetic history put together shortly after Cobbett's death June 18, 1835, largely from Cobbett's own writings.

99   No entry.

Other Cobbett Imprints

1796

100 A new Drawing Book, from the best masters, Price 1d.25 cts. Philadelphia. Printed for, and sold by, William Cobbett, opposite Christ Church. 1796. [Conjectural title. No copy known.] ¶ Evans 30844.

Advertised as 'just published' on p. [80] of the Political Censor for September 1796. (No. 20a.) Gazette of the United States, August 27, 1796: 'This day is published by William Cobbett...'

Account Book Sale Date September 29, 1796. Cobbett's accounts record 46 copies sold, first at $1.25 and later at $.75.

1797

101 Adams, John 1735–1826.
A | Defence | of the | constitutions of government | of the | United States | of | America, | against the attack of M. Turgot | in his | letter to Dr. Price, | dated the twenty-second day of March, 1778. | [rule] | by John Adams, L.L.D. | President of the United States. | [rule] | [one line from] Pope. | [rule] | In three volumes. | Vol. I [–III] | The third edition. | [rule] | Philadelphia: | Printed by Budd and Bartram. | for William Cobbett, opposite Christ Church. | 1797.

[π]¹[a]–e⁴,A–C3⁴=217 leaves, 8 vo.; (2)(3)4–6(1)ii–xxii(7)xxx–xxxiii(2)4–392(2). Portrait. A leaf is tipped to the first 'Contents' leaf entitled 'Addition to the List,' not included in above collation ¶ Evans 31689 ¶ Location of three volumes: MWA

Contents: blank, portrait, title, blank, account of the author [3]–6, preface [i]–xxii, Subscribers [xxiii]–[xxviii], Contents [xxix]–xxxiii, blank, Letters etc. [3]–392, blank leaf. The portrait of Adams, by Smither after Copley, has the legend: 'Philadelphia, publish'd Febr 15, 1797 by William Cobbett.' 'Vol. I' to left of signatures. Running titles. Catchwords except page 8; page xxii the catchword 'Contents' is misplaced; p. 4 catchword 'ETTER', for 'Letter'.

Vol. II A | Defence | of the | constitutions of government | of the | United States | of | America,... | [seven lines from] | Shaftesbury | [five lines quoted] | [rule] | in three volumes | Vol. II. | The third edition. | [rule] | Philadelphia: | Printed by H. Schweitzer, | for William Cobbett, opposite | Christ Church. | 1797.

[A]–3L⁴3M²=230 leaves, 8 vo.; (9)2–451(1) ¶ Evans 31690

Contents: blank leaf, half-title, blank, title, blank, contents, blank, A defence [1]–451, blank. 'Vol. II' to left of signatures. Running titles. Catchwords. Some errors noted. Running titles: Michiavel pp.19, 47, 59, 83, 85, 105, 129; p. 163 Guinchiardin. Catchwords: p. 109 'Candini' for 'candina'; p. 135 'no' for 'on'; p. 163 'brated' for 'lebrated'. P. 112 begins 'afterwads'; p. 317 begins 'Austria' for 'stria.' Page numbers 362 for 384, 448 for 441. Page number 446 in brackets.

Vol. III A Defence | of the | constitutions of government | of the | United States of America | ... Vol. III. | The third edition. | [rule] | [6 lines quoted from] | Johnson | [rule] | Philadelphia: | printed by William Young, | for William Cobbett, opposite Christ's Church. | 1797.

[A]¹B–4B⁴4C²=283 leaves, 8 vo; (3)2–528(36) ¶ Evans 31691

Contents: title, blank, A defence [1]–528, Index [1]–[36].

'Vol. III' to left of signatures, except R. Running titles except pp. 502–528; on these pages the numbers are centered in brackets. Catchwords, except p. 514. Some errors noted: in running titles, pp. 233, 351, 385 have 'axamened'; pp. 287, 331, 333 lack the comma; p. 415 begins 'tal' for 'al'.

Gazette of the United States, November 18, 1796, proposals by Cobbett to publish; February 23, 1797: 'This day is published...' Account Book Sale Date February 20, 1797. Cobbett's accounts record 382 copies sold at prices from $5 to $7. In the Censor for December 1796 (No. 26), next to last page, it is stated: 'Adam's Defence...is now in the Press and will appear on or before the 15th of February next...'

102   Burke, Edmund. 1729–1797.

Two letters | addressed to | a member | of | the present Parliament, | on the proposals for | peace | with the | regicide directory | of | France. | [rule] | By the Right Hon. Edmund Burke. | [rule] | Philadelphia: | printed for William Cobbett, in Second Street, opposite | Christ-Church, and J. Ormrod No. 41, Chesnut Street. | By Bioren and Madan. | [rule] | 1797.

[A]–H⁴;A–C⁴=32, 12 leaves, 8 vo; (3)4–64;1–22(2) ¶ Evans 31895 ¶ MWA; NN

Contents: title, blank, Letter I [3]–64; Letter II, 1–22, blank leaf. Note page 23 dated 'Downing Street, April 10, 1796.' Tailpiece second page 22.

Gazette of the United States, February 21, 1797: 'This day is published...' Account Book Sale Date February 23, 1797. Cobbett's accounts record 199 copies sold at 37½¢. Page 49 line 1 'straggered'; second page 13 last 'ar' for 'ar-'; second page number 12 underscored; second page 17 last 'despotickmeans.'

103   [Smith, William Loughton] [?] 1758–1812.

The pretensions of Thomas Jefferson to the presidency examined; and the charges against John Adams refuted. Addressed to the citizens of America in general; and particularly to the electors of the President. [Part first-second]. Philadelphia: published complete and for sale by William Cobbett, opposite Christ Church, 1797. [Conjectural title. No copy known. Compare Evans 31212, 31213 (John Fenno, November, 1796).]

¶ Evans 32853. S. T. Evans, page 788, col. 3, 'apparently a ghost of 31212'.

Advertised in Porcupine's Gazette for June 24, 1797: 'Published complete, | and for sale by William Cobbett, opposite | Christ | Church. | Phocion's | examination of the pretensions of | Thomas Jefferson | and his refutation of the charges against | John Adams.' Note that this is not a flat representation that Cobbett was the publisher. The advertisement continued into October.

Account Book Sale Date June 22, 1797. The Book shows sales of 117 copies at 50¢.

In Porcupine's Works, London 1801 (No. 59), Cobbett twice excerpted from Smith's work (Vol. I pp. 346–358 and Vol. XII pp. 192–217), but in neither case did he refer to a republication of his own, as it would have been most natural for him to have done had there been one. It is my guess that the 1797 advertisements were a warm-over of the 1796 edition, and that there was no Cobbett imprint.

104   An accurate plan of the blockade of Cadiz. Published by Peter Porcupine. Price 9D. [Conjectural title. No copy known.]

Evans 31943; Wheat and Brun, maps and charts published in America before 1800, no. 805.

Account Book Sale Date September 23, 1797. Cobbett's accounts record 882 copies sold at 12½¢. The Plan, 12.5 x 13.7 cm., with references and text, is printed in Porcupine's Gazette September 21, 1797. Advertised in the Gazette September 27, 1797 as 'just published by Peter Porcupine... on one sheet of superfine paper, suited for framing—price 12½ cents.' Wheat and Brun reproduces the Plan as printed in the Gazette.

105   Gifford, John [John Richards Green] 1758–1818.

A | Letter | to | the Hon. Thomas Erskine; | containing | some strictures | on his | view | of the | causes and consequences | of the present | war with France. | [rule] | By John Gifford, Esq. | author of a letter to the Earl of Lauderdale, &c. &c. | [rule] | [two lines from] Voltaire | [rule] | Philadelphia: | published by William Cobbett, opposite | Christ Church. | November, 1797.

[A]²B–R⁴=66 leaves, 8 vo; (5)2–128 ¶ Evans 32191 ¶ CTY; MWA

Contents: half-title, blank, title, blank, A Letter [1]–122, Postscript 123–128.

Account Book Sale Date November 3, 1797. The Book records sales of 607 copies at 50¢. Advertised in Porcupine's Gazette November 3, 1797, 'Peter Porcupine has this day published...'

106   Erskine, Thomas 1750–1823.

The | Speeches | of the | Hon. Thomas Erskine, | in the Court of King's Bench, | June 28, 1797, | before the Right Hon. | Lloyd Lord Kenyon, and a special jury, | on the | trial | The King versus Thomas Williams, | for publishing the | Age of Reason, | written by Thomas Paine; | together with | Mr. Stewart Kyd's reply, | and | Lord Kenyon's charge to the jury. | [rule] | Philadelphia: | printed for, and sold by William Cobbett, | opposite Christ Church. | [rule] | Nov. 1797.

[A]–C⁴=12 leaves, 8 vo; (3)4–23(1) ¶ Evans 32093 ¶ CTY; MWA

Contents: title, blank, The Speeches [3]–23, blank. Catchwords. Account Book Sale Date November 10, 1797. The Book records sales of 643 copies at 12½¢. Advertised in Porcupine's Gazette November 9, 1797 'Published by William Cobbett.'

107   Rules | and | Constitutions | of the | Society | of the | Sons of St. George, | established at Philadelphia, | for the | advice and assistance | of | Englishmen in distress | [rule] | Philadelphia: | Printed by William Cobbett, | opposite Christ Church. | [rule] | 1797.

[A]–C⁴[D]¹=13 leaves, 8 vo; (3)4(1)6–8(1)10–25(1) ¶ Evans 32683 ¶ NN

Contents: title, blank, At a meeting [3]4, Introduction [5]–8, Rules [9]–18, List of members 19–25, blank.

One of two United States works represented to have been printed by Cobbett. (The other is No. 32).

108   Russell, John Miller 1768–1840.

An | Oration, | pronounced at Charlestown, | July 4, 1797, | at the request of the | selectmen, artillery company, and trustees | of the school in said town, | in | commemoration | of the | anniversary | of | American Independence. | [rule] | By John Miller Russell | [rule] | second edition. | [rule] | Philadelphia: | printed for William Cobbett, | opposite Christ Church. | [rule] | Nov. 1797.

[A],B⁴=8 leaves, 8 vo; (5)6–15(1) ¶ Evans 32791 (Evans has 'Printed by') ¶ cty

Contents: title, blank, advertisement, vote of thanks, oration [5]–15, blank. Catchwords.

Eleven-line 'advertisement' for the work, written by Cobbett, dated Nov. 10, 1797.

1798

109a   [Lowell, John] 1769–1840.

The | Antigallican; | or, the | lover of his own country: | in a series of pieces partly heretofore published and | partly new, wherein | French influence, | and | false patriotism, | are | fully and fairly displayed. | [rule] | By a citizen of New England | [rule] | Philadelphia: | Published by William Cobbett, | opposite Christ Church | [rule] | December, 1797. [i.e. 1798]

[A]–I⁴K⁵L²=43 leaves, 8 vo; (the third leaf of K is tipped in); (5)6–44(1)46–71,71,73(2),74–82 (2) ¶ Evans 32393 ¶ cty; MWA

Contents: title; blank; dedication; blank; The Antigallican [5]–41; appendix, 42–44; The pseudo patriot [45]–71, 71, 73; Appendix to Ascanius (2); Hamilton versus Monroe 74–77; Letter 78–82; blank leaf. Catchwords, except pp. 11, 18, 41, 52, 73, 77. Page 70 first word 'if' is missing.

See Cobbett's Account Book, Appendix, at page   . Account Book Sale Date January 19, 1798. The Book records sales of 300 copies at 37½¢.

Advertised in Porcupine's Gazette February 26, 1798 as 'just published by William Cobbett.'

109b ———. Here the paging is 46–69, 67, 71–73. ¶ NN
Page 69 catchword 'if' not repeated on following page 67.

110   Kennedy, Patrick fl. 1797.

An | answer | to | Paine's letter | to | General Washington: | including | some pages of gratuitous counsel | to | Mr. Erskine. | [rule] | Impius, ingratusque, audax, scelerumque magister. | [rule] | By P. Kennedy, Esq. | [rule] | Philadelphia: | re-published by William Cobbett, opposite | Christ-Church. | Jan. 1798.

[A]²B–F⁴=22 leaves, 8 vo; (5)4–42 ¶ Evans 33947 ¶ ctY; MWA

Contents: title, blank, advertisement, blank, An Answer [3]–42. The two paragraph 'Advertisement' is signed 'P.P.' i.e. William Cobbett. See Cobbett's Account Book, appendix, at page 239. Account Book Sale Date January 19, 1798. The Book records sales of 321 copies at 25¢. Advertised in Porcupine's Gazette January 20, 1798 'Just published by William Cobbett...'.

Published London, 'For the author', 1797, 55 p., Bartlett 3888.

111   [Harper, Robert Goodloe] 1765–1825.

Speech | of | R. G. Harper, Esqr. | in the | House of Representatives, | Monday, the 29th day of May, 1797, | relative to the | unjust, cruel, insolent and perfidious | conduct of France | towards | the United States. | [rule] | Philadelphia: | published by William Cobbett, | opposite Christ Church. | [rule] | March, 1798.

[A]–E⁴,F²=22 leaves, 8 vo; (5)6–44 ¶ Evans 33844 ¶ ctY; MWA

Contents: half-title, blank, title, blank, speech [5]–44. Page numbers 24 and 34 have a parenthesis and a bracket. Account Book Sale Date March 27, 1798. The Book records sales of 594 copies at 50¢. Advertised in Porcupine's Gazette March 27, 1798 'This day is published by William Cobbett...'.

In Porcupine's Works (No. 59), Vol. IX, page 332, in the course of a severe attack on Harper at pages 326–333, Cobbett wrote: 'Harper is under greater obligations to me than to any man, or set of men in the world, his silly Carolinian constituents not excepted. His famous *speeches*, which he always *wrote out* for the press, cost me not less than two hundred pounds extraordinary expense, which was a dead loss to me. People accused me of writing these speeches myself, of which I was not, to say the truth, altogether innocent. I dictated alterations, and, in some instances, I made them myself.'

112   Robison, John 1739–1805.

Proofs | of a | conspiracy | against all the | religions and govern-ments | of | Europe, | carried on | in the secret meetings | of | free masons, illuminati, | and | reading societies. | collected from good authorities, | by John Robison, A.M. | professor of natural philoso-phy, and secretary to the | Royal Society of Edinburgh. | Nam tua res agitur paries cum proximus ardet. | The third edition. | To which is added a postscript. | [rule] | Philadelphia: | printed for T. Dobson, No. 41, South Second | Street, and W. Cobbet [sic], No. 25, North | Second Street. | 1798.

[A]–2A⁴,*2B⁴,*2C²,2B⁴–2U⁴,2V⁴,2X⁴–3A⁴,3B²=200 leaves, 8 vo; (5)6–17(2)20–204;197–391(1) ¶ Evans 34477 ¶ MWA; NN

Contents: title; blank; dedication; latin from Lucretius; introduc-tion [5]–17; blank; Proofs [19]–204, 197–366; postscript 367–391; blank. Running titles. Catchwords, except pp. 112, 204. Page 391 concludes with a note 'To the Binder' about the two starred signa-tures. In the running titles: Chap. I, II, iii, iv; page 35, 'CAAP'; page 362 no chapter number. Page 21 ends 'ceremo-' and page 22 begins 'monies'. Page 337 the catchword has a dropped letter 's'. The postscript is by the author. It seems that one printer did [1]–204 and another 197–[392].

Account Book Sale Date April 9, 1798. The Book records 93 copies sold at $1.75 in boards or $2.00 in leather. Advertised in Porcupine's Gazette April 6, 1798: 'Just published by T. Dobson and William Cobbett...'.

113   United States.

Instructions | to | Charles Cotesworth Pinckney, | John Marshall and Elbridge Gerry, | envoys extraordinary and ministers plenipo-tentiary | to the | French Republic, | referred to in the message of the President of the United | States of the third instant. | [rule] | Philadelphia: | published by William Cobbett, opposite | Christ Church. | 1798.

[A],B⁴=8 leaves, 8 vo; (3)4–15(1) ¶ S. T. Evans page 897 Col. 1 ¶ MWA

Contents: title, blank, Instructions [3]–15, blank. Page 12 last letter 'e' above the line.

Account Book Sale Date April 10, 1798. The Book records sales of 115 copies at 12½¢.

114   Watson, Richard 1737–1816.

An | address | to the | people of Great Britain | [rule] |. By R. Watson, | Lord Bishop of Landaff. | [rule] | Philadelphia: | published by William Cobbett, | opposite Christ Church. | [rule] | April, 1798.

[A]–E⁴=20 leaves, 8 vo; (5)6–40 ¶ Evans 34962 ¶ cty; MWA

Contents: half-title, blank, title, blank, An address [5]–40.

Account Book Sale Date, April 20, 1798. The Book records sales of 347 copies at 25¢. Advertised in Porcupine's Gazette April 19, 1798: 'This day is published by William Cobbett...'.

115   Allen, John.

Speech | of | John Allen, Esqr. | in the | House of Representatives, | Friday, the 20th day of April, 1798. | relative to | employing the armed vessels | as convoys. | [rule] | Philadelphia: | Published by William Cobbett | [rule] | May 3, 1798.

[A]–D⁴=16 leaves, 8 vo; (3)iv,v(2)8–32 ¶ Evans 33284 ¶ cty; MWA

Contents: title, blank, preface [iii]–v, blank, speech [7]–32. Catchwords. On page 21 lines 1, 2, end letters dropped down; page 26 the catchword is 'honourable' and page 27 begins 'honorable'. Account Book Sale Date May 4, 1798. The Book shows sales of 109 copies at 25¢. Advertised in Porcupine's Gazette, May 4, 1798, as 'just published by William Cobbett...'

116   Harper, Robert Goodloe 1765–1825.

Observations | on the | dispute | between the | United States and France: | addressed, | by Robert G. Harper, Esq. | of South Carolina, | to his | constituents, | in May, 1797. | With a preface and appendix by the author. | [rule] | Third American edition. | It has passed through five editions in England. | [rule] | Philadelphia: | published by William Cobbett, | Opposite Christ Church. | [rule] | May, 1798. | [Copy right secured according to law.]

[A]²,B–M⁴,N²=48 leaves, 8 vo; (3)iv(1)6–88(1)90–93(1)95,96 ¶ Evans 33841, Pearl 33 ¶ cty

Contents: title, blank, preface [iii]iv, Observations [5]–88, Appendix No. 1 [89]–93, Appendix No. 2 [94]–96. Running titles page iv and appendix.

Account Book Sale Date May 4, 1798. The Book records sales of 918 copies at 50¢. Advertised in Porcupine's Gazette, May 4, 1798, 'just published by William Cobbett...'.

The work was first published in June 1797 (by Bradford, Evans 32226). In Porcupine's Works, (No. 59) Vol. IX, pp. 326–333, Cobbett made a severe attack on Harper in which he had much to say about this work, especially p. 332: 'Of the pamphlet, which gained him so much renown in England, and which was quoted with high encomiums in both houses of parliament, I *furnished the materials, gave the hints, drew the plan*, and if my name had been put to the work, I should not have been so much of a plagiarist as he was..." As to the republication, Cobbett wrote (p. 333) '...there was nothing to do but purchase the copy-right [from Thomas Bradford], which Harper agreed to do with a note of hand for *two hundred dollars*, provided *I would pay the note when it became due*. This was done, I republished the pamphlet, and *lost the two hundred dollars with about one hundred more at the back of them*! Still I did not repine. I was convinced, that the pamphlet did great good to both countries, and great injury to France, which far outweighed with me, all the dollars in the world.' In his 'Harrison Gray Otis' (Boston 1913) Samuel Eliot Morison noted the great influence of the pamphlet, which he states went through at least 23 editions (Vol. 1, p. 67 note).

117   Muir, James 1757–1820.

A | sermon | preached in the Presbyterian Church | at | Alexandria, | on the 9th of May, 1798, | being | the day appointed for a | general fast. | [rule] | By the Revd. Doctor James Muir. | [rule] | Philadelphia: | published by William Cobbett. | [rule] | May 9, 1798.

[A]⁸=eight leaves, not signed, 8 vo; (5)6–14(2). ¶ Evans 34157 ¶ MBAt

Contents: half-title, blank, title, blank, sermon [5]–14, blank leaf. 'Finis' on page 14.

Some errors: page 6 line 9, last letter lowered; line 15 first letter lowered; page 7 lines 5, 6 and 13 last letters raised; page 9 line 8 'Babtist'.

Account Book Sale Date May 16, 1798. The Book records sales of 127 copies at 12½¢. In Porcupine's Gazette, May 15, 1798, Cobbett states: 'I have published it and have it for sale.'

118　Aufrère, Anthony 1756–1833.

The | cannibals' progress; | or the | dreadful horrors of French invasion, | as displayed by the republican officers and sol- | diers, in their perfidy, rapacity, ferociousness | and brutality, exercised to- | wards the in- | nocent inhabitants of Germany | Translated from the German, | by Anthony Aufrer, Esq. | [Cut 5.9 x 8 cm.] | [three lines quoted] | [rule]. | London: | Published by Wright, Cadel and others; and republished at | Philadelphia | By William Cobbett. | [rule] | Price only 6 cents. | 11 for half a dollar, 25 for a dollar, 56 for 2 dollars, | Three dollars and a half per hundred. [1798].

[A]²B–D⁶E⁴=24 leaves, 12 mo; (3)4(1)6–47(1). Third leaves signed B2–D2 ¶ Evans 33334, Pearl 39 ¶ cty; mwa

Contents: title, blank, introductory address [3]4, cannibal's progress [5]–40, 'Americans' 41–47, blank. Ornament page 47. Catchwords in text, except page 40. The introductory address is by Cobbett. Announced in Porcupine's Gazette in June as 'now printing.'

Under Evans 33338, a New Hampshire edition, Evans quotes from 'New Hampshire Gazette' July 31, 1798: 'Five thousand copies sold in Philadelphia in a few days—another edition of ten thousand copies is now in the press in that city.' Cobbett wrote his friend Edward Thornton of the British Legation August 27, 1798: 'The little pamphlet called the Cannibals' Progress I send you to let you see how I am working against the French. I have published 25 thousand of this work, and about as many more have issued, by my permission, from the German and other presses in the States.' (quoted in *Cole-Thornton*, page 4).

'The Cannibals' Progress...' is reprinted in Porcupine's Works (No. 59) Vol. VIII, pp. 259–320. A note on page 320 reads as follows: 'Of this pamphlet upwards of a hundred thousand copies were printed and sold in the United States of America, besides a large edition in the German language.'

Reprints, with the one and one-half page 'Introductory Address to the People of America' written by Cobbett, were published in 1798 at Albany, N.Y.; Boston; Charleston, S.C.; New London; Newburyport, Mass.; Portsmouth, N.H.; Vergennes, Vt.; and Walpole, N.H. (See Evans 33325, 7, 8, 33331, 2, 5, 7, and 8. Evans lists other editions which either do not have the Address or have never been located.) Only in the Charleston edition is Cobbett identified as author of the Address, which emphasizes the unhappy fate of Suabia. See also next entry.

Account Book Sale Date June 18, 1798. The Book shows sales of 6078 copies at 3½¢.

119 Aufrère, Anthony. 1756–1833.

Der Förtgäng | der | Menschenfresser. | oder die | greuel eines französischen Einfalls, | [four lines] | [vignette] | [three lines quoted] | [rule] | Philadelphia, | gedruckt bey Henrich Schweitzer, No. 85 | in der Rees-Strasse [1798].

[A]–E⁴F²=22 leaves, 8 vo; (3)4–32,25–32,41–44. (No known copy has pp. 9–12) ¶ Evans 33525 ¶ PHi (PPL)

Pp. [3]4 contain an introduction subscribed 'Peter Porcupein', i.e., Cobbett. German edition of 'The cannibals' progress...' (see preceding entry).

120 Snyder, G. W.

The | Age of Reason | unreasonable; | or, the | folly of rejecting | revealed religion. | In a series of letters to a friend. | [rule] | By G. W. Snyder, A.M. | [rule] | Philadelphia: | Published by William Cobbett, | opposite Christ Church. | [rule] | May, 1798.

[A]–S⁶=108 leaves, 12 mo.; (5)6–132,132–135,137–213(3). Third leaves signed A2–S2 ¶ Evans 34568 ¶ CtY; DLC

Contents: title, blank, recommendatory letter, blank, text [5]–132, 132–135, 137–213, blank, blank leaf. Text divided into seventeen letters. Page numbers 188 and 189 lack first parenthesis.

214th Pennsylvania District copyright issued to William Cobbett June 25, 1798. See Cobbett's Account Book, appendix, p. 238 for a discussion of the publication of this work. Account Book Sale Date July 25, 1798. Porcupine's Gazette June 26, 1798 advertised as 'This day is published and for sale by William Cobbett.'

121   Lewis, Matthew Gregory, 1775-1818.

Ambrosio, | or | the Monk: | a | romance. | [rule] | | by M. G. Lewis, Esq., M.P. | [rule] | Three volumes in two. | Vol. I. [Vol. II] | [rule] | The first American, from the fourth | British edition. | with considerable additions and alterations. | [rule] | [two lines quoted from 'Hor.', with two lines translation] | [rule] | Philadelphia: | printed for W. Cobbett, opposite | Christ-Church. | 1798. ¶ Evans Supp. B. 10383 ¶ MH

Vol. I. [A]⁴B–V⁶W–Bb⁶Cc²=162 leaves, 12 mo.; (3)iv,v(4)10–55 (1)57–128(1)130–184(1)186–279(1)281–323(1). 'Vol. I' to left of signatures. Third leaves signed B2–Bb2.

Contents: title, blank, preface [iii]–v, blank, table of the poetry, advertisement, The Monk [9]–323, blank. Tailpieces pp. 55 and 279.

Vol. II. [A]¹B–V⁶W–Cc⁶=163 leaves, 12 mo.; (3)4–291(1)293–325 (1).

'Vol. II' to left of signatures. Third leaves signed B2–Cc2.

Contents: title, blank, The Monk [3]–325, blank. Tailpieces pp. 48, 82, 121 and 231.

Account Book Sale Date July 16, 1798. The Book records sales of 432 copies at $2.00. Advertised in Porcupine's Gazette July 16, 1798: 'This day is published, and for sale by William Cobbett...'

122   Sorlie, Sholto.

A | treatise | on the | new sword exercise, | for cavalry. | [rule] | By Sholto Sorlie, | of the seventh (or Queen's own) regiment of | light dragoons. | [rule] | "Without discipline, soldiers are but an armed mob." | Marshal Saxe. | [rule] | Philadelphia: | republished by William Cobbett. | [rule] | 1798.

[A]–C⁴=12 leaves, 8 vo; (3)4–24. Second leaf signed B2 ¶ Evans 34572 ¶ MWA

Contents: title, blank, A Treatise [3]–24. Wood cuts on pages [3] and 22. Catchwords except p. 21. Account Book Sale Date August 1, 1798. The Book records sales of 263 copies at 25¢. Advertised in Porcupine's Gazette, July 31, 1798 'This day is published and for sale by William Cobbett...'

123   [Harper, Robert Goodloe] 1765–1825.

A short | account | of the principal | proceedings of Congress, | in the late session, | and a sketch of the state of affairs between the |

United States and France | in July, 1798: | in a letter from | Robert Goodloe Harper, | of South Carolina, | to one of his constituents. | [rule] | Philadelphia: | published by William Cobbett. | [rule] | August, 1798.

[A]–C⁴=12 leaves, 8 vo; (5)6–22(2) ¶ Evans 33838 ¶ cty; MWA

Contents: half-title, blank, title, blank, A Short Account [5]–22, blank leaf. Page numbers in brackets except pp. 15–17 in parentheses.

Account Book Sale Date August 1, 1798. The Book records sales of 564 copies at 25¢. Advertised in Porcupine's Gazette, August 2, 1798, 'This day is published by William Cobbett...'

1799

124a Gifford, William 1756–1826.

The | Baviad, | and | Maeviad, | By William Gifford, Esquire. | [rule] | [five lines of Latin] | [rule] | To which is prefixed, | A poetical epistle to the author, | by an American gentleman. [William Cliffton] | [rule] | A new edition revised. | [rule] | London— Printed– | Philadelphia: | re-printed for William Cobbett. | [sixteen dots] | M.DCC.XCIX.

[A]–O⁶=84 leaves, 12 mo; (5)vi–xi(2)xiv–xx(3)2–59(3)63–145(1). Third leaves signed A2–I2, H2, L2–O2 ¶ Evans 35546 ¶ cty; MWA; NjR

Contents: title; blank; dedication; blank; To | William Gifford, Esquire [v]–xi, signed 'C' and dated Philadelphia 13th May, 1799 on page xi.; blank; Introduction [xiii]–xx; The Baviad, blank. The Baviad [1]–59; blank; The Maeviad; blank; introduction 63–70; The Maeviad 71–145; blank. Thick paper.

Cobbett sent a copy to John Wright in London, June 10, 1799. (Reitzel p. 239n) Printed by John Ward Fenno. See Cobbett's Account Book, appendix, at page 244. Account Book Sale Date, May 17, 1799. The Book records sales of 178 copies at $1.50. Advertised in Porcupine's Gazette May 22, 1799 'William Cobbett has just published...'

124b ————. The transcription concludes: edition revised | [rule] | Philadelphia. | Printed for William Cobbett. | [rule] | M.DCCXCIX [no second period]. ¶ NjR

On page xi there is no date and no 'C' at the foot. Around page number 20 both brackets open to the left.

125   The | United States | Court Kalendar, | and | gentleman's | complete pocket-companion, | for the | year of our Lord | 1800, | [rule] | being the fourth after bissextile, | and the first of the 18th Century. | [rule] | New-York | published by William Cobbett. [1799].

[π]¹[A],B¹⁶[C],D¹⁶[E]²=67 leaves, 24 mo. Not paged ¶ Evans 36601 ¶ NN

Contents: title, blank, contents (2), Almanack (14). Sovereigns (1). Memorandums [blank pages ruled for each day] (24), Government of the United States (10), Officers in the Army (20), Navy (8), Foreign Ministers (1), Post Office, Mint, foreign monies, Bank of the United States, Duties, Bounties (36), the States (1), finances (5), British packet-boats, navy, ships captured, victories (10). Unusual in the British emphasis in the final ten pages.

See Cobbett's Account Book, appendix, at page 244. Account Book Sale Date, December 26, 1799. The Book records sales of 22 copies at 75¢ to $1.50.

1800

126   Polwhele, Richard 1760–1838.

The | unsex'd females; | a | poem, | addressed to the author of | the pursuits of literature. [Mathias, Thomas James] | [rule] | By the Rev. Richard Polewhele. [sic] | [rule] | to which is added, | a sketch of the private and public character of | P. Pindar. [John Wolcott, M.D.] | [rule] | New-York: | re-published by Wm. Cobbett. | 1800.

[π]³A–C⁹D⁶=36 leaves, 18 mo; (3)iv–vi(1)4–49(2)52–68. Second through fifth leaves signed A–C; also D2 D3 ¶ Evans 38293 ¶ MWA; NN

Contents: title, blank, preface [iii]–vi, The Unsex'd Females [3]–49, blank, A Sketch [51]–68. The preface is by Cobbett. The 'unsex'd females' are the French 'amazons'. Footnotes greatly exceed the text of the poem.

Advertised as 'just published' in the Rush-Light for 30th April 1800 (No. 55). Account Book Sale Date May 1, 1800. The Book records sales of 89 copies at 62½¢.

127 Some | account | of an | existing correspondence | now carrying on between | the inhabitants of the moon | and the | natives of old England, | to which is subjoined, a list of such articles as are | immediately wanted for the | export trade, | by some merchants just arrived from the planet. | Interspersed with several useful and valuable hints, | particularly adapted to the use of those | gentlemen who are fond of | speculation. | A work strongly recommended to the perusal of the | merchants, bankers, manufacturers, whole- | sale tradesmen, shopkeepers, under- | writers, insurance brokers, and | ladies of Great Britain. | [rule] | London: | printed and sold by H. Fry, Finsbury-place. | [rule] | New–York: | re-published by William Cobbett, | No. 141, Hanover Square. | 1800.

Colophon p. 23: Printed by | G. & R. Waite.

[A],B⁶=12 leaves, 12 mo; (3)4–23(1). Second and third leaves signed ¶ Evans 38530 ¶ MWA

Contents: title, blank, Some Account [3]–23, blank. Catchwords, except pp. 9 and 13. Ornamental tailpiece. Curious, heavy-handed satire, answering to the title. The London edition was 1800.

128 Tansillo, Luigi 1510–1568.

The | Nurse, | a poem. | translated from the Italian of | Luigi Tansillo. | [rule] | By William Roscoe [of Liverpool]. | [rule] | –London– printed– | New York: | re-printed for William Cobbett, | By John Furman. | 1800.

[A]–I⁶=54 leaves, 16 mo; (5)6–30;(3)4–7(1)9–20(1)22–44;(3) 4–28(3)32–34. Third leaves signed A2–I2 ¶ Evans 38604 ¶ MWA; NN; PHi(PPL)

Contents: half-title, blank, title, blank, re Tansillo [5]–30; sonnet, blank, The Nurse [3]–20; Canto II [21]–44, Notes, blank, notes [3]–28, Inscription, blank, inscription [31]–34.

The discussion of Tansillo pp. [5]–30 is by the translator, as is the sonnet.

129 No entry.

1795

130   [Callender, James Thomson] 1758–1803.

The | Political Progress | of | Britain: | or, an | impartial history | of | abuses in the government | of the | British Empire, | in | Europe, Asia, and America. | from the revolution, in 1688, to the present time: | the whole tending to prove the ruinous consequences of | the popular system of | taxation, war, and conquest. | [rule] | "The world's mad business." | [rule] | Part First. | Third Edition. | [rule] | Philadelphia: | Printed by and for Richard Folwell, No. 33, Mulberry-street. | [rule] | 1795. | [Price half a dollar]

[A]–P⁴=60 leaves, 8 vo; (3)4–6(1)8(1)10–27(1)29–120 ¶ Evans 28379; Sabin 10066 ¶ CtY; MWA

Contents: title, copy-right secured; advertisement [3]–5 dated Philadelphia, November 14, 1794; Postscript 5, 6 signed James Thomson Callender and dated Philadelphia, 3d of March 1795; Contents [7] 8; Introduction [9]–27; The |Political Progress | of | Britain [28]–120. On page 120 'The end.'

The work was first published in London and Edinburgh in the fall of 1792, resulting in Callender's flight to America in 1793. A second edition was published in Philadelphia in November 1794 (Evans 26725). Another printing was made in Philadelphia with a preface dated March 31, 1795 (Evans 28380) and a second part was published in the Fall (Evans 28381).

Errors noted: p. 26, l. 35 're' for 'are'; p. 109 heading 'Guin a'.

The work, written from the Scottish viewpoint, answers to its title. The second edition had been noticed by Cobbett in A Bone to Gnaw (No. 3a), in a large part of the first dozen pages. The work mentions Bone in the Postscript (p. 5), but says only: 'The author is offended at my presumption in having predicted a Scots revolution.'

131   Anonymous.

The | Philadelphia Jockey Club; | or, | mercantile influence weighed, | consisting of | select characters | taken from the | Club of

Addressers. | [rule] | By Timothy Tickler. | [rule] | [seven lines quoted from Proverbs] | [rule] | printed for the purchasers. | 1795.

[A]–C⁴=12 leaves, 8 vo; (3) iv–vi(1)8–20(1)22,23(1) ¶ Evans 29638, Sabin 95799 ¶ MWA

Contents: title; blank; advertisement, subscribed 'The Proprietor' [iii]–v; author's address, subscribed 'A Philadelphian', vi; The Philadelphia Jockey Club [7]–20; appendix [21]–23, subscribed p. 23 'A Philadelphian'; blank.

Some errors noted: p. iv, l. 19 'personaiity'; p. 16, next to last line, 'benifit'; p. 22, l. 13, 'religiou'.

The work consists principally of short sketches, mainly very uncomplimentary, of 45 Philadelphians, identified only by initials, who signed an address in support of the treaty with Great Britain negotiated by John Jay. (In the MWA copy the names are filled in). The general thrust is that they were motivated by self-interest. Cobbett comes in for notice in two instances: page iv, third full paragraph, that an attack on individual reputation 'is authorized by the precedent of the infamous Peter Porcupine and the literary outlaw SNUB [John Swanwick] whose political squabbles have involved the characters of many respectables.'; and page 17, on 'T–B– [Thomas Bradford]...it will only be necessary to review his private professional endeavors to propagate the obnoxious principles of monarchy and aristocracy, speciously disguised by Peter Porcupine. After almost every printer in the city had objected to publishing that baneful performance...the city has been deluged by the copious overflowings of that author's brain.'

The work was answered in 'The Democratiad...', Evans 28853, 4, attributed to Lemuel Hopkins. In the preface, p. iv, the printer, Thomas Bradford, defends himself, but Cobbett is not otherwise defended. 'The Democratiad' is attributed to Cobbett in Sabin 13879, 95799, but it seems impossible to believe Cobbett could have written this and remained silent as to the attacks on him.

132a [Dallas, Alexander James] 1759–1817.

Letters | of | Franklin, | on the conduct of the | executive, | and the | treaty | negociated, by the | Chief Justice of the United States | with the | Court of Great Britain. | [rule] | Philadelphia: | printed by E. Oswald, No. 156, Market-Street, South. | [rule] | M,DCC,XCV.

[A]⁴[B]–G⁴=28 leaves, 8 vo; (7)8–56 ¶ Evans 29256, Sabin 25640 ¶ MWA

Contents: title, blank, address, dated 18th June 1795 [3, 4]; Advertisement, blank, Letters [7]–53; letter of Philo-Franklin dated June 12, 1795, 54–56. Running titles. In the MWA copy the advertisement precedes the address.

This work was considered in detail by Cobbett in 'A Little Plain English...' (No. 7a), which see for a discussion of its publication and authorship. Evans attributed it to Oswald, the printer of the work, but Dallas seems more likely, as Cobbett evidently thought. Thus in his Porcupine's Works (1801) (No. 59), Volume II page 355, where 'Plain English' is reprinted, there is a note appended in reference to 'Franklin': 'The vile Dallas, Secretary, of the state of Pennsylvania.'

132b ———. Signature B is printed. ¶ CTY

133a [Randolph, Edmund Jennings] 1753–1813.

A | vindication | of | Mr. Randolph's | resignation | [rule] | Philadelphia: | Printed by Samuel H. Smith. | No. 118, Chesnut Street. | [rule] | M,DCC,XCV.

[A]²B–N⁴,O²=52 leaves, 8 vo; (5)6–98(1)100–103(1) ¶ Evans 29384, Sabin 67817, 99797+ ¶ MWA

Contents: title, copyright notice, nine line errata note, blank, statement of facts &c. [5]–98, appendix [99]–103, blank.

Cobbett made a strong attack on this pamphlet in his 'A New-Year's Gift to the Democrats...' (No. 10a) published in January 1796. Cobbett wrote (page 7) that the 'Vindication' was published December 18, 1795. 116th Pennsylvania District Copyright issued to Samuel Harrison Smith as proprietor, November 9, 1795. (Only a title page had to be presented to obtain copyright). Gazette of the United States, December 14, 1795: 'This day is published...'

133b ———. Same transcription and contents. Same collation and pagination except that signature K is preceded by a dagger mark † to indicate resetting. ¶ MWA

133c ———. Same transcription and contents.

[A]²†B–†N⁴†O²=52 leaves, 8 vo; (5)6–98(1)100–103(1) ¶ Evans 29385 ¶ CTY; MWA

Here the errata note is followed by four lines beginning: 'Extract of a letter from Mr. Randolph to the printer.' The second erratum

is corrected. Signatures †B through †I reset and the † added to signatures L–O. Example of change: on page [5], in the caption, No.
133b has '&c' and No. 133c has '&c.'

134   [Swanwick, John] 1740–1798.

A | rub from snub; | or a | cursory analytical | epistle: | addressed
to | Peter Porcupine, | author of the Bone to Gnaw, Kick for a |
Bite, &c. &c. | [rule] | containing, | glad tidings for the Democrats,
and a word of | comfort to Mrs. S. Rowson. | [rule] | wherein the
said Porcupine's moral, political, | critical and literary character is |
fully illustrated. | [rule] | Philadelphia, | printed for the purchasers. |
1795.

[A]–K⁴=40 leaves, 8 vo; (5)vi(1)8–80 ¶ Evans 29594 ¶ cty;
MWA

Contents: half-title, blank, title, blank, preface [v]vi, Epistle [7]–
72, A Word of Comfort to Mrs. Rowson, 72–80. Subscribed p. 80
'Citizen Snub'. Page 80 and part of 79 in smaller type. The page
numbering is unusual: the numbers 8 to 80 are underlined; p. 8 has
a single parenthesis to the right; the other pages have a single
bracket on the inner side of the number.

Some errors noted: p. 10 l. 4, 'indeliable'; p. 32, l. 11 'where' for
'were'; p. 41 note, 'Delagate'; p. 63, l. 11, 'uless'. In the preface the
author says he has 'undertaken the chastisement of Peter Porcupine
...' He devotes pp. [7]–38, 64–65 and 72–80 to this task, in not a light
manner. Pp. 66–72 are devoted to King George, with a doggerel
parody of 'God Save the King' in 14 stanzas, which no doubt an-
noyed Cobbett more than the attack on him. Cobbett frequently
derided Swanwick, as the Index will show. In the Political Censor
for September (No. 20a) p. 53, he identified 'Snub' as being the
same man as the author of 'A Roaster...by Sim Sansculotte' (No.
150) identified as Swanwick, 'the blunderbuss author, who disgusted
the city with *Rub from Snub*.' Cobbett bitterly attacked Swanwick in
his 'Letter to Citizen John Swanwick' annexed to MacKenzie's 'An
Answer to Paine's Rights of Man' (No. 22).

135   Anonymous.

A | Twig of Birch | for a | butting calf; | or, | strictures | upon re-
marks on the emigration of | Doctor Joseph Priestley, &c. &c. |
[rule] | By 'A brother of the birch'. | [rule] | to which is added, | an
historical anecdote. | translated from the French. | [rule] | [four

lines quoted from] | M'Fingal | [rule] | New-York: | Printed by J. Buel, No 152, Water Street | M,DCC,XCV.

[A],B⁴D⁴D–F⁴=24 leaves, 8 vo; (3)4–39(2)42–46(2) ¶ Evans 29965 ¶ MWA; NN (repro.)

Contents: title; blank; To the author [3]–39; copyright secured; Historical anecdote [41]–46; blank leaf.

An answer to Cobbett's 'Observations on the emigration of Dr. Joseph Priestley...' (No. 2a). It is scholarly and comparatively restrained. The anecdote concerns Archimedes. The work is attributed to Priestley in Bulletin, British Association for American Studies, No. 2, new series, March 1961, p. 25, note 9.

On page 5 line 7 reference is made to 'your third edition', so the work followed Bradford's Philadelphia edition of 1795 (No. 2h).

A few errors noted: p. 6, l. 2 'lest' for 'least'; p. 7, l. 3 'unvail'; p. 26, l. 2 'insiduously'.

1796

136a   [Bradford, Samuel F.] 1776–1837.

The | impostor detected, | or | a review | of | some of the writings | of | "Peter Porcupine." | [rule] | By Timothy Tickletoby | [rule] | [two lines from] | Pope. | [rule] | To which is annexed | a refreshment for the memory of | William Cobbet [sic], | by | Samuel F. Bradford | [rule] | Philadelphia: | from the free and independent | political & literary | press of | Thomas Bradford, | printer, bookseller & stationer, | No. 8, South Front Street. | [rule] | 1796.

[A]–I⁴K²=38 leaves, 8 vo; (3)iv–xvii(2)20–51(4)4–23(1) ¶ Evans 30019 ¶ MWA; NN (repro.)

Contents: title, blank, To the reader [iii]–xvii, dated at the end 'Philadelphia, August 26, 1796.'; blank; The impostor detected, &c. [19]–51, 'copy right secured according to law' at foot of page 51; blank; second title, with type-ornament rules above and below; blank; A refreshment, &c. [3]–23, subscribed Samuel F. Bradford; blank. Pages 21–23 contain a letter to Mr. Bache from 'a correspondent' [i.e., Cobbett] dated 'Burlington, June 2, 1795.' Running title pp. iv–xvii.

Some errors noted: p. 30, l. 24 'Serjeant'; p. 37, l. 8 and p. 38 l. 11 'Priestly'; p. [3] l. 18, p. 11, l. 3, and p. 18, l. 23 'Cobbet'; p. 4, ll. 27, 28 'and and'; p. 5 ll. 4, 5 'on on'; p. 7, ll. 15, 16 and p. 11 ll. 24, 25 'in in'; and p. 22, l. 10 'raiise'.

The two works are almost entirely a long tirade against Cobbett by the son of Thomas Bradford, Cobbett's one-time printer. Much space is devoted to the Life and Adventures (No. 19a). Pages v–vii give extracts from the Centinel of Boston favorable to Cobbett as evidence of the workings of a British faction. Pages 39–41 contain a footnote subscribed by T. Bradford. Samuel speaks of Cobbett publications by the Bradfords. At page 14 lines 10–12 he says of the first edition of 'Observations on Doctor Priestley' (No. 2a, no copy known) that the imprint was 'Philadelphia: printed by Thomas Bradford, No. 8, South Front Street'. On page 15, lines 23–25 he states that five times as many copies of the first edition of Bone to Gnaw were sold as of the Observations. On page 17 he writes that Cobbett abandoned the name 'Prospect from the Congress Gallery' (No. 11) in order to break his contract with Thomas and avoid his copyright. On pages 21–23 appears Cobbett's anonymous letter to Bache in which he writes a severe criticism of his own Bone to Gnaw, part II. (No. 6) Bache did not publish this.

149th Pennsylvania District Copyright issued to Thomas Bradford, as proprietor, September 3, 1796. Gazette of the United States, September 2, 1796 'on Monday [Sept. 5] will be published...'

The work was considered at length on pages 61–79 of the Political Censor for September (No. 20). At page 61 Cobbett writes as to the two parts of the work: 'It is evident...that both are by the same author' i.e. Samuel F. Bradford. At page 66 he says he wrote the letter signed 'A Correspondent.' 'The letter, as now printed by Bradford, may, for ought I know, be a very correct copy.' It 'is what is called a *Puff indirect*' and was written at the instance of Bradford. There are precedents in Addison, Phillips and Pope, Cobbett writes.

136b   [Bradford, Samuel F.] 1776–1837.

The | Impostor detected, | or | a review | of | some of the writings | of | "Peter Porcupine" | [rule] | By Timothy Tickletoby. | [rule] | [two lines from] | Pope. | [rule] | To which is annexed | a refreshment for the memory of | William Cobbett, | By | Samuel F. Bradford. | [rule] | second edition. | [rule] | Philadelphia: | from the free and independent | political & literary | press of | Thomas Bradford, | printer, bookseller & stationer, | No. 8, South front street. | [rule] | 1796.

[A]–I⁴K²=38 leaves, 8 vo; (3)iv–xvii(2)20–51(4)4–23(1) ¶ Evans 30120 ¶ DLC

Contents: As in first edition.

A new setting of type. See p. [19]: has '&c' for '&c', second rule is shorter than the first, page 39 last line begins 'ed', for 'ded'; second page [1] first and last rules were type ornaments; page [3] last line 'me.'; pages 4–20 are much altered.

137   [Callender, James Thomson] 1758–1803.

British Honour | and | humanity; | or, | the wonders | of | American patience, | as exemplified in the modest publications, and universal applause | of Mr. William Cobbet [sic]; including a variety of anecdotes | and remarks, personal and political, and a survey of | the modern state of American newspapers: | by | a friend to regular government. | [rule] | Philadelphia: | printed for and sold by Robert Campbell No. 40, South | Second Street. | [rule] | 1796.

[A]²B–D⁴D⁴F,G⁴H³=29 leaves, 8 vo; (2)3,4(1)6–58 ¶ Evans 31255, Sabin 94022+ ¶ MWA; NN (repro.)

Contents: title; Preface [2]–4, dated 'Philadelphia, Octob. 8, 1796'; British Honour, &c. [5]–58.

Errors noted: p. 10, ll. 7, 8 'the the'; p. 16, ll. 12, 13 last letter dropped; p. 41, last line 'termitate'; p. 55, l. 30 'editorail', l. 39 'uarrel'. Cobbett's name is always misspelled except p. 8, l. 1 and p. 46, l. 1

This is a long work, with 42 lines or more to a page and numerous notes in microscopic type. It is a defence of John Swanwick, whose name is mentioned no less than 36 times, an attack on Cobbett and on Great Britain and a defence of France. Mentioned and extracted from are ten or more of Cobbett's pamphlets, from Observations on Dr. Priestley to the Political Censor for September 1796.

In the postscript to Mackenzie 'An Answer to Paine's Rights of Man' (No. 22) Cobbett replied to this work (pp. [93]–96) and charged that Swanwick had paid the 'Scotch Runaway' [i.e. Callender] to write it. Cobbett quotes from page 47, lines 1–3, that Swanwick's 'disbursements to foundations of various kinds have amounted to a considerable sum' as evidence of Swanwick's participation. The work is reminiscent of Callender's 'The Political Progress of Britain' (No. 130) and may be considered a sequel. In fact the incident concerning Mrs. Caldwell of Connecticut Farms, at page 15, is a repetition of the same story at page 118 of Political Progress.

Evans attributed British Honour to John Swanwick, but it is evident from the note to Evans 30727 that he had confused British Honour and Rub from Snub (No. 134). Callender as much as claimed the authorship of British Honour in his American Annual Register (No. 151) page 196 lines 34, 35 and note. In the latter work, the Caldwell incident is mentioned again, page 268, lines 4, 5.

Claypoole's American Daily Advertiser, October 11, 1796: 'This day is published...'

138 [Carey, James] d. 1801.

A | Pill for Porcupine: | being a | specific | for an | obstinate itching | which that hireling has long contracted for lying and calumny. | containing, | a vindication | of the | American, French, and Irish characters, | against his scurrilities. | [rule] | By a friend to political equality. | [rule] | [seven lines quoted from] | Miles in answer to Burke's address to the Duke of Bedford. | [rule] | Philadelphia: | Printed for the author [by Stewart and Cochran] | [rule] | September 1, 1796.

[A]²B–L⁴=42 leaves, 8 vo; (3)iv(1)6–83(1) ¶ Evans 30155, Clark p. 190 ¶ MWA; NN (repro.)

Contents: title; blank; Preface [iii]–iv, with 2 line errata at the foot of p. iv; A Vindication [5]–83; blank. Catchwords. Running title p. iv.

Some errors noted: p. 22, next last 'panygeric'; p. 52, l. 28 'ones's'; p. 53, third from last 'unlimitted'; p. 57, ll. 17, 18 are garbled; p. 78, l. 13 'heirs' for 'hairs'.

In spite of the title, the work is a stronger attack on Alexander Hamilton than on Cobbett. Pages 13–24, 26–33, 43–5 and elsewhere are devoted to Hamilton, or more than one fourth of the text. The writer goes pretty low too. Thus on page 21 he asserts 'that Mrs. Maginnis was among the number of those ladies, which Mr. Hamilton let into the secrets of the funding system...' [i.e. leaked to her U.S. Treasury secrets]. Mrs. Maginnis was evidently a brothel keeper (see also page 62, lines 23, 24). On page 44, lines 24, 25 he writes as to Hamilton 'he has a wonderful itching after other men's wives,' even 'an African' (line 30). Cobbett receives his share of abuse. At pages 56 and 57 he is accused of seducing a young girl— specifically 'the girl who lived with him as his wife.' (57 note). On page 62 line 9 the writer fabricates an obscenity and states it comes from the May Political Censor (No. 17). Pages 33–41 defend the Irish, and there is much in praise of John Swanwick.

In the Political Censor for September (No. 20a) Cobbett devoted three pages (58–61) to the Pill, 'this quacks compound of filth', quoting the attack on his wife and answering vigorously.

'Tit for Tat; or a Purge for a Pill' by Benjamin Davies (No. 141) is an answer to this in detail, although not much related to Cobbett. Davies identifies the author as Irish and devotes a paragraph and a half of the Preface (pp. iv, v) to the publisher 'a sober old gentleman, with the phiz of a covenanting elder'. Concerned in the distribution he writes were [James] Carey, [Henry and Patrick] Rice and [Robert] Campbell (p. iv, l. 26).

Mathew Carey in his 'To the Public' (No. 140) gives the publication date of 'The Pill' as 'about the first of September.' Claypoole's American Daily Advertiser, September 3, 1796: 'this day is published and to be sold by Stewart and Cochran...'

139   [Carey, James] d. 1801.

He wou'd be | a poet; | or, | "nature will be nature still." | an | heroic poem: | to which is annexed | a thanksgiving epistle | on | electioneering success. | [rule] | By Geoffrey Touchstone | [rule] | Philadelphia: | printed for the author. | [rule] | 1796.

[A]–C⁴[D]²=14 leaves, 8 vo; (5)6–24(1)26–28 ¶ Evans 30154; Clark pp. 54, 190 ¶ MWA

Contents: title, blank, argument [3] [4]; He wou'd be a poet [5]–24, A Thanksgiving epistle. [25]–28. Running title on p. [4]. Error noted p. 12, l. 1 'rien' for 'rein'.

Gazette of the United States, October 26, 1796: 'This day is published...'

The work is a mock heroic poem on John Swanwick as a poet, educator, merchant and legislator. The epistle celebrates his re-election to Congress. He is identified as 'John S—K' on page 9 line 9 and again on page 24 last line.

Cobbett (or Porcupine rather) receives brief mention on page 12 lines 16–20 and page 13 lines 1–6, in a mild way. Carey gives himself a puff (page 13, lines 3, 4): 'The Pill's great author, so replete with wiles, | at first (I'm told) gave Porcupine the piles...', referring to Carey's 'A Pill for Porcupine...' (see preceding entry).

140   Carey, Mathew 1760–1839.

[rule] | To the Public. | Philadelphia, November 14, 1796. [caption title].

[A]²=two leaves, 8 vo; (1)2–4. ¶ Evans 30160 ¶ NN (repro.)

Error noted: p. 4, l. 5: 'rotrospect'.

Carey writes to disclaim authorship of 'A Pill for Porcupine' (No. 138), attributed to James Carey, who was Mathew's brother (see 'Plumb Pudding' (No. 160) page 14, line 1.) He quotes a letter to Cobbett of September 6, 1796, disclaiming any intention of a controversy, and Cobbett's concurring reply of September 7. He gives facts about his flight from Ireland and his beginnings in this country in humble circumstances.

141   [Davies, Benjamin] fl. 1774–1806.

Tit for Tat; | or, | a purge for a pill: | being | an answer to a scurrilous pamphlet, | lately published, entitled | "A Pill for Porcupine." | to which is added, | a poetical rhapsody | on | the times. [by William Cliffton] | describing | the disasters of an emigrant. | [rule] | [6 lines of verse] | [rule] | By Dick Retort. | [rule] | Philadelphia: | printed for the author. [1796].

[A]¹[B]–E⁴;[A]–C⁴[D]¹=30 leaves, 8 vo; (3)iv,v(2)8–34;(3) 4–25(1) ¶ Evans 30314, Clark pp. 75, 100 ¶ MWA; RPJCB (repro.)

Contents: title; blank; Preface [iii]–v; blank; Tit for Tat, &c [7]–34; second title; blank; Rhapsody on the times [3]–25; blank. Running title pp. iv, v.

Some errors noted: p. [7], ll. 19, 20 'by by'; p. 8, l. 1 'polititics'; p. 20, l. 3 'intersprerse'; l. 32 'Pampheteer'; second p. 11, l. 23 'hey' and 'the' for 'they'; p. 24, l. 15 'setpent'. Davies answers James Carey's 'Pill for Porcupine' (No. 138). Though he was Cobbett's friend, he makes only brief passing references to Porcupine on pages [iii], [7], 8, 10 and 24. In the second part Cliffton tells of Paddy's flight from Ireland and reception here. There is a brief mention on page 22, lines 1–16, of an encounter with 'the keen, bright, quills of Porcupine.'

The work is attributed to Davies in Mathew Carey's 'To the Public' (No. 140) and the publication date given as November 7, 1796. Claypoole's American Daily Advertiser, November 7, 1796: 'this day is published, for the author...and sold by B. Davies.'

142   [Henderson, A.]

The | Adventures of a porcupine; | or, | the villain unmask'd: | being the | genuine memoirs of a notorious rogue | lately in the British army, | and | ci-devant member of an extensive | light-fingered association | in England. | containing a narrative of the most extraordinary and | unexampled depravity of conduct perhaps | ever exhibited to the world. | in a letter to a young gentleman in New-York. | "These things are strange, but not more strange than true." | [rule] | To which is added, | a postscript to Peter Porcupine; | being | remarks | on a pamphlet lately published by him, entitled, his | "Life and adventures." | By Daniel Detector. | "I'll tell the bold fac'd villain, that he lies." | embellished with a likeness of the Porcupine | [rule] | Philadelphia, | printed for, and sold by A. & J. G. Henderson; | also, by the different booksellers. | September, 1796.

[π]¹[A]–D⁶=25 leaves, 8 vo; (2)(5)6–32(1)34–47(1). Second and third leaves signed A–C, also D3 ¶ Evans 30553 ¶ DLC

Contents: blank, plate, title, copy-right secured according to law, preface [3] [4]; The | Adventures of a Porcupine | [rule] [5]–32; A | postscript to Peter Porcupine | [rule] [33]–47; Advertisement, for a History of France (Evans 30489). The plate shows: lower right, a porcupine erect, with a balloon reading in part 'give me but Guineas & the Independence of the United States shall sink beneath my venom'; upper left, a crowned figure with a balloon reading in part: 'we could not do it by force—let him have the Guineas'; below, a legend 'The Contract'. Running title page [4].

The DLC copy has endorsed on the title page in ink 'spurious wrote by A. Henderson T. Condie' (Thomas Condie was a Philadelphia bookseller when the pamphlet was published). Gazette of the United States, September 7, 1796. 'This day is published...'

There are many errors in the text of which a few: p. [5] beginning the first paragraph 'At' is above the line of type; p. 9, l. 10 'proyerty', ll. 20, 21 'whose whose'; p. 20, l. 7 'immediatly'; p. 43, l. 15 'ther' for 'there', l. 21 'in in'.

The 'Adventures' of course bear no resemblance to that facts of Cobbett's life. In the postscript an attempt is made to discredit Cobbett, mainly on the ground of unaccountable financial resources. In the September Political Censor (No. 20) Cobbett took note of this work in sixteen lines (pp. 57, 58) under the heading 'The History of a Porcupine', beginning: 'This pamphlet is, I am told, copied, *verbatim*, from a chap-book, containing the lives of several men who were executed in Ireland some years ago.'

143   [Hopkinson, Joseph ?]1770–1842.

A | Congratulatory Epistle | to the | redoubtable "Peter Porcupine." | on his | "complete triumph | over the | once towering but fallen and despicable faction, | in the United States:" | A poem, | [rule] | By Peter Grievous, Junʳ. | [rule] | [two lines quoted from] | Swift. | [rule] | To which is annexed | The Vision, | A dialogue | between Marat and Peter Porcupine, | in the infernal regions. | [rule] | Philadelphia: | from the free and independent | political & literary | press of | Thomas Bradford, | printer, bookseller & stationer, | No. 8, South Front Street. | [rule] | 1796.

[A]²[B]–F⁴=22 leaves, 8 vo; (5)6–39(2)42–44 ¶ Evans 30593, Sabin 14025 ¶ MWA

Contents: half-title, blank, title, blank, 'A | Congratulatory Epistle, &c.' [5]–39; on p. 39 'The End', 'Copy right secured according to law'; blank, The Vision [41]–44; on p. 44 'The End', 'In the free and independent press a new edition of Porcupine's Plain English.'

Some errors: p. 8, l. 8 'allusion' for 'illusion'; p. 23, l. 2 'griding'; p. 26, l. 18 'expidition.'

There are sharp attacks on Cobbett at pages 38–39 and 43–44. Pages 8–19 contain a satire on the American Revolution and 22–30 on the French Revolution and Bonaparte. Mention is made (p. 30) of the Scare-crow (No. 18a) published in late July and of the Independent Gazetteer of July 20, 1796. The work is not noticed among other anti-Cobbett publications in the September Censor (No. 20a), published in late September. Gazette of the United States, October 4, 1796: 'This day is published by T. Bradford...'

158th Pennsylvania District Copyright issued to Thomas Bradford as proprietor, October 3, 1796.

The work is ascribed to Hopkinson by Evans (but not the short title Evans) and by Sabin. Francis Hopkinson his father used the pseudonym 'Peter Grievous'. In the biography of the son, 'Joseph Hopkinson 1770–1842' by Burton A Konkle, Philadelphia 1931, there is no mention of this work.

144   [Lee, Richard]

Political | Curiosities, | including | an account of the state of | political affairs | in | Europe | by a society of patriots. | [vignette] |

printed for | Richard Lee, | No. 84 Mulberry-street, near the corner of Third-street. | Philadelphia. [1796].

8 vo ¶ Evans 31010 ¶ MWA

Contents: title page; dedication: "To | His sublime excellency, | Peter Porcupine, Esq. | minister plenipo' | from the | sacred, mighty and immaculate | British Court, | to the now free and independent | Republic of America, | This volume is presented | with the greatest | &c. &c. &c. | By the editor."; followed by a motley collection of pamphlets, mainly English 1795, and some Lee advertising.

145   A caricature of Cobbett, untitled. Anonymous [1796].

Broadside, 24.7 x 30.8 cm.

Cobbett is pictured as a porcupine trampling on Randolph's "defence," Paine's works, Madison, Gallatin, Swanwick, Volney and Wolcott. Opposite is a crowned British Lion, with a jay on his back holding a treaty in its beak, behind him the Devil with a money bag. The lion is saying, 'Go on dear Peter; my friend and I will reward you.' (printed upside down). Below the cartoon are two couplets side by side, the first reading: 'See Porcupine in coulours just portray'd | urg'd by old Nick to drive his dirty trade...'

Evans 30820 ¶ PHi (PPL)

Gazette of the United States, September 2, 1796, and Claypoole's American Daily Advertiser, September 3, 1796: 'Porcupine a print to be had at Moreau de St. Méry's book store.' Cobbett commented on the print in the Censor for September (No. 20), page 57, that it came from the same quarter as the Blue Shop (see next entry), published by Moreau de St.-Méry. Evans entered the item under Moreau de St. Méry. Reproduced, under date of [1799], in Nevins, Allan and Weitenkampf, Frank, 'A Century of Political Cartoons... 1800–1900', New York, 1944, page 22.

146   [Puglia, Santiago Felipe (James Philip)] b. 1760.

The | Blue Shop | or | impartial and humorous observations | on the | Life and Adventures | of | Peter Porcupine, | with the | real motives which gave rise to his | abuse of our distinguished | patriotic characters; | together with | a full and fair review of his late | Scare-Crow. | [rule] | By James Quicksilver. | [rule] | Philadelphia: | Printed by Moreau de St.-Méry, N° 84, Corner of | Front and Walnut Streets. | [rule] | August 1796.

[A]⁴A–E⁴F²=26 leaves, 8 vo; (3)iv–viii(1)10–48(1)50–52. Second leaves signed A2, A2–E2 ¶ Evans 31065, Clark p. 190 ¶ NN (repro.) PHi (PPL)

Contents: title; blank; Preface [iii]–viii; The Blue Shop [9]–48, with 'Copy right secured according to law' at the foot of p. 48; Postscript [49]–52, with an advertisement at the foot of p. 52. Running title pp. iv–viii. On page [9] at top, row of type ornaments between rules; page 48 'FINIS' ornamented. Catchwords at the end of each signature. Rule above each footnote.

Some errors noted: p. 12, l. 15 'Porcurpine'; p. 21, l. 27 'contended' for 'contented'; p. 23, l. 1 'militar'; p. 26, l. 17 'cautions' for 'cautious'; p. 28, l. 10 'wich'; p. 29, l. 12 'breathen'; p. 39, l. 7 'endued'.

Claypoole's American Daily Advertiser, and Gazette of the United States, August 30, 1796: 'just published'.

The work considers the Life (No. 19a) in detail, with many page references, in a style much lighter than most. Pages 38–48 are devoted to the Scare-Crow (No. 18). On page [iii] the author says that on August 8th he purchased a copy of the Life at the 'Blue Shop', i.e. Cobbett's shop. On p. 51 note he repeats the publication date as the 8th and writes that he put the present work to the press on the 17th. On page 52 he writes that in three weeks he will publish 'The Disappointment or Peter Porcupine in London, a comedy in three acts written by James Quicksilver.' On page [30] of the 'Political Massacre...' by the same author (see next entry), the same title is advertised as 'shortly will be published.' Evans 32731 includes such a title as published in 1797, but locates no copy and none is known. For the present work, 145th Pennsylvania District Copyright issued to Moreau de St. Méry as proprietor, August 22, 1796.

Cobbett commented on the 'Blue Shop' in the Censor for September (20a) in 16 lines on pp. 53, 54, deriding the use of the word 'humorous' in connection with it.

Mathew Carey wrote in his autobiography in 1833 (ed. Brooklyn, N.Y. 1942, p. 30): 'a certain Joseph Scott [Philadelphia gazetteer] wrote a pamphlet against Cobbet [sic] entitled the Blue Shop, in allusion to the colour of his windows and shutters.' Carey does not mention the 'Political Massacre'. (next entry).

147   [Puglia, Santiago Felipe (James Philip)]. b. 1760

The | Political Massacre, | or | unexpected observations | on the | writings of our present | scribblers. | [rule] | By James Quicksilver, |

author of the Blue Shop. | [rule] | [ornament] | Philadelphia: | printed by Moreau de St. Méry, N° 84, corner of | Front and Walnut Streets. | [rule] | September 1796.

[A]–D⁴=16 leaves, 8 vo; (3)iv–vi(1)8–29(3). Second leaves signed. Folded plate 18 x 17 cm ¶ Evans 31066, Sabin 67166 ¶ PPL

Contents: title; blank; preface [iii]–vi; The Political Massacre [7]–29, 'copy right secured according to law' foot of page 29; advertisements (2); blank. The plate has six men grouped around a porcupine, with the head of Quicksilver at the door right, all crudely drawn. Running titles pp. iv–vi. Catchwords at the end of each signature. Rule above each note. Ornaments on pp. vi and 29 and row of printer's ornaments between rules at the top of p. [7]. Gazette of the United States, September 20, 1796, 'Just published from the press of Moreau de St. Méry...'

Some errors noted: p. v, l. 24 'commissionned'; p. 10, l. 31 'is' for 'it'; p. 13, l. 2 'yon' for 'you'; p. 17, l. 18 'Gobbett'; p. 26 note 'Blue Sop'.

Cobbett is mentioned here and there and discussed on pages 19–28. 'Daniel' or 'Daniel Detector' (i.e. A. Henderson, see No. 142) is discussed on pp. iv and 17–18; 'Doctor' (i.e. James Carey, see No. 138) on pp. 7–10; the Bradfords, Thomas and Samuel, and the Impostor Detected (No. 136) on pp. 10–17, 18, 19, 21; and John Fenno and B. F. Bache on pp. 23, 24. The advertisement on page [30] is for 'The Disappointment' and on page [31] for the 'Blue Shop'—see the preceding entry as to both of these.

151st Pennsylvania District Copyright issued to Moreau de St.-Méry as proprietor, September 17, 1796. Claypoole's American Daily Advertiser, September 21, 1796: 'just published.'

148   Select pamphlets: | viz. [8 titles of which No. 3 is] 3. A Bone to Gnaw for the Democrats—or | observations on a pamphlet, entitled, The Political | Progress of Britain... | [rule] | Philadelphia: | published by Mathew Carey, | No. 118, Market-Street. | [rule] | 1796. | (Price two dollars.)

The pamphlet 'Bone to Gnaw' included is the second edition, revised, printed by Thomas Bradford, 1795 (No. 3b).

¶ Evans 31173 ¶ MWA

149   Select Pamphlets: | viz | [eight titles listed of which No. 4 is] 4. New Year's Gift for the Democrats... | [rule] | Philadelphia: |

published by Mathew Carey, | No. 118, Market-Street, | [rule] | 1796. | (Price two dollars.)

The pamphlet 'A New Year's Gift...' is the 'second edition' printed by Thomas Bradford, 1796 (No. 10f).

¶ Evans 31174 ¶ MWA

150 [Swanwick, John] 1760–1798.

A | roaster; | or, | a check to the progress | of | political blasphemy: | intended | as a brief reply to | Peter Porcupine, alias Billy Cobler. | [rule] | By Sim Sansculotte. | [rule] | Philadelphia: | Printed by J. Johnson. | M.DCC.XCVI.

[A]–C⁴=12 leaves, 8 vo; (3)4–21(3) ¶ Evans 31256, Sabin 94025 ¶ cty; MWA

Contents: title, blank, A Roaster, &c. [3]–21, blanks (3) 'FINIS' on page 21.

Errors noted: p. 8, l. 6 'wouderful'; p. 12, note l. 2 'villancies'; p. 15, last 'pourtray'; p. 20, l. 23 'trajic.'

Claypoole's American Daily Advertiser, August 8, 1796: 'just published by T. Stephens'.

A number of Cobbett's works are discussed, principally the Scare-Crow but including Bone, Kick, Observations on Priestley and Bloody Buoy. At page 15 line 8 Swanwick says he will 'anticipate the speedy publication of his life' (No. 19a), which came out in August 1796. Since the Scare-Crow (No. 18a) came out in late July, the present work must have issued in early August 1796. Swanwick charged that Cobbett was an 'aristocratic tool...pensioned by the British despots...', and indulged in a lot of name-calling.

In the Political Censor for September (No. 20a) (p. 53) Cobbett gave four lines to a reply to this: 'What can I say worse of this blustering performance, than that it bears all the internal evidence of being written by the blunderbuss author who disgusted the city with *Rub from Snub?* [No. 134]'.

1797

151a [Callender, James Thomson] 1758–1803.

The | American Annual Register, | or, | historical memoirs | of the | United States, | for the year 1796. | [rule] | Philadelphia: |

printed and sold by Bioren & Madan, No. 77, Dock-Street | [rule] | January 19th, 1797.

[π]⁴A–Nn⁴=148 leaves, 8 vo; (3)iv–vii(2)2–288 ¶ Evans 31905, Sabin 10062 ¶ CTY

Contents: title; entered according to law; contents [iii]–vii; blank; The | American Annual Register, | for the year 1796, [1]–288. Postscript on page 288 noting two errata, followed by 'The end.' Running title pp. iv–vii.

Some errors noted: p. v, l. 2, 'and' for 'an'; l. 6 'Governs' for 'Govern-'; p. 93, note, 'Randolp.'; p. 281, l. 3 'house of representatives,' in lower case, and compare the table of contents, p. vii.

Cobbett or his works are mentioned or discussed on pages 160–5, 178, 203, 205, 213–4, 217, 247, 249 and 252. Page 178 lines 34–39 quote from the Political Censor for September (No. 20a) as an example of violence of style and conclude 'This is the stile of the most popular writer now in America.'

167th Pennsylvania District copyright issued to Bioren & Madan as proprietors, January 19, 1797. Gazette of the United States, January 28, 1797: 'This day is published...'

Callender's 'History of the United States for 1796', Evans 31906, noted for its disclosure of the relationship of Alexander Hamilton and Mrs. Reynolds, is a new work and not a new edition of the Register, as Evans thought. In the History, Cobbet [sic] receives mention on pages vii, viii, 25 and 223, note.

151b   ———. A variant in which the errors noted on page v have been corrected ¶ MWA

152   [Carey, James] d. 1801.

Anticipation! | [rule] | Peter Porcupine's | Descent into | Hell: | or, | an elegy | on his death. | [rule] | a mock-heroic poem |[rule] | By Henry Hedgehog. | [rule] | The second edition, corrected. | [rule] | Philadelphia: | Printed by James Carey, No. 83, North Second-street | [rule] | September 25, 1797.

[A]⁴=4 leaves, 8 vo; (3)4–8 ¶ Evans 31914, Clark p. 104 ¶ DLC

Contents: title, blank, Anticipation! [3]–8. At the top of page [3] a three-line rule; subscription page 8: 'Henry Hedgehog', followed by 'Finis,' ornamented (the ornament looks identical with that used by Moreau de St. Méry in 'The Blue Shop' (No. 146) the previous year).

Errors noted: in the title the word 'Descent' is badly misaligned; page number 4, the bracket is not closed. In another copy 'INTO' in the title is misaligned.

No copy of the first edition appears to have survived.

The poem celebrates Peter's death, burial, trip to the infernal regions, welcome there and the mourning for him. He is called some harsh names in the process. A sample couplet (page 7):

'No more will he Columbia's children drench
With cruel falshoods father'd on the French.'

Porcupine's Gazette October 6, 1797 states this work was advertised by James Carey in Merchant's Daily Advertiser September 15, 1797.

153a   Fauchet, Joseph 1761–1834.

A | sketch | of the | present state | of our | political relations | with the | United States of North-America. | [rule] | By Joseph Fauchet, | Ex-Minister of the | French Republic | at Philadelphia. | [rule] | Translated by the Editor of the Aurora. [B. F. Bache] | [rule] | Philadelphia; | Printed by Benj. Franklin Bache, No. 112, Market-Street. | M,DCCXCVII. [sic].

[A]–D⁴=16 leaves, 8 vo; (3)4–31(1) ¶ Evans 32115, Sabin 23921 ¶ CTY

Contents: title, blank, 'A Sketch, (a) &c.' [3]–31, blank. One line 'Errata' on page 31. A note, pages 23,24, quotes from a speech made May 22, 1797.

Some errors noted: p. 14, fourth last 'nation' for 'nations'; p. 18, l. 3 'tht'; p. 27, fourth last 'wh le'. P. 25, ll. 18–23, Cobbett is singled out for special mention on anti-French writings: 'A writer, publicly known to be in the pay of the British legation, publishes periodically in Philadelphia, the most atrocious libels against us; and it is almost certain that this libeller is encouraged by all those who compose the administration.' A note identifies the writer: 'His name is Cobbel [sic], and he writes under the name of Peter Porc-Epic [sic]'.

153b   ———. A variant in which the error noted on page 27 has been corrected ¶ MWA

154a   Anonymous.

The | last confession | and | dying speech | of | Peter Porcupine, | with | an account of his dissection. | [rule] | Philadelphia: | printed, and sold by the booksellers, | May 22, 1797. Title within mourning border.

[A]–D⁴=16 leaves, 8 vo; (3)4–32 ¶ Evans 32353 ¶ cty

Contents: title, blank; The confession... [3]–24; Execution and dissection... 25–31; glossary 31, 32.

Evans notes the printing was by William T. Palmer.

Some errors noted: p. 4, l. 3, 'ignominous'; p. 10, ll. 5, 6 'iniquites', l. 13 'were' for 'where'; p. 12, ll. 12, 22, p. 13, l. 9 'Priestly'; p. 21, l. 9 'catatlogue'; p. 26 next last 'folloing'.

Using sentences and phrases from the Life and Adventures... (No. 19), the work depicts a career of crime and deceit. In Philadelphia, Porcupine receives from an English agent a subsidy, house rent and a fund to start his daily paper, all with support of the Administration. He is ultimately hung for treason and dissected, the description of which is nauseous.

154b ———. Same transcription except after 'dissection': | [rule] Second edition! |; and except dated May 27, 1797. Same collation, pagination and contents, etc ¶ Evans 32354 ¶ cty; DLC

The errors noted are not corrected except that on page 21. Pasted to first leaf verso is an advertisement for 'Cannibals' Progress. No. 2, this day published.

154c ———. Same transcription as 154b except dated 'June 1797'.

[A]–C⁶=18 leaves, 17.5 cm. (trimmed); (3)4–36. Third leaves signed A2–C2 ¶ Evans 32355 ¶ DLC

Contents: title, blank, The confession [3]–26; death and dissection 27–34; glossary 34–36.

154d The | last confession | and | dying speech | of | Peter Porcupine, | with | an account of his dissection. | [rule] | New-York: | printed and sold--price one shilling | [rule] | 1797.

[A],B⁶C²=14 leaves; (3)4–28. Third leaf A3; ninth leaf B2 ¶ Evans 32356 ¶ NHi (repro.)

Contents: title, blank, The Confession... [3]–28. Subtitles pages 23 and 27. Ornament foot of page 28.

1798

155a [Carey, James] d. 1801.

The | House of Wisdom | in a | bustle; | A poem, | descriptive of
the noted | battle, | lately fought in C–NG---SS | [rule] | By Geof-
frey Touchstone | [rule] | Philadelphia: | printed for the author. |
[rule] | 1798. | [price 25 cents.]

[A]–C⁴D²=14 leaves, 8 vo; (3)4–27(1) ¶ Evans 33490 ¶ MWA

Contents: title, blank, The House of Wisdom... [3]–27, blank. A
small blow at 'Porcupine' occurs on page 4, lines 2–4. The poem
deals with the fracas on the floor of the House between Matthew
Lyon of Vermont and Roger Griswold of Connecticut, in which the
former spat and the latter used a cane.

155b The | House of Wisdom | in a | bustle. | A poem, | descrip-
tive of the noted | battle | lately fought in C–NG—SS. | [rule] | By
Geoffry [sic] Touchstone. | [rule] | New-York: | printed for the
purchasers. | [rule] | 1798. | [price 25 cents.]

[A]–C⁴=12 leaves, 8 vo; (3)4–24 ¶ Evans 33492 ¶ MWA

Contents: title, blank, The House of Wisdom... [3]–24. 'The end'
on page 24.

156 [Carey, James] d. 1801.

The | Life of skunk Peter | Porcupine | and his two uncles the cob-
bler and salm-singer | [rule] | [twelve lines of verse] | [rule] | [rule] |
Printed at Constantinople. | At the sign of the heads of traytors,
Arnorld [sic], Gob- | bet [sic], and Blount and next door to the
knights of | "the last ditch". [Phila. 1798 ?]

[A]⁶=six leaves, 20.5 cm; (3)4–12 ¶ Evans 33493 ¶ NHi

Contents: title, a fragment, A short sketch [3]–12. In the title
page verse, eighth line, 'satesmen'; page [2] third from last line
'Brititish'; page 11 l. 14 'jumpping'.

A fanciful tale. 'bones to knaw' are attacked on page 5. There are
other references that fit Cobbett.

157 [Carey, James] d. 1801.

A | Nosegay, | for the | young men | from 16 to 24 years of age. |
A true picture of the King of England. | dedicated to his hireling

skunk Porcupine, | with his petition to the corporation, of the city |
of Philadelphia, | &c. &c. &c. | [rule] | [seven lines quoted] | The
substance of Mr. Ames's speech on the B. Treaty | [rule in nine
parts] | Printed at Philadelphia, next door to Porcupine's | coat of
arms, a bull's eye, a baboons head, and a lions tail. | sold at the
book-stores,–price one shilling. [1798]

[A]⁸=eight leaves, 8 vo; (3)4–16. Page no. 6 obliterated ¶ Evans
33494 ¶ DLC

Contents: title, Dedication to Skunk Porcupine, with note; Mr.
Grey's letter [3]–7; A monument 7, 8; attack on Cobbett 9, 10;
British Clemency 10–12; attack on the administration 12, 13; the
petition of Skunk Peter Porcupine 14; his epitaph, etc. 15, 16.

This is slovenly, a mish-mash of types, with many errors of
grammar and spelling. A sampling of the latter: p. [3], l. 14 'Chis-
tian'; p. 5, l. 19 'contemptiple'; p. [6], l. 6 'ownly'; p. 8, note last
'dow'; p. 13, l. 25 'affars', l. 26 'dermination'.

Cobbett is a target, as is Alexander Hamilton and the British
generally. Evans notes that the printing was by James Carey.

158   [Murdock, John] 1748–1834.

The | Politicians; | or, | a state of things | [rule] | a dramatic
piece. | [rule] | written by an American, | and | a citizen of Philadel-
phia. | [rule] | Philadelphia: | printed for the author. | [rule] | 1798.

[A]–E⁴=20 leaves, 8 vo; (3)4–37(3) ¶ Evans 34160 ¶ DLC (repro.); MWA.

Contents: title; dramatis personae; The | Politicians &c. [3]–37;
three blanks. Running titles.

Peter Porcupine is mentioned once: p. 4, l. 4. A heavy-handed
work.

1799

159a   Carey, Mathew 1760–1839

A | plumb pudding | for the | humane, chaste, valiant, enlight-
ened | Peter Porcupine. | [rule] | by his obliged friend, | Mathew
Carey. | [rule] | [line from] | Gen. xvi. 12. | If "blessed are the peace-
makers"—accursed be Porcupine, the apostle of blood | "hated by
knaves, and knaves to hate, | "be this my motto—this my fate." |

[rule] | [vignette] | Philadelphia: | printed for the author. | [copy right secured acccording [sic] to an act of Congress.] [1799] The vignette, an oval 4.5 x 5.8 cm., depicts a street scene with a large porcupine hanging from a lamp post.

[A]²B,C⁴D²E–G⁴=24 leaves, 8 vo; (5)6–48. Second leaves signed B2,C2,F2 ¶ Evans 35272 ¶ cty

Contents: title; Federalism of Peter Porcupine; Preface, dated January 16, 1799; Dedication; A | Plumb Pudding | for |Peter Porcupine [5]–48; The END on page 48. Catchwords beginning page [5], except pp. 13, 18, 24.

Some errors noted: p. 8, last 'Infam'; p. 17, last 'nstance'; p. 22 catchword ''Th'; p. 33, l. 13 'examplary'; p. 40, l. 11 'ʌuarter'; p. 41, l. 6 'June', should be January; page 45 l. 8 'Cobbet'.

This is a severe attack on Cobbett, which probably had an effect judging from the number of editions as well as from the text. Some extracts of interest:... 'This reptile dictates to the government in a style infinitely more authoritative than that of either the last or present president of the United States' [page 7]; 'A man who circulates two thousand papers daily...' [page 8]; 'Those who know him, will judge whether a man who has once seen his carotty head and Drawcansir* face, could ever forget him.' [page 10]. On page 11 Carey details his purchases from Bradford of 63 copies of Cobbett's Observations on the Emigration of Dr. Joseph Priestley (No. 2a), beginning with 36 copies on August 23, 1794. On pages 11 and 12 Carey gives details on his own publishing career, with business to the amount of 300,000 dollars and employment given to 150 persons in all its aspects. At pages 12 and 13 he republishes the letters from his 'To the Public...November 14, 1796' (No. 140). In his 'To the Public...Feb. 5, 1799' (No. 161), page 2 line 35, Carey wrote that the Plumb Pudding was published January 21, 1799.

219th Pennsylvania District copyright issued to Mathew Carey as author, January 19, 1799. As stitched the work has a plain blue wrapper.

159b ———. A variant in which the vignette has been reworked, and a sun now appears in upper right. The errors noted, including that on the title page, have not been corrected. ¶ Sabin 10881 ¶ cty; mwa

---

*A blustering braggart in Buckingham's play 'The Rehearsal' (1671).

159c ———. Second edition, in which a rule and the words 'The Second Edition' are added after 'Carey.' The vignette is in the second state. ¶ Evans 35273 ¶ MWA

The errors noted in the title and on pages 8, 17 and 41 have been corrected. Page number 9, parenthesis not closed. Includes No. 161.

160   [Carey, Mathew] 1760–1839.

Just Published, | by Mathew Carey, | No. 118, Market Street, | (price a quarter dollar.) | A Plumb Pudding | for the humane, valiant, chaste, enlightened | Peter Porcupine. | [rule] | To the puplic [sic] | A retailer of snuff, whom I formerly knew...[1799] [caption title].

Broadside 22.4 cm. ¶ S. T. Evans page 133, col. 3 ¶ NN

The body of the advertisement quotes two paragraphs, which are taken from the 'Plumb Pudding' (No. 159) pages 33, 34 and 47, 48, including the following, as a sample (page 47): 'Cowards and rascals are dangerous enemies. I would, therefore, rather have a contest of any sort whatever, with *ten gentlemen*, than with one Cobbett.'

161   Carey, Mathew 1760–1839.

[rule] | To the Public. | Philadelphia, Feb. 5, 1799. [caption title].
A⁴=4 leaves, 8 vo; (1)2–8 ¶ Evans 35274 ¶ CtY; PPL; RPJCB (repro.)

Subscribed at the end, Mathew Carey. On page two, Cobbett's name appears six times and is spelled 'Cobbet' three times. The work is primarily an attack on John Ward Fenno, editor of the Gazette of the United States, with Cobbett receiving incidental mention on all pages except 4.

162a   Carey, Mathew 1760–1839.

The | Porcupiniad: | a | Hudibrastic poem. | in four cantos. | addressed to | William Cobbett, | by | Mathew Carey. | [rule] | Canto I. | [rule] | [six lines quoted (the first beginning 'Republican ingratitude is proverbial') from four issues of] Porcupine's Gazette | [rule] | Philadelphia: | printed for and sold by the author. | March 2, 1799. | (copy-right secured according to Act of Congress.)

[π]¹[A]–F⁴G²=27 leaves, 8 vo; (2)(3)iv–vi(1)viii(1)10–52. ¶ Evans 35275 ¶ PHi (PPL)

Contents: blank, frontispiece, title, Federalism of Peter Porcupine, preface [iii]–vi, Observations on Hudibrastic poetry [vii]viii, The Porcupiniad [9]–52. The frontispiece is a sketch of the frontispiece and title page of the Bloody Buoy, with two lines of poetry below. 'Federalism' is the same, reset, as in Carey's 'Plumb Pudding' (No. 159). The preface is dated March 2d, 1799. On page 52, 'End of Canto I.' Running titles. Canto I is in 262 lines numbered every five lines except 145 and 195 and except irregular numbers 197, 204, 213, 224, 247, 254, 259 and 262. The notes outmatch the poetry.

Errors noted; p. 22, l. 12 'BEEORE'; p. 49, note l. 11 'Cobbet's' Universal Gazette, March 7, 1799: 'just published...'

162b The | Porcupiniad: | a | Hudibrastic poem. | in three cantos. | addressed to | William Cobbett. | by | Mathew Carey. | [rule] | Canto I. | [rule] | [rule] | second edition improved. | [rule] | [six lines quoted (the first quotation begins 'Thank Heaven...') from four issues of] Porcupine's Gazette | [rule] | Philadelphia: | printed for and sold by the Author. | April 22, M,DCC,XCIX. | (copy-right secured according to Act of Congress.)

[π]¹[A]–D⁴E²=19 leaves, 8 vo; (2)(3)iv–vi(1)viii(1)10–21(1) 23–35(1) ¶ Evans 35277 ¶ ctY; MWA

Contents: blank, frontispiece, title, Federalism of Peter Porcupine, preface [iii]–vi, Observations on Hudibrastic poetry [vii]viii, The Porcupiniad [9]–21, Appendix [22]–35, blank. The frontispiece and preliminaries as in the first edition, but a new setting of type throughout. The preface is dated March 2d, 1799. 'FINIS' at foot of page 35. Running titles except on page viii. Canto I of the Porcupiniad is in 262 lines, numbered every five lines except 145 and 225 and except that the concluding numbers are 247, 254 and 259. There are copious notes. The appendix contains extracts from Porcupine's Gazette designed to show the arrogance, vulgarity and violence of which Cobbett was capable and his contempt for republicanism. Found in a faded blue wrapper printed on the front recto with a title resembling that of No. 164.

Some errors noted: p. iv fifth last 'consideted'; p. 10 last "respectivele'; p. 11, note l. 7 'contary'; p. 18, note l. 7 'Ellizabeth' and l. 27 'difficuty'; p. 23, l. 31 'briug'; p. 24, first note † for *; p. 32 sixth and eleventh notes blank.

163 [Carey, Mathew] 1760–1839.

To the Public. | It is difficult to account for the rancour which the weak and wicked | John Ward Fenno displays against me...[1799] [Caption title].

Broadside. 21.5 cm ¶ S. T. Evans p. 134, col. 2 ¶ PPL

In the PPL copy the foot of the text has been trimmed off by the binder. Attributed to Carey by PPL.

The main target is Fenno, but Cobbett gets notice in one paragraph: 'That Cobbett, a low-bred alien, emerging from the dregs of the people, after serving six or seven years for sixpence a day, should publish a prostitute paper, open for the reception of the vilest abuse, and that he should enjoy and feast on the frightful repast of torn, mangled reputations, cannot astonish. But that John Ward Fenno...should, in the course of four or five months, have sunk nearly as low, by scurrility, abuse, and malignity, as Cobbett has been able to do in as many years, must surprise as well as afflict...'

164   Carey, Mathew 1760–1839.

The | Porcupiniad: | a | Hudibrastic poem. | In three Cantos. | addressed to | William Cobbett, | by | Mathew Carey. | [rule] | Canto II & III. | [rule] | [six lines quoted from four issues of] | Porcupine's Gazette | [rule] | Philadelphia: | printed for and sold by the author. | April 15, 1799.

[A]¹[B]⁶C–F⁴=23 leaves, 8 vo; (2)(3)iv(1)6,7(1)9,01,11–29(1) 31–38(1)40–44 ¶ Evans 35276 ¶ CtY; MWA

Contents: blank, frontispiece, title, blank, preface [iii]iv., the Porcupiniad | Canto II [5]–7(1)9–29; The Porcupiniad | Canto III [30]–38; appendix [39]–44. Page 10 numbered 01.

The frontispiece shows a man running from a crowd, with a gallows in the background, and two lines of verse below. (See frontispiece herein). The preface is dated April 15, 1799. Canto II is in 584 lines numbered every five lines (with several omissions) omitting to count a line between 210 and 215, line 212 numbered 211. Many footnotes with notes to footnotes. Canto III the numbering begins with 165 and continues each five lines, except lines numbered 184 and 204. The Appendix contains quotes from Porcupine's Gazette. The first quotation on the title page begins 'Republican ingratitude...' Running titles, with, however, 'The Porcupiniad' instead of 'Appendix.''

On page 38 'End of the third and last canto.' Found in faded blue wrapper printed on the front recto with a title closely approximating the title page, beginning, however, 'No. II' and ending '(copyright secured according to Act of Congress).'

Some errors noted: p. [5], note l. 2 and p. 9 note l. 2 'Cobbet'; p. 15 last note symbol missing.

The work is a sustained and bitter attack on Cobbett.

165   [Freneau, Philip] 1752–1832.

Letters | on | various interesting and important subjects; | many of which have appeared | in the | Aurora. | corrected and much enlarged.. | [rule] | By Robert Slender, O.S.M. | [rule] | [two lines from] | Pope's Essay. | [rule] | Philadelphia: | printed for the author. | from the press of D. Hogan- | and sold at his store, No. 222, South Third-street, and at | the office of the Aurora. | [rule] | December 30, 1799.

[A]–G⁴F⁴I–S⁴=72 leaves, 8 vo; (3)iv–viii (1)10–142(2) ¶ Evans 35516, B.A.L. 6450 ¶ MWA

Contents: title, entered according to Act of Congress, Fellow Citizens [iii]–viii, Slender's Letters [9]–142, advertisement, blank. Catchwords except pp. viii and 142. Page 47 for 74. B.A.L. notes a second state with page 47 correctly paged.

There are twenty-four letters, on current topics, mainly political. Cobbett is mentioned or discussed by name or as Porcupine on pages 28–30, 38, 41, 43, 55, 56, 105–6, 133, 136 and 142.

166   Anonymous.

To the freemen | of the | Northern-Liberties, | Fellow-Citizens, | The young men of our district have been addressed by an anonymous incendiary...[Philadelphia 1799] [caption title].

Broadside, 33.2 x 20.3 cm. ¶ Evans 36429 ¶ DLC

Subscribed at the foot 'BRUTUS.'

Peter Porcupine is identified as the author of the address objected to: 'There is a stamp of wickedness and a sanguinary disposition impressed upon all his transactions, which designate him as clearly as if Peter Porcupine was written upon his forehead.' '...wretch... foul leper of iniquity...hireling of a British minister...' etc., etc. The citizens are called on to shun the federalists and the British faction.

167   Anonymous.

[rule] | To the | independent electors of Pennsylvania. | Friends & fellow citizens. [1799] [caption title].

[A]⁴B²=6 leaves, 8 vo; (1)2–11(1) ¶ Evans 36432 ¶ PPL

Contents: text [1]–11, blank. Subscribed at the foot of page 11 'An American'. Catchwords.

The work attacks as members of a 'British party' General Edward Hand and Charles Smith, who issued an address from Lancaster favoring James Ross for Governor. Included as a prominent member of the 'party' is Cobbett, who receives mention on pages 4, 6–8 and 9. Reproduced at page 7 is the letter of W. Short August 6, 1792 to Jefferson introducing Cobbett, and at page 8 Cobbett's transmittal letter to Jefferson of November 2nd, 1792. These letters are substantially the same as the originals, the word 'days' in a P.S. to Cobbett's letter being changed to 'weeks', and emphasis supplied. At page 4 the loyalist 'anchor club' is described: 'Wm. Cobbett, a noted English emissary, was admitted and cooperated with them...' At page 6 Cobbett is represented as having deceived Jefferson as to his intention to become a citizen: '...this most base, most flagitious and most insolent foreign printer, is the intimate, the colleague, and the instrument of that British diplomatic corps...'

The Short and Cobbett letters appeared in the Philadelphia Aurora of August 1, 1799 and Cobbett replied in five and one-third columns of his Porcupine's Gazette August 12, 1799 (repeated August 19), in a 'Letter from William Cobbett to Thomas Jefferson.' In this, Cobbett charged a 'scandalous breach of confidence' on the part of Jefferson in making the letters available for publication and questioned his motive in so doing.

168   Priestley, Joseph 1733–1804

Letters | to the | inhabitants | of | Northumberland | and its | neighbourhood, | on subjects interesting to the author, | and to them. | Part I. [Part II] | [rule] | By Joseph Priestley, L.L.D. F.R.S. &c. | [rule] | —Nunquamne reponam? | Juvenal. | [rule] | Northumberland: | printed for the author by Andrew Kennedy. | [rule] | MDCCXCIX.

Part I: [A]²B–G⁴=26 leaves, 8 vo; (5)2–48 ¶ Evans 36161 ¶ CtY

Evans notes some copies dated MDCCLXLIX.

Contents: title, blank, contents, blank, 'To the inhabitants...' [in seven letters] [1]–48. Five errata on page 48. Running titles, catchwords. Final letter dated, p. 43, 'Nov. 1, 1799.'

Some errors noted: p. 10, l. 16 'impossibie'; p. 15, l. 13 'thiug'; p. 16, l. 12 'peculicar'; p. 18, l. 24, 1788 for 1798. Cobbett (always spelled Cobbet) is the subject of Letter VI, pp. 30–37, entitled 'of the style of abuse in the writings of Mr. Cobbet, alias Peter Porcupine'. He or his writings are mentioned also on pages 2, 4, 12, 29, 38, 41, 43 and 45.

Part II: [A]–E⁴[F]²=22 leaves, 8 vo; (3)4–32(1)34–42(2) ¶ Evans 36162 ¶ cty; MWA

Contents: title, blank, 'to the inhabitants...' [letters viii–xii] [3]–32; 'Maxims of political arithmetic...' [33]–42; The contents; blank. Running titles, catchwords. The 'Maxims' are reprinted from the Philadelphia Aurora. 'Cobbet' is discussed briefly at pages 6 and 7.

The Letters were reprinted at Philadelphia in one volume in 1801, pp. (3)ii,iii,v(3)2–96. (A.B. 1188). There is a new preface, which begins with a paragraph on the 'low scurrility of Mr. Cobbet...'. In the footnote to page 44 it is stated that the second part was originally published about a month after the first. 'A letter to a friend in Paris' is added, dated January 1801, in which Cobbett is mentioned in a footnote. (No copy is known of the Letters, Evans 38332, (1800)).

1800

169   [Macdonald, Thomas].

A | brief statement | of | opinions, | given in the | Board of Commissioners, | under the sixth article of the treaty of amity, | commerce, and navigation, with Great Britain: | with | an appendix, | containing | certain articles of the treaties with Great- | Britain;-the commissions under the said sixth | article of the treaty of amity;– and | references to | opinions delivered by judges | of the supreme and circuit courts of the | United States: | By one of the commissioners | under the said sixth article. | [rule] | Philadelphia: | printed by James Humphreys, No. 106, South Side of Market-Street. | [rule] | 1800..

[π]⁴A–I⁴=40 leaves, 8 vo; (5)vi(1)viii(1)2–54(3)58–71(1) ¶ Evans 37869, Sabin 7904 ¶ cty; MWA

Contents: half-title, blank, title, blank, advertisement [v]vi, Contents [vii],viii; a brief statement [1]–54; appendix, blank, appendix

[57–]71, blank. Appendix in smaller type. Running titles pp. vi, viii. Catchword p. 54.

The British Commissioners under the Jay Treaty were in the United States from 1797 to 1800 but were unable to conclude any business because the two United States Commissioners, Thomas Fitzsimons and Samuel Sitgreaves, seceded. The present work recounts the proceedings from the British viewpoint. Macdonald, a British commissioner, was a friend and customer of Cobbett's. Cobbett attributed authorship to him in Porcupine's Works (No. 59) Vol. XII page 64. The attribution to Fitzsimons suggested by Evans 37428 clearly is not correct because Fitzsimons was on the other side of the fence. In Cole-Thornton page 58, Professor Cole states that Cobbett helped Macdonald write the pamphlet.

170   [Webster, Noah]. 1758–1843.

A | letter | to | General Hamilton, | occasioned by his letter | to | President Adams. | [rule] | By a federalist. | [rule] | Sir, | It has long been known... [New York 1800?] [caption title].

[A]⁴=4 leaves, 8 vo; (1)2–8.

A Bibliography of the Writings of Noah Webster, E.E.F. Skeel, New York, 1958, Nos. 727–732, give the various printings. ¶ cty; MWA

An attack on Cobbett occupies more than half of page 3, that he was a British agent.

171   Webster, Noah. 1758–1843.

Ten letters | to | Dr. Joseph Priestly [sic], | in answer | to his letters | to the inhabitants | of Northumberland. | [rule] | from Noah Webster, Jun. | [rule] | New Haven: | printed by Read & Morse. | 1800.

[A]–C⁴[D]³=15 leaves, 8 vo; (3)4–29(1) ¶ Skeel (see preceding entry) 722 ¶ cty; MWA

Contents: title, blank, Letters [3]–25, Postscript 26–29, blank. Note on page 29. On heavy, water-marked paper.

Errors noted: p. [3], l. 9, 'apppear'; p. 4, l. 17 'bull-bog'; p. 28, l. 1, 'theroists'.

Cobbett is aspersed pages 3, 4, 9, 15 and 17. '...it is all one whether a dog barks or Cobbett writes.' (page 4).

1801-1819

172 [Bruce, David].

Poems | chiefly in | the Scottish dialect, | originally written | under the signature | of the Scots-Irishman, | by | a native of Scotland. | with | notes and illustrations. | [rule] | Washington [Penna.]: | printed by John Colerick, | and sold by the booksellers. | [rule] | 1801.

[A]⁶[B]–M⁶N⁴=76 leaves, 12 mo; (3)iv–vi(1)viii,ix(1)xi,xii (1)2–126(14). Second and third leaves signed A–M except B2 for C2; second leaf of N signed N2 ¶ A.B. 244; Sabin 8730 ¶ MWA; PU

Contents: title; blank; Preface [iii]–vi; Note [vii]–ix; Dedication [x]–xii; Poems [1]–126; Glossary (8); Index (2); errata; blank (3). Running titles.

Pages 106–110 contain a poem: To | Peter Porcupine, in twenty, six-line verses. On page 106 is a footnote on 'Cobbet' on the whole favorable to him. Both men hate 'A Jacobin'. The poem concludes: '...God save your life | to be the axe an' pruning knife | O' these wild o'er grown times !'

173 [Brackenridge, Hugh Henry]. 1748-1816

Modern Chivalry, | containing | the | adventures | of a | Captain, &c. | Part II | [rule] | [line of Latin] | [rule] | published for the author. | [rule] | Carlisle [Pa.]: | printed by Archibald Loudon. | [rule] | 1804.

16.6 cm ¶ MWA

See B.A.L., Vol. I., pp. 265–268, for a description of this and subsequent editions. Pages 6–34 contain a tale of a contest between Peter Porcupine (identified on page 34 as 'Cobbet' [sic]) and a man who moved in next door with a pole-cat. Brackenridge had no high opinion of Cobbett: 'The truth is, he had been bred in the barracks, and had at his finger ends, the familiar phrases of the common soldiery, with that peculiar species of wit, which is common with that occupation of men, and in that grade.' (page 6)

Reprinted 1953, Columbia U.P., as 'Porcupine and the pole-cat.'

174 Freneau, Philip. 1752-1832

A | collection of | poems, | on | American affairs, and a variety of other subjects, | chiefly moral and political; | written between the

year 1797 and the pre- | sent time. | [rule] | By Philip Freneau...Vol.
I | [rule] | New-York: | published by David Longworth, | at the
Dramatic Repository, | Shakespeare-Gallery. | [rule] | 1815.

Sabin 25892, B.A.L. 6454 ¶ MWA

B.A.L. gives pagination and collation, and notes publication on
thick and on thin paper.

Pages 76–78 contain the poem 'On the departure of Peter Porcupine for England.', consisting of fifteen three-line stanzas. There
are two notes. The first and last stanzas will give the flavor:

> A bird of night attends the sail
> that now towards us turns her tail
> with Porcupine, escaped from jail.

*

> He took his leave from Sandy-Hook,
> and parted with a surly look
> that all observed and few mistook.

175   Birkbeck, Morris.

Extracts | from a | supplementary letter | from the Illinois, | dated
January 31st 1819. | [rule] | Address | to | British emigrants | arriv-
ing in the Eastern ports. | July 13th, 1819. | [rule] | reply | to | Wil-
liam Cobbett, Esq. | July 31st 1819. | [rule] | By Morris Birkbeck |
[rule] | New-York: | published by C. Wiley and Co. 3 Wall-street |
J. Seymour, printer. | 1819.

[1]–3⁴4³=15 leaves, 21.2 cm.; (3)4–8(1)10–12(1)14–29(1) ¶ A.
B. 47365 ¶ PPAMP

Contents: title, copyright, Extracts [3]–8, To British emigrants
[9–]12, to William Cobbett, Esq. [13]–29, blank. Cobbett is characterized as 'an eminent caricaturist' whose 'credit as an honest
writer suffers.' Cobbett is answered on some of his agricultural observations in his 'Year's Residence.' (No. 77). Marginal numbers
refer to paragraphs in that work. Birkbeck concludes '...There is
something in your character, as a writer, which is greatly in favour
of those whom you attempt to villify.'

Items
Sometimes Associated with Cobbett

Attributions to Cobbett already mentioned which are not accepted in the present work are the Antigallican (No. 109), by John Lowell, and the Democratiad (see No. 131), attributed to Lemuel Hopkins in Evans 28853 and Dictionary of American Biography 9: 215. Others follow.

176 Anonymous.

Christianity | contrasted with | Deism: | or the | present religion of France...The second edition corrected, with notes and additions. By Peter Porcupine. Philadelphia: | Printed for the booksellers | [by Thomas Stephens–Evans] 1796. Pp. (3)iv–vii(2)10–83(1) ¶ Evans 30192 ¶ DLC (Also the same, 64 p., Evans Supp. B9510; S.T. Evans 47734.)

Running title page 8: 'contrstaed'.

Although Cobbett's pseudonym is used here, Cobbett specifically disowned it: '...by a masterpiece of baseness...my assumed name, Peter Porcupine, was inserted in the title page, in order to give currency to the pernicious production.'—The Democratic Judge...(No. 37a), page 52. And see Porcupine's Gazette for March 7, 1797 to the same effect.

177 [Hopkins, Lemuel] 1750–1801.

The Guillotina, or a democratic dirge, a poem. By the author of the 'Democratiad'...Philadelphia: sold at the political book-store, South-Front-Street, No. 8 [Thomas Bradford 1796].

8 vo., 14(2)p. ¶ Evans 30591; D.A.B. 9:215. Sabin 13885 attributed this to Cobbett. Gazette of the United States, January 13, 1796: 'This day is published...' See S. T. Evans, page 365, Col. 3, to the effect that there are no known copies of an 8 page edition, Evans 30590.

178 Fennell, James. 1766–1816.

Philadelphia, July 6th, 1798. | To Mr. William Cobbet [sic], | Sir, | I shall ever think myself obliged by any person | ...[caption title].

Broadside 44 x 30.5 cm. ¶ S. T. Evans page 264, col. 3 ¶ PHI (PPL)

Text in four columns. Signed at the foot 'James Fennell | 129 Chestnut Street.' It is in answer to a letter subscribed James Walker, 76, North Fourth St. in Porcupine's Gazette of June 28th, 1798 commenting on Fennell's treatise advocating a plan for obtaining salt from sea water (Evans 33729). There is no indication Cobbett had any connection with the letter. S. T. Evans has 'Corbet' for 'Cobbet'.

179   Anonymous.

The | Little Innocent | Porcupine Hornet's Nest. | [rule] | [five lines of poetry] | [rule] | United States of America | printed for the author. [1800?]

[A]–C⁶=18 leaves; (5)6–32(1)34,35(1) ¶ Sabin 14028; Evans Supp. B11080 ¶ PHI (PPL)

An anti-slavery tract, written after the death of George Washington. (See p. 31). It does not relate to Cobbett.

180   Anonymous.

[rule] | The | Republican Rush-Light. | By William Cobbet [sic]. | [rule] | No. VII.–being the first number of volume II. | [rule] | [four lines quoted from] | Sedley. [1801?] [caption title].

B–G⁴=24 leaves, 8 vo; (1)2–48 ¶ A.B. 1236; Evans 37198, 38378 ¶ CTY

Catchwords. Second leaves signed. 'Vol. II' to left of signatures, except F. Attributed to Cobbett by Evans. However, this is not in Cobbett's style and espouses views opposite to his. For examples, it slights Fenno and Hamilton (p. 4), commiserates with Lyon, Callender and Cooper (p. 10), contends for a militia (p. 18), refers to the 'miserable and crazy government of England' (p. 33), and to the 'aristo-federalists, during their long, disastrous reign of twelve years...' (p. 40). Since the work refers to 'the administration of Mr. Jefferson...' (p. 47), it is probably not earlier than 1801. (Jefferson was chosen President in February). It is written as if by a resident of the United States—see p. 8 'Here', 'this country', etc.

SECONDARY BIBLIOGRAPHY

Selected in relation to the United States

Binger, Carl, M.D.
> Revolutionary Doctor Benjamin Rush, 1746-1813. New York. Norton. 1966.
>
> Pages 217-247 are valuable for an understanding of the Rush-Cobbett controversy.

Bowen, Marjorie [ie. Mrs. G. M. V. Long]
> Peter Porcupine. A study of William Cobbett, 1762-1835. London. Longmans. 1936. xii, 312 p.
>
> Only pp. 62-72 relate to the U.S. 'A Bone to Gnaw' has become 'A Bolder Law.'

Bowers, Claude G.
> Jefferson and Hamilton. Boston. Houghton. 1925.
>
> Cobbett is characterized at pages 259, 356-357 and 369. He is quoted on pages 350, 353-355, 359, 361, 370 and 371, and cited on pages 374-377 and 384.

Brant, Irving
> James Madison ... 1787-1800. Indianapolis. Bobbs-Merrill [1950].
>
> Cobbett receives brief mention at pages 417 and 427.

Butterfield, Lyman H., editor
> Letters of Benjamin Rush. Vol. II. Princeton. 1951.
>
> There is much valuable information in the appendix pp. 1213-18 on 'The Cobbett-Rush Feud.'
>
> Pp. 816-18 contain a letter of Rush to Brockholst Livingston concerning the trip of John Rush to New York to attack Cobbett.
>
> P. 1133, Rush to John Adams, May 5, 1812, concerning 'a just tribute' to Adams 'from your and my old enemy Cobbett.'

Callender, Tom
> Letters to Alexander Hamilton, King of the Feds ... New York ... 1802. Pp. (3)4-63(1).
>
> Cobbett is assailed, pp. 32-48, for an article critical of Washington which Cobbett published in London after his return there; mentioned pp. 8, 59, 60. Pro-Jefferson.

Carey, Mathew
> Autobiography. Brooklyn. 1942.
>
> Carey's controversy with Cobbett is described pp. 30-39.

Carlile, Richard

> The Republican. No. 19, Vol. 13 London. May 12, 1826. Life of William Cobbett. pp. [577]-608.

> Cobbett had attacked the radical reformer Carlile in his Political Register April 15, 1826 (See G. D. H. Cole, Life, p. 285). Carlile replied in his paper—a distorted account.

Carlyle, E[dward] I[rving]

> William Cobbett. A study of his life as shown in his writings. London. 1904 xii, 318 p.

> Pp. 43-74 relate to the United States. Brief bibliographical note 305-308. Unexciting.

Carroll, John A. and Ashworth, Mary W.

> George Washington (volume seven of Freeman biography) New York. Scribners. 1957.

> Cobbett is mentioned pages 224, 225, 248 note (inaccurate); discussed 225 note; on Randolph 336 and note; on death of Washington 642 and note.

Chesterton, Gilbert Keith

> William Cobbett . . . London. Hodder. 1925. 4 p. leaf 3-277 p.

> Valuable for an understanding of Cobbett's place in history and letters; trenchant and quotable descriptions of Cobbett and his style.

Clark, Mary Elizabeth

> Peter Porcupine in America. The Career of William Cobbett, 1792-1800. Philadelphia. 1939. v, 193 p.

> This is the best Cobbett source for the period covered; a valuable and informative work.

Cobbett, John M. and James P.

> Selections from Cobbett's political works . . . with notes, historical and explanatory. London. 1835. 6 vols.

> Vol. 1 pp. 1-211 contain 'American writings' from 1794 to 1800. The notes are mainly to acquaint English readers with American persons and events.

Cole, George Douglas Howard

> The Life of William Cobbett. New York. Harcourt. [1924] x, 458 p.

> The best 'life'. Not too much on the U.S. directly, but see pp. 48-69, and pp. 216-235, 272 on his second sojourn here. Brief critical bibliography pp. 438-47.

Cole, George Douglas Howard, editor

> Letters from William Cobbett to Edward Thornton written in the years 1797 to 1800. Oxford U.P. London. 1937. xlvi, 127 p.

Very valuable for the period covered. Thornton was secretary to the British Legation at Philadelphia. Prof. Cole has a long introductory note.

Cole, George Douglas Howard, ed.
Life and adventures of Peter Porcupine with other records of his early career in England & America. London. Nonesuch Press. 1927.
The Introduction, pp. 1-8, by Prof. Cole contains an appreciation.

Conway, Moncure Daniel
The Life of Thomas Paine. New York. 1892. 2 vols.
Cobbett quoted 1:58; Washington on Cobbett 1:175; mentioned 2:63, 238, 336, 423, 424, 427. Sketch of Cobbett and Paine: 2:429-433. Cobbett's 'Thomas Paine', 2:433-459.

Conway, Moncure Daniel
Omitted chapters of history disclosed in the life and papers of Edmund Randolph. New York. 1888.
271 n. on Cobbett and Fauchet. 347 and note, Cobbett and Randolph's 'Vindication', quoting James Madison to Thomas Jefferson, January 10, 1796.

Corner, George W., editor
The autobiography of Benjamin Rush. Princeton. 1948. (8) 399 p.
Cobbett is characterized page 1; mentioned pp. 18, 99 and note, 103-4 and note, 122 note, 279 note and 366.

Dauer, Manning J.
The Adams Federalists. Baltimore. Johns Hopkins Press. 1953.
Cobbett quoted pp. 34, 88, 129; mention 181, 2, 206; cited 28, 63, 149, 150, 159, 193, 232.

Davis, C. Rexford
William Cobbett. Philadelphia bookseller and publisher. Journal Rutgers University Library. Vol. XVI, December 1952, pp. 16-26.
Mainly a discussion of Cobbett's business relations with Congressman Robert Goodloe Harper, including the fact Harper charged no fee in the Rush case.

De Conde, Alexander
(a) Entangling Alliance. Durham. Duke U.P. 1958.
Cobbett is mentioned pp. 412n, 475-476; works cited 103, 125.
(b) The Quasi-War. New York, Charles Scribners Sons. 1966.
Cobbett is quoted pp. 84, 86-7, 116, 168; mentioned p. 278; discussed in notes pp. 400, 405.

Dos Passos, John
The Men Who Made the Nation. New York. Doubleday. 1957.

Cobbett is sketched pp. 341-342; the Rush affair pp. 406-409; mention 349, 370, 398; quoted 392.

[Duane, William John]
Politics for American farmers . . . free government . . compared with . . . British monarchy . . . Washington City . . . R. C. Weightman. 1807. 8⁰, (2) 96 p.; also 12⁰ (2) 200 p.

Cobbett is attacked pp. 12, 18, 23 and 33-35: 'British spy', etc.

Dunlap, William
The Diary . . . New-York Historical Society. 1930.

Vol. II p. 409. Cobbett and Thomas Moore are blasted together— 'malignant falshoods of a ruffian like Cobbet [sic]'.

Fay, Bernard
The Two Franklins. Boston. 1933.

More than a chapter is devoted to Cobbett versus Benjamin Franklin Bache, Philadelphia Republican editor. See especially pp. 278-9, 285, 288, 321.

Genzmer, George Harvey
William Cobbett, in Dictionary of American Biography. Vol. 4, page 248.

Good, short account of Cobbett's American career.

Hazen, Charles Downer
Contemporary American opinion of the French Revolution. 1964 reprint.

Cobbett is discussed and works cited pp. 241-43, quoted pp. 175, 205.

Hazlitt, William
Table Talk; or, Original Essays. London. John Warren. 1821. Essay VI. Character of Cobbett, pp. [115]-134.

Complimentary, in general. His appearance, p. 134. ' . . . the most powerful political writer of the present day . . . one of the best writers in the language.", p. [115]

Hildreth, Richard
The History of the United States of America. Revised edition. 6 vols. New York. 1879.

Cobbett is discussed Vol. V pages 120-121, 164-174, 368-370; Vol. VI page 269. Particular attention to the suits against him.

Huish, Robert
Memoirs of the late William Cobbett, Esq. M.P. for Oldham. London. 1836. 2 vols.

Because of inaccuracy it is not worth much.

Jack, Ian

> English Literature 1815-1832. Oxford History of English Literature Vol. X. Oxford. 1963.

> Cobbett is discussed and analysed pp. 312-19; mentioned pp. 43, 269, 354, 422, 429; quoted p. 433.

Konkle, Burton Alva

> Joseph Hopkinson. 1770-1842. Philadelphia. U. of Penn. Press. 1931.

> Rush vs Cobbett is discussed pp. 58-68. Hopkinson was chief counsel for Rush.

Link, Eugene Perry

> Democratic—Republican Societies 1790-1800. New York. 1942.

> Cobbett is quoted pp. 10, 12; characterized pp. 76, 189; mentioned pp. 199, 223 and note.

Lodge, Henry Cabot

> Studies in History. Boston. 1884.

> Contains an excellent brief study of Cobbett, pages 110-131.

McMaster, John Bach

> A History of the people of the United States. Vol. II. New York. 1921.

> Cobbett is discussed at pp. 206, 207, 352, 353; mentioned or quoted pp. 252, 253, 301, 309, 317, 346, 350.

Malone, Dumas

> Jefferson and the Ordeal of Liberty. Boston. Little, Brown. 1962.

> Cobbett is characterized pp. 449, 520; quoted p. 414; cited pp. 302, 346, 378.

Malone, Dumas

> The public life of Thomas Cooper, 1783-1839. Columbia. Univ. of So. Car. Press. 1961.

> Cobbett's attacks on Joseph Priestley are described pp. 84-86 and Priestley's reply p. 106. Cobbett is mentioned pp. 80, 87, 88.

Melville, Lewis [ie. Lewis S. Benjamin]

> The Life and Letters of William Cobbett in England & America. 2 vols. London. John Lane. 1913.

> Vol. 1, Ch. 14, pp. 84-116 relate to the United States. Uneven, but with some facts of interest. Vol. 2, pp. 267-275, contain an early listing of Cobbett's U.S. publications to 1801, and other Cobbett U.S. publications appear thereafter.

Miller, John C.

> Crisis in freedom. The Alien and Sedition Acts. Boston. Little, Brown. 1951.

Cobbett is discussed pp. 66n, 92, 229, 230; quoted pp. 39-40, 51-52, 55, 60-61n, 167-8.

Mitchell, Broadus
Alexander Hamilton ... 1788-1804. New York. MacMillan. 1962.
Cobbett is quoted pp. 223, 227, 394.

Mitchell, Stewart, ed.
New Letters of Abigail Adams. 1788-1801. Boston. 1947.
Cobbett is mentioned p. 95 and note and p. 101; quoted pp. 132, 143, 183; characterized pp. 143, 4 and 169. Mrs. Adams evidently was a steady reader of Porcupine's Gazette.

Muirhead, Arnold M.
An introduction to a Bibliography of William Cobbett. The Library. Fourth Series. Vol. XX, pp. 1-40 (1939).
This is a very useful article, particularly for Cobbett's English publications.

Neilson, Winthrop and Frances
Verdict for the doctor. The Case of Benjamin Rush. New York. Hastings. 1958. ix, 245 p.
About one-fifth of the text is devoted to the trial of Rush vs. Cobbett. Something less than half of the remainder is on Cobbett.
Though somewhat fictionalized and sympathetic to Rush, it is generally fair and accurate.

Nevins, Allan
American social history as recorded by British travellers. New York. Henry Holt. 1923.
Cobbett is discussed pp. 23, 24 and 87, 88, extracted pp. 88-94, mentioned pp. 4, 12, 15, 20. Not entirely accurate. For example, I find no evidence Cobbett ever went to Illinois.

Newell, L. C.
'Peter Porcupine's Persecution of Priestley.' Journal of Chemical Education, Mar. 1933, pp. 151-159.

Nichols, J. Horatio
Jefferson and Liberty; or celebration of the fourth of March. A patriotic tragedy . . . 1801. 8 vo. 28 (1) p.
A dialogue between Porcupine and Liston (British Minister) occupies half of page 10 and most of page 11, followed by comments on the two by Duane (Philadelphia publisher) ending with six lines on page 12.

Nye, Russel Blaine
The cultural life of the new nation. 1776-1830. New York. Harper. 1960.
Cobbett is cited pp. 108, 129; mentioned p. 113.

Oberholtzer, Ellis P.
    Literary history of Philadelphia. Philadelphia. 1906.
    Cobbett receives brief mention pp. 130-132.

Osborne, John W.
    William Cobbett: his thought and his times. Rutgers. 1966.
    Not of use in the present context.

Palmer, R. R.
    The age of the democratic revolution. The struggle. Princeton.
    1964.
    Cobbett is quoted (not admiringly) pp. 52, 531; mentioned 532,
    539, 541, 542.

Pearl, M[orris] L[eonard]
    William Cobbett. A bibliographical account of his life and times.
    Oxford U.P. 1953. Foreword G. D. H. Cole.
    Bibliographical details are given for all Cobbett works in the Cole
    Collection at Nuffield College, England, and many other works are
    noted. Valuable, especially for Cobbett's English publications, but
    does not purport to be definitive.

Pemberton, W. Baring
    William Cobbett. Penguin Books [1949].
    Pp. 24-37 are devoted to his career in the United States. A highly
    readable account over-all, with much information.

Potter, J.
    Cobbett in North America. Bulletin, British Association for Ameri-
    can Studies, No. 2, new series, March 1961, pp. 4-28.
    Contains a discussion of a number of Cobbett's United States pub-
    lications, with quotations.

Reitzel, William
    William Cobbett and Philadelphia Journalism: 1794-1800. Penn.
    Mag. of Hist. and Biog. Vol. LIX (1935) pp. 223-244.
    Valuable for a description of Cobbett's literary activities in Phila-
    delphia and for a rationale of them.

Reitzel, William, ed.
    The progress of a ploughboy to a seat in Parliament. London. 1933;
    new edition: The Autobiography of William Cobbett. London
    [1947]. 272 p.
    Prepared by extracting the autobiographical parts of Cobbett's own
    writings. His life in the United States pp. 56-79 [1st ed.]; 153-168
    [2d ed.]

Renwick, W. L.
English Literature 1789-1815. Oxford History of English Literature. Vol. IX. Oxford. 1967.

Cobbett is briefly discussed pp. 33-34 and note and 268; mentioned pp. 22, 35 and 189.

Reports of Cases adjudged in the Supreme Court of Pennsylvania. Jasper Yeates. Philadelphia. 1818.

(a) Benjamin Rush against William Cobbet [sic]. 1798. Vol. II, p. 275. In the libel action Cobbett petitioned for removal to the U.S. Circuit Court on the ground he was a British subject. Petition denied; a tort action is not removable. (not the law today).

(b) Mathew Carey against William Cobbet [sic]. 1798. Vol. II. p. 277. Same petition and same result.

(c) Respublica against William Cobbett. 1798 Vol. II, p. 352. Same petition and same result. And see 3 United States Reports 467, 1882 edition, pp. 467-476, for commentary by Frederic C. Brightly, and see (d) below.

(d) Respublica against William Cobbet [sic]. 1800. Vol. III, p. 93. Cobbett had been put under $2000 bond by M'Kean, Pennsylvania C. J. to maintain good behavior (not defame Pennsylvania officials). The action is to forfeit the bond for libel. Prosecution by M'Kean, now Attorney General. Verdict for the commonwealth. The animus of Shippen, C. J., is obvious.

Roberts, Kenneth and Anna M., translators and editors.
Moreau de St. Mery's American Journey [1793-1798]. Doubleday. 1947.

At page 211 is a contemporary appraisal of Cobbett, with a brief footnote on his American career by the editor.

Rowe, Kenneth Wyer
Mathew Carey. A Study in economic development. Baltimore. Johns Hopkins. 1933.

Pages 25, 26 on Carey's defeat of Cobbett.

Saintsbury, George
Essays in English Literature 1780-1860. Second series. N. Y. 1895. William Cobbett, pp. 38-80.

Cobbett's sojourns in the United States, pp. 47-49, 54; American works 65-66.

Schachner, Nathan
The Founding Fathers. New York. Putnam. 1954.

Cobbett is sketched pages 357-359 and 429-431—highly colored and inexact; quoted 422; mentioned 83, 178, 466, 485, 518 and 542. At 518 Rufus King, Ambassador to England, is quoted to the effect that Porcupine's Gazette had been accepted by the British 'as the most authentic source of information respecting the United States.'

Scharf, J. Thomas and Westcott, Thompson
History of Philadelphia. 1609-1884. 3 vols. Philadelphia. 1884.
There is considerable on Cobbett, in no friendly vein: pp. 482n, 485, 490, 493, 497-499, 919, 1960, 1961, 1979.

Smith, Edgar F.
Priestley in America 1794-1804.
Newspaper attacks on Cobbett in defence of Priestley quoted (1796) pp. 41-45, (1801) p. 143. Mention pp. 96, 97. Quoted, without naming him, pp. 103, 104.
Letter of Thomas Jefferson to Priestley Jan. 18, 1800 quoted ' . . . dishes of abuse against you as high-seasoned as Porcupine's were.' p.110.

Smith, Edward
William Cobbett: a biography. 2 vols. London. Sampson Low. 1878.
Cobbett's United States career is discussed Vol. 1, pp. 100-246; Vol. 2, pp. 195-214. Still valuable though partial. There is much bibliographical material, mainly English. Smith was author of an article on Cobbett in Dictionary of National Biography.

Smith, James Morton
Freedom's Fetters. The alien and sedition laws and American civil liberties. Ithaca. Cornell. 1956.
Cobbett is discussed pp. 175, 190n, 411n; quoted pp. 25, 26, 101, 102, 160, 190, 191, 192, 193, 194, 195, 222, 223, 224, 279, 337.

Smith, Page
John Adams, Vol. II, 1784-1826. Garden City. Doubleday. 1962.
Cobbett is quoted and discussed page 956; mentioned pp. 883, 1000, 1001, 1025.

Stewart, Donald H.
The opposition press of the Federalist Period. Albany. State Univ. of New York Press. 1969.
The opposition view of Cobbett as a journalist in Philadelphia; not complimentary, although it does speak of a 'faction headed by Hamilton, Cobbett and Pickering . . ' 334. Cobbett appraised 264, 271, 299; and alien law 465; and cockades 303,4; and Franklin 611; and 'German Porcupine' 580; mentioned 257, 259, 260, 288, 317, 350, 402, 404, 489, 499, 549, 556, 568, 581, 586, 623, 857, 861, 863; opposition quoted 292, 387, 623; quoted 362, 3, 635. Porcupine's Gazette: circulation (perhaps second largest) 17, 610, 653; deficits 18; mentioned 111, 300, 412, 483, 497, 582, 633, 852.

Tinkcom, Harry Marlin
The Republicans and Federalists in Pennsylvania 1790-1801. Penn. Hist. and Mus. Com. Harrisburg. 1950.

Cobbett is quoted and discussed pp. 143, 144, 176, 177.

Tolles, Frederick B.
George Logan of Philadelphia. New York. Oxford. 1953.

Cobbett is quoted and characterized (unfavorably) at pp. 156, 165, 171, 172, 173; mentioned p. 182.

Tuckerman, Henry T.
America and her commentators. New York. Scribners. 1864.

Pages 208-211 contain an appreciation of Cobbett, particularly in regard to his second stay here.

Walters, Raymond Jr.
Alexander James Dallas. Philadelphia. U. of Penna. 1943.

Cobbett's attacks on Dallas described page 85; mentioned pp. 90, 116. On page 63 is a reference to Porcupine's Gazette as of a time more than two years before it commenced.

Warfel, Harry R.
Noah Webster schoolmaster to America. New York. MacMillan. 1936.

Cobbett is quoted and discussed page 234; mentioned pp. 118, 160, 224, 237, 253, 265, 266, 291.

Warfel, Harry R., ed.
Letters of Noah Webster. New York. Literary Publishers. 1953.

Cobbett is discussed page 148 (letter to Jedidiah Morse) and pp. 205-207 (letter to Joseph Priestley). He is mentioned pp. 183, 208, 531, 537.

Warren, Charles
Jacobin and Junto...diary of Dr. Nathaniel Ames. Cambridge. Harvard. 1931.

Cobbett is quoted pp. 63-64, mentioned p. 81, discussed and quoted pp. 90-91, discussed pp. 92n, 93n, 95.

Watson, George, editor
The new Cambridge bibliography of English literature. Volume 3. 1800-1900. Cambridge. Cambridge University Press. 1969.

Columns 1199-1210, by M. L. Pearl, list Cobbett bibliographies, collections, works and biographical material in great detail. There are quite a few differences between the list of works here and the list there which there was no opportunity to reconcile.

Wharton, Francis

State trials of the United States during the administrations of Washington and Adams. Philadelphia. Carey and Hart. 1849.

Pages 322-8 give the judge's charge and the indictment in the grand jury proceedings November 1797 involving the Spanish envoy, Yrujo, in which Cobbett was discharged. A note on Cobbett, pp. 328-332; mentioned pp. 9, 23; quoted pp. 338, 343 on Matthew Lyon.

Winsor, Justin, editor

Narrative and critical history of America. Boston. Houghton, Mifflin. 1888.

Vol. VII. Cobbett is characterized page 314 and note, page 515 and note; mentioned pages 349 (on Jackson), 422 (War of 1812), 517 note (Randolph) and 158 note (Jay Treaty).

Vol. VIII, mentioned pages 493, 499.

Woodbury, Margaret

Public opinion in Philadelphia 1789-1801. A dissertation. Durham. 1919.

Of some help in giving the setting. Discussion of Cobbett: in general pp. 13-15; Rush 15-20; Jay Treaty 81-87, 89; France 93-96; Alien and Sedition Acts 104; Disunion 104,5. Cobbett quoted pp. 81, 124; mentioned 103, 127.

SHORT TITLE LIST

INDEX OF NAMES

References are to pages

Adams, Abigail. letters 212, quoted xiv.
Adams, John. author 67, 159; criticized 95, 104, 112; defended 76, 83, 161; election 75; Hamilton on 113; life 215; mention 110, 118, 166, 207, 209; message 239; Senate address 75, 79.
Addison, Joseph. mention 179.
Adet, Pierre. attacked 68, 69, 75; correspondence 64, 65; mention 76.
Albrecht (or Albright), Johann (or John) & Co., publisher 77.
Allen, John. speech 166.
Allen, Thomas. bookseller 239.
An American. author 38, 118, 200.
American Daily Advertiser, see Claypoole.
An American farmer. author 116, 117.
An American gentleman. author 171.
Ames, Fisher. mention 71, 109; speech 194.
Ames, Nathaniel. diary 216.
Anchor Club. mention 200.
Anthing, Johann Friedrich. author 96.
Anti-Jacobin Review. extracted 113.
Archimedes. mention 178.
The Argus (N.Y.). mention 43.
Arnold, Benedict. mention 193.
Ascanius. mention 164.
Aufrère, Anthony. author 111, 168, 169.
The Aurora (Phila.). mention 10, 43, 53, 89, 199; reprint 65, 200, 201.

Bache, Benjamin Franklin. attacked 10, 21, 53, 66, 75, 83, 88(2), 89; legatee 79; letter to 179; mention 23, 188; printer 191; translator 191; vs. Cobbett 210.
Bank of England. subject 155.
Baylis, T. printer 108.
Beckley, John J. attacked 51; mention 110.
Bedford, Duke of (Francis Russell) and Burke 49, 181.
Belden, J. and Co. publisher 119, 120.
Benbow, Mr. of Manchester. 136.
Benbow, William. printer, publisher 126.
Bensley, B. printer 135, 136.
Bergami, Baron Bartolomeo. imputations 138.
Berkley, George [ie. Berkeley]. mention 110.
Binger, Carl. author 207; cited xiii.
Binns, John. printer 104, 148.
Bioren and Madan. copyright 190; printers 161, 190.
Birkbeck, Morris. addressed 131, 133; author 204.
Bishop, Abraham. quoted 118.
Bishop, Samuel. mention 118.
Blanck, Jacob. cited 106.
Blomfield, Charles James, Bishop. Dedication to 157.
Blount, William. conspiracy 111; mention 193.
Bonaparte, Napoleon. mention 120, 185; peace 113, 114.
Booksellers—See Appendix, C.
Bowen, Marjorie (Mrs. G.M.V. Long). study of Cobbett 207.
Bowers, Claude G. author 207; quoted xiv.

Tolles, Frederick B. author 216.
Torrey, Jesse. author 141.
Touchstone, Geoffrey—See Carey, James.
Tuckerman, Henry T. author 216; cited xiii.
Tracy, Uriah. customer 241.
Tull, Jethro. quoted 147.
Turgot, Anne Robert Jacques, Baron. answered 159.

Ulster Register Office. printer 135.
United Irishmen. conspiracy 85, 86; proceedings 20.
United States. banking 153; Congress 34, 42, 43; 44, 45, 50, 51, 71, 75, 113, 170, 193; constitutions 159; emigration to 149; envoys 165, 166; free press 56, 85, 86, 96; map 154, 155; officials, etc. 172; slavery 141; Spanish America 127; tariff 148; year's residence 129-136. And see France, Great Britain, etc.
Universal Gazette. quoted 197.

Vail, R.G.W. cited 17.
Valerius. author 110.
Van Norden & Mason. printers 151.
Van Winkle & Wiley. booksellers 120; printers 119, 120, 123.
Vaublanc. defence of Lafayette 3.
Vaughan, Benjamin. attacked 94.
Virginia, Commonwealth of. attacked 46, 48.
Volney, Constantin Franc. mention 186.
Voltaire, F.M.A. de. attacked 35.

Waite, G. and R. printers 96, 98, 173.
Walker, James. mention 206.
Walters, Raymond Jr. author 216.
Waree. bookseller 18.
Warfel, Harry R. author 216, editor 216.
Warren, Charles. author 216.
Washington Benevolent Societies. attacked 119.
Washington City. burning 119.
Washington, George. address 71; death 95, 112; defended 24, 34, 72, 73; description 34; life 208; mention 35, 44, 51, 61, 69, 70, 87, 105, 109, 110, 164, 206, 207; message 34; quoted xiii, 72.
Watson, George. editor 216.
Watson, Bishop Richard. author 166, mention 61.
Watts, Dr. Isaac. grammar 137.
Webster, Noah. attacked 78, 99; author 119, 202, 203; a Federalist 202; legatee 79; letters 216; life 216; praised 51.
Wellington, Duke of (Arthur Wellesley). dedication 156.
Wharton, Francis. compiler 217.
Wheat, James C. & Brun, Christian F. cited 49, 162.
White, James. bookseller 241.
Whiting, D. & S. publishers 115.
Whitney, Charles. bribery 34.
Wiley, C., and Co. publishers 204.
Wilkie, G. & T. publisher 39.
Willcox, Mark. papermaker 241.
Williams and Mason. printer 123; publisher 123.
Williams, Thomas. defendant 162.
Winsor, Justin. editor 217; quoted xiv.
Witmer, Henry. printer 41.

Cobbett's Account Book*

THE American Antiquarian Society has in its library the account book used by William Cobbett as a bookseller in Philadelphia and New York from June 1796 to June 1800. The account book thus covers the full span of Cobbett's book-selling and publishing activities in this country (leaving aside his second sojourn here in 1817-1819).

The account book is large folio with 160 double pages and some miscellaneous single pages, including an index. A single page measures approximately 15½ x 9¼ inches. On each double page the left hand has the customer's name and debits and the right hand credits, and in some cases addresses or other identification. The entries are by Cobbett and at least two others. The customers' names, in large flowing script, may well have been written by Cobbett, who had a copybook hand when he chose to use it. Some customers' accounts ran to several pages, while some pages contain as many as four accounts. Some pages have over forty entries and others only a handful.

Frequent references in the accounts to a "day book" indicate that transactions were entered there first in detail and then posted to the account book when customer credit was being extended. In general, there appear to be no cash transactions, and cash sales to customers who visited the shop would not be reflected in the account book.

As to the books which Cobbett dealt in, about 340 titles are represented, a good many by only a copy or two which may have been ordered specially for customers. There are many English imports in the latter category. As might be expected,

---

*Reprinted in substance from Proceedings of the American Antiquarian Society, Volume 78, Part 2.

the books and pamphlets which were sold in quantity were mainly Cobbett imprints. Annexed marked A is a chronology of these as derived from the accounts, within the limitations noted. Schedule B gives sales data for these imprints similarly derived. It may be observed that the sales prices roughly correspond with the size of the pamphlet or book, and the dealer discounts with the sales prices. One exception is Cannibals' Progress, which Cobbett priced very low as an anti-French propaganda document.

Parenthetically, it appears that Cobbett once took in trade for books one 'Pointer Dog', valued at $52.50 (fol. 49).

Some of Cobbett's publishing ventures as disclosed in the accounts are deserving of special mention. One of these was his publication in May 1798 for the Reverend G. W. Snyder of Fredericktown, Maryland, of his work in 213 pages: 'The Age of Reason unreasonable; or, the folly of rejecting revealed religion. In a series of letters to a friend.' (No. 120) This was scarcely a dashing success, but is interesting for the publishing details (fol. 103). The printing was by Budd & Bartram, the binding in boards by [David] Patton and the binding in sheep by [Phillip] Limeburner, all of Philadelphia. 500 copies were printed of which 305 were in sheets at 50 cents, 97 in boards at 56 cents and 98 in sheep at 75 cents. The costs were as follows:

9 reams printing paper	$ 31.50
Cash paid for 'coppyright'	1.20
Advertising of D° 10 times	2.75
Printing	72.00
Binding in boards at six cents	5.82
Binding in leather at 13 cents	12.74
	$126.01

Cobbett sold one copy in boards at 56 cents (two reported sold elsewhere in the accounts must have been returned). The Reverend Snyder paid $80 in cash. 36 copies in boards and 98 in sheep were delivered to his order, leaving 60 copies in boards and 305 in sheets. Since the Reverend was also charged with the advertising costs at $2.75 for another Cobbett imprint (Kennedy, Patrick. An answer to Paine's letter to General Washington . . . No. 110), his deficit was $47.64, upon payment of which Cobbett was ready to deliver the remainder. On June 20, 1799, the firm of Isaac and John Mentz of Snyder's Fredericktown received the remainder in exchange for their 'note of hand payable in 4 months' in the amount of $47.64 (fol. 74). Presumably this was arranged by Snyder.

John Lowell had Cobbett print 'The Antigallican . . . (No. 109) on a commission basis (fol. 75). Printing costs were $78.20 for 300 copies of 86 pages each, February 5, 1798. The sale price was 37½ cents. Cobbett credited himself with commissions of $9.37½ on '100 Antigallican retailed at Philadelphia', at 25%, and of $22.55 (sic) on 200 'sent to correspondents in different parts', at 30%. There seems no basis for the suggestion which has been made that Cobbett was actually author of this work.

Timothy Pickering, the Secretary of State, evidently in the interest of person and party, had Cobbett arrange a reprint (by John Ward Fenno) from his Porcupine's Gazette of January 24, 1799, of 1682 copies of the 'Message from the President of the United States accompanying a report of the Secretary of State' regarding France, dated January 21, 1799 (Evans 36548). The charge was $28.00 (fol. 104).

Bibles and prayer books were evidently important staples. In April 1798 Cobbett purchased of John Cross 44 folio bibles at eight dollars each, less 25% (fol. 99). In May of that year he received from Thomas Allen, bookseller of New York, on commission of 25%, 54 prayer books as follows: 32 plain at 62½ cents, 6 in red 'morroco' at $1.75, 2 do. with clasps at $2.00, 2 in blue do. at $1.75, 3 in calf gilt at $1.50, 3 in green 'morroco' at $1.75 and 6 in sheep gilt at $1.25.

Cobbett made a significant investment in the United States Court Kalendar . . . (No. 125) in December 1799 and January 1800 by the purchase from John Morgan, Philadelphia, of 398 copies for $367.50. The bindings were interestingly varied: 36 in morocco with locks at $1.50; 14 in do. but locks not put on, not priced; 183 in morocco with tucks at $1.25; 129 in red sheep at $.75 and 36 in red sheep with locks at $1.00. (fol. 153)

Booksellers of course did not confine themselves to books. Cobbett sold writing paper, sealing wax, tooth powder, quills, brushes and red ink. He purchased from Robert Field of New York 174 prints at 75 cents and another 86 at 37½ cents or 25 cents (fol. 119, 133). He purchased from Morgan & Wigmore, 'pocket book makers', in 1798 and from John Morgan in 1799 and 1800 $693.16 worth of pocket books (fol. 60, 153). On February 10, 1798 he purchased from Dr. William Burrell of New York 20 Godboldt's Balsam* at $4 per bottle. One of the purchasers from Cobbett was the eminent geographer Rev'd Jedidiah Morse (fol. 100).

An extraordinary amount of money was spent for lottery tickets, which varied in price from $6 to $14, with the bulk Cobbett sold in the range $6.50 to $8. Over the period June 2, 1797 to March 7, 1799 the account book records sales of 263 tickets for just over $1900. Some of the lotteries are designated as 'Canal', 'Canal No. 2' or 'Washington.'

As to customers, the account book shows 229, of which 75, or one-third, can be identified with some certainty as fellow booksellers because so noted in the accounts, or in book-trade lists, or simply because of the quantities billed and discounts allowed. Schedule C lists the latter arranged by geographical distribution, which was not inconsiderable. Also, the accounts with some of them show fairly large sums, indicating that Cobbett did a substantial business. Thus the account with Archibald Drummond in New York ran to a total of $2943.25 and was settled May 2, 1799 by a bill on London for $1373.30 (fol. 134). James and Andrew Duncan of Glasgow received

*Buchan's *Domestic Medicine*, Hartford 1789, pp. 723, 725, lists six kinds of balsams or balsamic compositions, good for rheumatic complaints, dysentery, haemorrhages, wounds, coughs, ulcers, colic, etc. etc.

£148/10/6 to settle their balance (fol. 139) and John Wright of London received a bill of exchange for £600 December 5, 1799 (fol. 147). Asbury Dickens of Philadelphia ran a total of $754.85, George Hill of Baltimore $1928.85, William Pritchard of Richmond $1748.66, James White of Boston $987.36 and William P. Young of Charleston $562.85.

There were individual customers of some distinction. Among these were the British Minister, Robert Liston, Cobbett's friend Edward Thornton, Secretary to the British legation, Messrs. MacDonald and Rich, British Commissioners under the Jay Treaty, Richard Soderstrom, Swedish Consul, Uriah Tracy, Senator from Connecticut, Samuel Sitgreaves, Representative from Pennsylvania, and Robert G. Harper and William Laughton Smith, Representatives from South Carolina.

Firms and individuals who did work for Cobbett appear throughout the accounts: Bookbinders include [John] Cameron, Michael Conrod, [William] Derickson, and John Rain; employees were James Douglas, Edward Mitchell, William Mitchill and Ezra Sergant (Sargeant); folder and sewer, Hannah Kesler. Paper makers in the accounts give an idea of the scope of Cobbett's publishing activity (although it does not appear what if any paper was purchased for Porcupine's Gazette). For the period June 15—November 7, 1797 George Hirst sold him 325 reams of paper at $3.50, or a total of $1137.50, paid for in large part by the delivery of about 9000 pounds of rags at 5 cents per pound. From April 4, 1797 through June 23, 1798 Mark Willcox (located on Chester Creek near Philadelphia) sold him $3088.39 worth of paper as follows: 98 reams at $4.50; 42 reams at $4.00; 52 demy at $3⅓; 536 F[oolscap?] Royal at $4.00 and 54 reams at $3.00. From June 4 through Sept. 24, 1799, Cobbett purchased of Thomas Meeteer & Sons (of Baltimore) 518 reams of paper at $3 each 'for my works.'*

---

*Cobbett issued a proposal in 1799 (No. 45) for publishing his works in a collected edition and printing had begun when Cobbett left Philadelphia for New York and the Benjamin Rush judgment was entered against him in December 1799. The proposed edition was junked as waste paper to help satisfy the judgment.

On May 13, 1800 he purchased 134 reams for the same purpose. Lesser purchases were made during 1798 from William Young (of Philadelphia), William Levis (of Philadelphia, who owned a paper mill in Upper Darby, Penna.) and one Pepper.

Budd & Bartram, just down the street from Cobbett's shop in Philadelphia, was his principal printer appearing in the accounts. On December 17, 1798, the firm acknowledged receipt of $744.04 representing the balance due of an account stated in the amount of $3949.53. A further bill of $171.54 was paid February 20, 1800. John Furman, of New York, had a bill of $33.75 March 10, 1800 'for printing Rush Light No.1' (No. 51). John Ward Fenno of Philadelphia charged $84 June 4, 1799 for printing Gifford's The Baviad and Maeviad (No. 124). On August 11, 1798, Samuel Sansom, Junr. also of Philadelphia received $294 'cash on acct. for printing History of Jacobinism', by William Playfair (No. 24).

There has been a question over the years whether or not Cobbett ever actually did his own printing (but see Nos. 32 and 107). It does appear from the account book that Cobbett owned a printing press, which was sold probably in 1800 to Hugh Maxwell, printer of Philadelphia, for $130.00 (unnumbered page).

A

CHRONOLOGY OF COBBETT IMPRINTS
DERIVED FROM EARLIEST SALES
IN ACCOUNT BOOK*

Short Title	Number	Sale Date
1. *The Scare Crow*	18	July 23, 1796
2. *The Life . . of Peter Porcupine* . . .	19	August 8, 1796
3. *The Political Censor* . . [for September, 1796] . . .	20	September 26, 1796
4. *A New Drawing book* . . .	100	September 29, 1796
5. Mackenzie, Henry: *An Answer to Paine* . . .	22	October 18, 1796
6. *The Gros Mousqueton Diplomatique* . . .	23	November 25, 1796
7. Playfair, William. *The History of Jacobinism*	24	November 28, 1796
8. *An Antidote for Tom Paine's . . . Poison* . . .	20b	December 5, 1796
9. *Porcupine's Political Censor for November, 1796*	25	December 20, 1796
10. *Porcupine's Political Censor for December 1796*	26	January 24, 1797
11. Adams, John. *A Defence of the Constitutions* . . .	101	February 20, 1797
12. Burke, Edmund. *Two letters addressed to a member* . . .	102	February 23, 1797
13. *Porcupine's Political Censor for Jan. 1797* . . .	29	March 10, 1797
14. *Porcupine's Political Censor for March, 1797*	31	April 24, 1797
15. Erskine, Thomas. *A view of the . . . war with France* . . .	32	May 18, 1797
16. [Smith, William L.] *The pretensions of Thomas Jefferson* . .	103	June 22, 1797
17. *An accurate plan of the blockade of Cadiz* . . .	104	September 23, 1797
18. Gifford, John. *A Letter to the Hon. Thomas Erskine*	105	November 3, 1797
19. Erskine, Thomas. *The speeches of . . . in . . . King's Bench*	106	November 10, 1797
20. [Lowell, John] *The Antigallican*	109	January 19, 1798
21. Kennedy, Patrick. *An answer to Paine's letter . . Washington* . .	110	January 19, 1798
22. *The Democratic judge . . . equal liberty of the press* . . .	38	March 22, 1798

*The earliest entry in the Account Book is for June 22, 1796. Cobbett's break with Bradford as publisher occurred in March of that year. The chronology does not reflect the works published by the latter or by Benjamin Davies, who succeeded him briefly. In a few instances it was necessary to disregard entries which from their timing and isolation were evidently advance orders and not sales. There are many entries in the Account Book for 'Porcupine's Works', but it cannot be determined what imprints are involved. A number of Cobbett imprints are not found in the Account Book, although published during the period covered by it.

Short Title	Number	Sale Date
23. Harper, Robert G. *The Speech* . . . *House* . . *29th of May, 1797.*	111	March 27, 1798
24. Robison, John. *Proofs of a conspiracy* . . .	112	April 9, 1798
25. *Instructions to* . . *Pinckney* . . . *envoys* . . .	113	April 10, 1798
26. Watson, Richard. *An address* . . *people of Great Britain* . .	114	April 20, 1798
27. Allen, John. *Speech* . . *in the House* . . *20th* . . *April 1798* . .	115	May 4, 1798
28. Harper, Robert G. *Observations* . . *dispute* . . *United States* . . .	116	May 4, 1798
29. Muir, James. *A sermon* . . *Alexandria* . . *9th of May 1798* . .	117	May 16, 1798
30. *French arrogance; or, the cat let out of the bag* . . .	41	May 25, 1798
31. Aufrere, Anthony. *The cannibals' progress* . . *French invasion.*	118	June 18, 1798
32. Lewis, Matthew G. *Ambrosio or the monk: A romance*	121	July 16, 1798
33. Snyder, G. W. *The age of reason unreasonable* . . .	120	July 25, 1798
34. Harper, Robert G. *A short account* . . *Congress* . . *in a letter* . .	123	August 1, 1798
35. Sorlie, Sholto. *A treatise on the new sword exercise* . .	122	August 1, 1798
36. Gifford, William. *The Baviad, and Maeviad* . . .	124	May 17, 1799
37. *United States Court Kalendar* . . .	125	December 26, 1799
38. Anthing, J. F. *History of the campaigns* . . *Prince* . . *Suworow*	50	February 10, 1800
39. *The Rush-Light* 15th Feb. 1800 . . .	51	February 25, 1800
40. *do.* 28th Feb. 1800 . . .	52	March 10, 1800
41. *do.* 15th March, 1800 . . .	53	March 24, 1800
42. *do.* 31st March 1800	54	April 14, 1800
43. Polwhele, Richard. *The unsex'd females; a poem* . . .	126	May 1, 1800
44. *The Rush-Light* 30th April 1800 . . .	55	May 21, 1800

B

COBBETT IMPRINTS
SALES DATA FROM ACCOUNT BOOK

Item	Copies[1] Sold	Prices to Public	Pages	Dealer Discount
1. *Scare Crow*	425	12½¢	23	25%
2. *The Life . . . Porcupine*	513	31¢	60	do.
3. *Censor* [September]	664	31¢	80	do.
4. *Drawing Book*	46	Began at $1.25 Reduced to 75¢	Unknown	do.
5. MacKenzie . . . *Paine*	399	37½¢	96	do.
6. *Mousqueton*	400	25¢	76	do.
7. Playfair . . *Jacobinism* 2V.	259	$2.50-sheets; $3-boards; $3.50-leather; $3.75-gilt.	384 352	1/6 —
8. *Antidote . . .* Paine	56	$1.25 plus 20¢ for binding	80	20%
9. *Censor . . . November*	2305	25¢	80	25%
10. *Censor . . . December*	1228	25¢	72	do.
11. Adams . . . *Defence* 3V.	382	$5-boards; $6-bound; $7-calf gilt.	430, 487, 566	20%
12. Burke . . . *Two letters*	199	37½¢	86	25%
13. *Censor . . January*	628	25¢	56	do.
14. *Censor . . . March*	1160	25¢	76	do.
15. Erskine . . . *View*	528	37½¢	100	do.
16. [Smith] *Jefferson*	117	50¢	Unknown	do.
17. *Blockade of Cadiz*	882	12½¢	do.	do.
18. Gifford . . . *Erskine*	607	50¢	132	do.
19. Erskine . . . *Speeches*	643	12½¢	23	do.
20. [Lowell] *Antigallican*	300[2]	37½¢	86	do.
21. Kennedy . . . *Paine*	321	25¢	44	do.
22. *Democratic Judge*	1618	50¢	102	do.
23. Harper . . *Speech*	594	50¢	44	do.
24. Robison . . . *proofs*	93	$1.75-boards; $2-leather.	400	20%
25. *Instructions . . envoys*	115	12½¢	15	25%
26. Watson . . . *address*	347	25¢	40	do.
27. Allen . . *speech*	109	25¢	32	do.
28. Harper . . . *Observations*	918	50¢	96	do.
29. Muir . . . *sermon*	127	12½¢	14	do.

[1] Copies are before returns.

[2] Fol. 75 shows 300 copies printed and sold. The printing costs were $78.20 and Cobbett received commissions from Lowell of $31.92, out of which dealer discounts were payable on about ⅓ of the copies.

Item	Copies Sold	Prices to Public	Pages	Dealer Discount
30. *French arrogance . . .*	90[3]	25¢	31	—
31. *Cannibals' progress . .*	6078	3½¢	47	—
32. Lewis . . *the monk* 2V.	432	$2.00	323, 325	1/6
33. Snyder . . *Age of reason*	3[4]	50¢-sheets; 56¢-boards; 75¢-sheep	213	—
34. Harper . . *account . . Congress*	564	25¢	22	25%
35. Sorlie . . *sword exercise*	263	25¢	24	do.
36. Gifford . . *Baviad*	178	$1.50	167	20%
37. *Court Kalendar*	22	75¢-sheep; $1.25-morocco with tucks; $1.50-morocco with locks.	134	1/6
38. Anthing . . *Suworow* 2V.	428	$2.50	192, 219	25%
39. *Rush-Light No. 1*	1618	25¢	48	25%[5]
40. do. 2	1742	25¢	68	do.
41. do. 3	1269	25¢	52	do.
42. do. 4	1659	25¢	48	do.
43. Polwhele . . *females*	89	62½¢	72	25%
44. *Rush-Light No. 5*	551	25¢	52	25%[5]

[3]88 of the copies were sold to one Peyton it would appear (fol. 119).
[4]See the preceding text. 500 copies printed. Copies were delivered to Snyder, and a remainder of 365 copies was sold for the balance owing.
[5]Large buyers got 33⅓%, such as Asbury Dickins who bought 1245 copies.

C
BOOKSELLERS

CONNECTICUT

New Haven,
    Beers, Isaac & John   1796–7, 1800

GEORGIA

Savannah,
    Miller, Thomas   1798–1800

MARYLAND

Baltimore,
    Campbell, Conrad & Co.   1799, 1800
    Hill, George   1796–1800
    Rainbow [See Norfolk]   1797
Chestertown,
    Arthur, James   1797, 1798
Easton,
    Cowan, James   1798
    Neale, Greenbury   1796, 1797
Fredericktown,
    Menby, J & J.   1798
    Mentz, Isaac & John   1797–1800
Georgetown Crossroads,
    Lathim, George   1796, 1797
Williamsport,
    Byus, Stanley   1797

MASSACHUSETTS

Boston,
    Nancrede, Joseph   1798–1800
    West, David   1797
    White, James   1796–1800
Newburyport,
    Blunt, Edmund   1797–99
Pittsfield,
    Van Schaak, W.   1798, 1800
Salem,
    Cushing, Thomas C.   1798

NEW JERSEY

Trenton,
    Dunham [David?]   1798

NEW YORK

Albany,
    McDonald, John   1797
New York City,
    Allen, Thomas   1798–1800

Brown & Stansbury	1800
Campbell, Samuel	1796–1800
Caritat, Hocquet	1800
Davis, Cornelius	1800
Davis, George	1797
Drummond, Archibald	1797–99
Fenno, John Ward [See Philadelphia]	1800
Herring, Abraham	1798
Rivington, James	1798
Somerville, Alexander	1797–1800
Swords, Thomas & James	1799
Waite, George & Robert	1800

PENNSYLVANIA

Carlisle,	
Loudon, Thomas	1797, 1798
Lancaster,	
Albright, John	1798
Philadelphia,	
Bradford, Thomas	1796, 97
Campbell, Robert & Co.	1796–99
Carey, Mathew	1796, 97
Davies, Benjamin	1796–99
Dickins, Asbury	1800
Dickins, John	1798
Dobson, Thomas	1796–1800
Fenno, John Ward [See New York City]	1798, 99
Morgan, John	1798–1800
Morris, Bs Wm	1798
Ormrod, John	1796–99
Rice, Henry & Patrick	1796–99
Stephens, Thomas	1796
Young, Mills & Son	1796–97
Young, William	1797, 1800
Pittsburgh,	
Scull, John	1798
Reading,	
Jungmann, Gottlob	1798

SOUTH CAROLINA

Charleston,	
Young, William P.	1797–1800

VIRGINIA

Alexandria,	
Price, Ellis	1797, 98
Chambersburg,	
Riddle & Lahn	1797, 98
Fredericksburg,	
Henderson, David	1797–1800
Norfolk,	
Hannah, Andrew	1797–99
Pollard, B. & Co.	1800
Rainbow & Hannah	1796–97

Petersburg,
    Bacchus, Eleazer F.   1796–1800
Richmond,
    Prichard, William   1799, 1800
    Pritchard & Davidson   1796–98

CANADA

Halifax,
    Henry, Anthony   1797, 1798, 1800
    Hodge   1796, 97
Montreal,
    Edwards, Edward   1800

GREAT BRITAIN

London,
    Wright, John   1799
Glasgow,
    Duncan, James & Andrew   1797, 98

JAMAICA

    Stevenson, Aikman & Smith   1800

NOT LOCATED

    Anthony, J & Co.   1798
    Helmouth, Henry K.   1799
    Stevenson   1797, 98
    Storey, Elizabeth—Wilmington   1797
    Spencer   1798
    Taylor, J. B.   1798
    Urquhart, William   1798